AF279454

MYSTERY TORNADO
S/FX
GTO
by PONTIAC
"For those who think young"
HEADERS & BILL WARD
CAM & ISKENDERIAN
TIRES & BRUCE
PLUGS & CHAMPION
IGNITION & MALLORY
LUBRICATION & VALVOLINE
— STP
DRIVER PHIL BONNER
ARCHWAY FORD, BALTO. MD.
AL MEANS Ford
Decatur, Ga.
GEORGIA PEACH
HORSEPOWER SALES
STP
TEAM

Ar...
"The F...
BES...

Arnie "The Farmer" Beswick

DEAN FAIT

CarTech ®

CarTech®

CarTech®, Inc.
6118 Main Street
North Branch, MN 55056
Phone: 651-277-1200 or 800-551-4754
Fax: 651-277-1203
www.cartechbooks.com

Edit by Wes Eisenschenk
Layout by Connie DeFlorin

ISBN 978-1-61325-530-8
Item No. CT664

Library of Congress Cataloging-in-Publication Data Available

Written, edited, and designed in the U.S.A.
Printed in China
10 9 8 7 6 5 4 3 2

PUBLISHER'S NOTE: In reporting history, the images required to tell the tale will vary greatly in quality, especially by modern photographic standards. While some images in this volume are not up to those digital standards, we have included them, as we feel they are an important element in telling the story.

DISTRIBUTION BY:

Europe
PGUK
63 Hatton Garden
London EC1N 8LE, England
Phone: 020 7061 1980 • Fax: 020 7242 3725
www.pguk.co.uk

Australia
Renniks Publications Ltd.
3/37-39 Green Street
Banksmeadow, NSW 2109, Australia
Phone: 2 9695 7055 • Fax: 2 9695 7355
www.renniks.com

Canada
Login Canada
300 Saulteaux Crescent
Winnipeg, MB, R3J 3T2 Canada
Phone: 800 665 1148 • Fax: 800 665 0103
www.lb.ca

TABLE OF CONTENTS

DEDICATION

By Arnie Beswick

TO EVELYN, MY DARLING WIFE IN HEAVEN. You were always there for me, and you faithfully supported me throughout my farming and racing careers. Even when times were tough, you never left my side. You were the one who got me through each and every day. You were the rock of this family and the one on whom we all depended. I miss you terribly.

TO MY FOUR DAUGHTERS AND THEIR FAMILIES. I know I missed many family dinners, birthday celebrations, and sporting events, but not a day goes by that I don't think or worry about you. You are my true success stories, and no one is more proud of each of you and all your many accomplishments than I am. I love you all dearly. And a special shout-out to my grandson Ryan. I am honored that you are following in my racing footsteps. Seeing you go down the track and win some races brings me such gratification. I am your biggest fan, and I'm so proud of you.

TO MY MOTHER IN HEAVEN. You have shaped my life from the time I was a small boy, and you will continue to do so until I see you in heaven. Thank you for instilling in me the importance of working hard and being passionate and for the courage to never give up no matter the obstacles. Despite the hardships encountered over the years, it was your influence that kept me strong.

TO DEAN. You have been a dear friend and big part of my life over the years. You are family to me. Thank you for taking the time to write this book. I'm humbled by the amount of time you dedicated and detail you've included. I'm especially touched knowing you worked with Evelyn on this endeavor. Although she didn't get the opportunity to read the final version of the book, it means the world to me that you involved her in the making.

TO THOSE (BOTH PAST AND PRESENT) WHO DEVOTED THEIR TIME, TALENTS, AND RESOURCES TO MAKE MY RACING CAREER POSSIBLE. The list of individuals, organizations, clubs, companies, and vendors is too numerous to call out and would fill many more pages of this book. Whether you provided parts and pieces; worked on the race car, truck, or trailer; sold merchandise; or drove to and from events, I appreciate your willingness to help, and I am forever indebted to you.

TO MY FANS. You have been loyal, supportive, and so very kind to me throughout my career. I am always so moved by the constant outpouring of love and appreciation in your cards and letters, emails, phone calls, and Facebook posts that I've received over the years. The effort that each of you make to reach out to me brings me pure joy, and I genuinely cherish each and every moment I get to spend with you. If I have put a smile on your face, please know that you have put an even bigger one on mine.

Thank you for taking the time to read this book. Each and every one of you have made an impact in my life. Words cannot express how truly blessed and eternally grateful I am.

Arnie "Farmer" Beswick

By Dean Fait

THIS BOOK IS DEDICATED TO EVELYN BESWICK. She passed away on November 11, 2019, while I was writing the chapters of this book that were around 1968. I'm sure I told her when she was alive, but I have to again say thank you to Evelyn for all of the photos, letters, and scrapbooks full or articles that she saved. Although this undertaking is a labor of love, I would have had a lot tougher job had she not taken the time to save all the related articles out of *Drag News* and, more importantly, *Drag World*. *Drag News* magazine was without a Midwest correspondent for several years. As Arnie's number-one fan and stalwart companion for 65-plus years, Evelyn saved all of the *Drag World* articles that provided a lot clearer picture of those years. Thank you, Evelyn. We miss you, Mom.

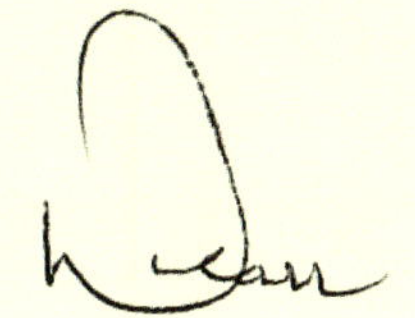

ACKNOWLEDGMENTS

The list of people to personally thank is long, so I will begin with the photographers and artists. Again, first and foremost, Evelyn took many of the photos in this book. Mike Garland, the current photographer for Cordova International Raceway, was the first one to say, "Yes." Then, there was Gary Beard. Longtime friend and fellow author, Don Keefe openly shared his great images and provided technical help. Mark and Laura Bruderle, former track photographer from Great Lakes Dragaway in Union Grove, Wisconsin, openly shared photos along with older images from Ray-Mar. A number of very early images came from the scrapbooks of the late Bob Slaymaker. There are promotional posters that were compliments of Ken Forster Jr. of reproracingposters.com. Thanks to Harlan Tiesman and Jim Wangers. Bob D'Olivo and the late Grey Villet supplied two photos that I colorized. Thanks to Bob Nelson, also known as "Slatts." We have Forrest Bond to thank for many images from Texas, not to mention the main cover photo, along with F. E. McKinzie for some Southern track photos. Brian Hatton was a great source for photos from 1964–1968. Many thanks go to the late Red Lawler, Dwight Garnhart, Robert Goldstein, Harry Pinkard, George Houraney, the late Jere Aldadeff, Joe Kerr, Jim Demmitt Jr., Jim Orloff, William Zinkhan, and the late Skip Norman. Laverne Zachary and Marvin T. Smith not only supplied some cool pictures, they told me interesting tidbits about the races that they attended. Ted Pappacena is another person who helped out beyond supplying photos. A thank you goes out to Jim Caputo, Brian Harmon, Mike Rutherford, Steve Reyes, John Asher, Marty Johnson, Dennis Scott, and Mark Van Osdol. Bill Blair was so very instrumental at showing his pictures of Arnie's return to racing in 1986. There's Mike Caretto, plus Roger and Judy Mac Zura who must be thanked along with Janette Holmes, Fred Simmons, Bill Vantuono, Chad Starbuck, Mike Kelm, Dave Bonaskiewich, Carrie Shenuk, Dennis Mothershed, and Arvid Svendsen.

There are a number of paintings in this book. Joel Naprstek, Tim Frederick, and James Ibusuki all must be thanked, not to mention my talented wife, Chrissie, for taking on my commission of the race between Arnie and Ronnie Sox.

Bret Kepner was a huge help. So were Ben Brown, Eric Carlson, Donnie Speer, Bill Stoermer, Charlie Carter, Tom Stephens, Rich Sawyer, Dave Boncosky, Bill Ege, Fred Coopman, Ed Abbott, Dave Jamison, Spencer Knox, Bob and Dawn Bartel, "Legal" Lee Smith, Don Bennett, Bill Wirges, Andy Perry, Marvin Panch, Gary and Glenn Dyer, Jim Wangers, Jim Andrews, Willie Harder, Fred Simmonds, Jim Mattison, Carl Brandt, Terry Kuchel, John "Woody" Bramm, Pete McCarthy, Bob "Super Duty" Lendman, James Renegar Jr., Bruce Larson, Paul Zazarine, Maurice Mauer, Larry Quinn, Frank Spittle, Dick Estevez, Randy Adler, Mark Kuykendall, Alan Ranz, Mike Guarise, Donnie Reeves, Craig Power, Ron Leek, Eric Larson, and Mike Garblik. Arnie's career wouldn't have been as successful as it was if it wasn't for competing against these legends: Richard Petty, Dick Brannan, "Jungle" Jim Liberman, Phil Bonner, Mr. Norm's Grand Spaulding Dodge, and the Chi-Town Hustler.

I certainly need to thank my proofreaders: Ken Moffett and my sister, Rachel.

Last but certainly not least, thanks to Wes Eisenschenk for giving me the opportunity to tell Arnie's story.

Thank you to all for helping!

CHAPTER 1

THE EARLY YEARS

The year 1930 was not very good in American history. The nation was entering the Great Depression after the stock market crash the previous year. On May 7 that same year, Arnold Wayne Beswick was born just west of the farming community of Morrison, Illinois. He was the first son of second-generation farmers Paul Raymond and Marie. Three years later, Arnie's younger brother, Jim, was born. As siblings, the brothers had their first taste of competition.

Raymond had polio and suffered from injuries that left him severely handicapped, which meant that Marie was saddled with the bulk of the farm chores. It also meant that as soon as they were old enough, Arnie (mostly) helped out with the seemingly endless daily chores. Jim played sports while he was in school. These chores, including herding the cows for milk (by hand at first) and feeding and caring for all of the other animals, helped the Beswick farm be self-sufficient. It was a common way of life in rural America, especially during the Great Depression.

Starting School with Mechanical Aptitude

Wind-up toys were a favorite pastime of Arnie as a small boy. After playing with them for a few weeks, his mom was a little more than disappointed when she found these Christmas gifts broken. How-

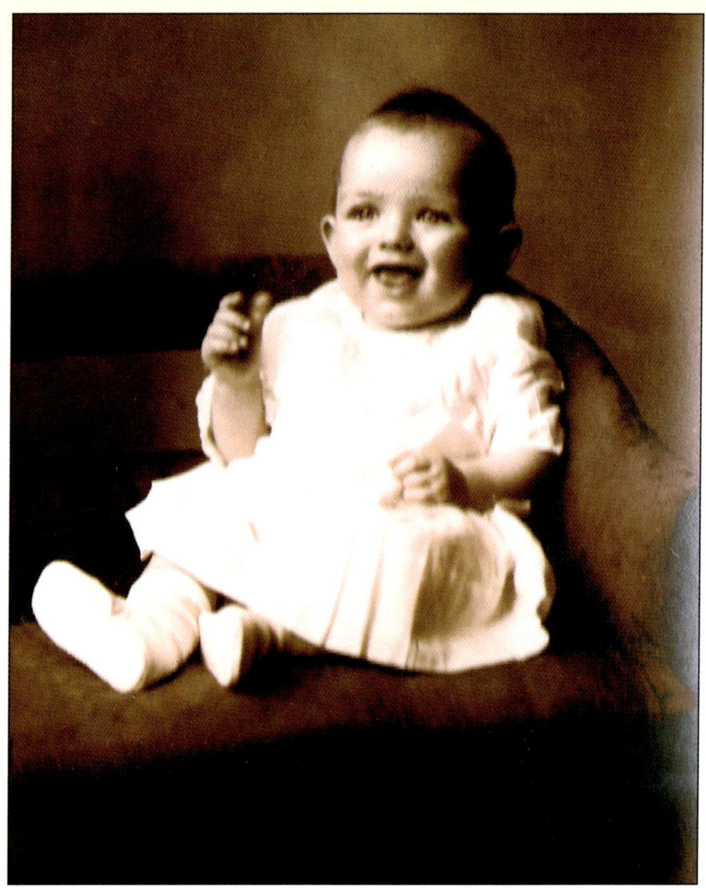

In one of the first photos ever taken of Arnold Wayne Beswick, he was probably 5 to 6 months old. He is wearing the traditional baby clothes of the day.

ever, she was amazed when Arnie fixed them again, showing aptitude with mechanical things at an early age.

Those of us who are old enough and grew up in rural America know that country kids received an education in one-room schoolhouses. Arnie's old schoolhouse still stands. He studied there from first through eighth grade with seven other students. When Arnie began his freshman year of high school in town, there were no buses to take him to school. Arnie recalled that the neighborhood parents shared carpooling or bus route duties until he was old enough to buy his first car.

Despite his disabilities, Raymond couldn't have been prouder of his young son. Here, Raymond and 2- or 3-year-old Arnie are on the farm.

Already a handsome young man, Arnie is in the correct farming attire while starting grade school. The ladies would say he was cute as a bug.

When this unknown professional portrait studio snapped this memory, Arnie was in second or third grade and 7 or 8 years old, and Jim was roughly a kindergartner.

The boys were just goofing around when Marie took this photo of her two sons. While Arnie admits that he often rode their horse, it's interesting that he's on the mechanical device while Jim isn't.

The brothers pose at home while dressed in their Sunday best. Arnie is around junior-high age and old enough to have one of his first suits, complete with necktie, while Jim had a few years to go.

Taken right around his junior or senior year, this photo was probably a little too informal to be used as a senior picture for the yearbook. It's still a keeper.

When Arnie entered his teenage years, the family tractor (a Farmall H) was in need of more power because of the increasing size of equipment. Arnie convinced his dad that he could remedy that, and Raymond gave the go-ahead.

Upon removal of the cylinder head, Arnie saw how choked up it was. He borrowed a little grinder and a few extra grindstones to open up and port match the intake and exhaust manifolds. He already knew that more compression couldn't hurt. He also had the head milled, taking off about 0.0075, before putting everything back together.

Naturally, all of this didn't happen in one day, and Raymond was eager for his son to be done because the tractor was needed for farm work. He kept after Arnie to hurry up. Once the red tractor was operational, the difference, according to Arnie, was "phenomenal."

"Before the engine work, the tractor had a hard time in third gear, especially in dirt that had a lot of clay," Arnie explained. "After the valve job and head work, the tractor flew over everything in that same gear. On level ground with the good black soil that is common to the area, they could even use fourth. That simple procedure alone was thought to have given the Farmall close to an additional 25 hp.

"From that point on, I was sold. I was going to tweak any motor I got my hands on to get a little more out of the stock configuration."

His First Car

While farm kids could obtain a driver's permit at age 14, Arnie got his driver's license at 15. His first car was an old four-door 1936 Chevy that was well used and pretty beat up. The previous owner had no respect for the old jalopy and had almost driven it into the ground. Raymond agreed to loan Arnie the money to buy it, taking the cost out of Arnie's farm wages. There was also money to be earned by bailing hay. Raymond was one of the few farmers in the immediate area who had a baler. Arnie was paid a penny per bale to stack them. It was extremely hard work.

The car was short-lived, as Arnie was still learning how to control one at higher speeds. The main incident that almost killed the car was when Arnie failed to negotiate a turn one night. He was traveling too fast when he came to a T in the road and hit ice. Rather than attempting a turn, he merely went straight, wrecking the car's front end. After it was fixed, he was still able to drive the car, but that incident and others made the car so rickety that the doors wouldn't stay closed on their own. The ever-present baling wire helped fix that until something more suitable was found.

The Second Car and a Growing Reputation

Arnie's next car was a hand-me-down from his parents. In 1947, Raymond decided that the family needed a newer car. When he found something newer, he gave the family's 1937 Plymouth to Arnie. With this car, Arnie developed a reputation as a fast driver. One of his favorite pastimes was to take the elevated railroad crossings and other cross streets to main roads at a good clip. His hope was that his passengers would hit their heads on the inside of the car's roof, just like a carnival ride. As his reputation grew, so did the list of friends who actually wanted to go on this roller-coaster ride.

Ed Abbott was Arnie's friend and neighbor who lived just up the road. He was on Arnie's carpool list. Ed was also on the staff of the high school newspaper. Almost 50 years later, he recalled Arnie's love for fast cars. As Ed put it, "The best place to be seated in a car that Arnie was driving was in the center of the front seat, close to the emergency brake!"

An Exciting Time in America

In 1948, Arnie graduated from Morrison High and had his picture taken with the rest of the class. It was published in the school newspaper. It was tradition for the senior class to list items that they were handing down to underclassmen. Arnie's name was the sixth one listed. It read: "ARNIE BESWICK – his careful driving to Merle Stralow."

The paper also listed some prophecies about what the graduating class members would accomplish. His classmates surely couldn't have known how accurate they were when the writers foretold that "Arnold 'Speed' Beswick—entered his hot rod in the annual race in California."

The year he graduated coincided not only with the first edition of *Hot Rod* magazine but also the founding of NASCAR. Late that year, General Motors produced 90-degree overhead-valve V-8s, first for Cadillac and then for Oldsmobile. Arnie began reading and studying *Hot Rod* and other car magazines, gleaning information that included tips and trends. The *Moline Dispatch* in Illinois carried all of the stock car race results, and that was the first section Arnie would read.

After graduation, there was always farmwork, but that wasn't enough income for Arnie, especially in the quiet of winter. One of his first jobs to supplement his income was working as a pinsetter at the Rock Falls bowling alley. This job was done by hand. He needed money to buy a new or newer car.

Arnie's First Brand-New Car

In 1949, Arnie began looking for a new or newer ride. The Plymouth was functional but hardly anything to be especially proud of, and the 201-ci

If you've ever bought a brand-new car off the showroom floor, you know the pride that Arnie had for his first new one. As was often the case, he spent extra money, optioning them up for resale. Fully loaded cars always brought more money when they went to the second owner, regardless if it was used for street or strip.

The appearance of Arnie's cars was always important, but never so much as his first. It's shown here complete with wheel covers (not just hubcaps) and fender skirts in the back.

engine wasn't big on performance, especially given Arnie's style of driving.

Cars that were exciting were the new Oldsmobiles equipped with their Rocket engines. They had 303-ci engines, and in 1949, they won six out of nine races at NASCAR events.

Arnie went to McEleny Motors in Clinton, Iowa, and ordered a dark blue, two-door 88, complete with the mighty Rocket engine and a Hydra-matic transmission. Gone was the need to shift gears for the 20-year-old Mr. Beswick. Arnie paid $828 for his first brand-new car.

Arnie immediately applied his hot rodding knowledge to his powerful new ride. He changed the jets on the carburetor, curved the distributor, advanced the cam, and added dual exhaust with lower-restriction glasspack mufflers to the car. Since he was already there, he decided to port match the exhaust manifolds as well. Arnie was now a force to be reckoned with on the local roads.

Thrills on the Highways

Arnie's new favorite thing to do, especially since nobody's car seemed as fast, was to come up behind an unsuspecting friend and literally push

The Mississippi Modified car club had its own cards. This is the front of Bob Slaymaker's card. (Photo Courtesy Bob Slaymaker)

The back of the card shows their good intentions as hot rodders. Notice how polite the card insinuates they were. Looking back, I'm sure they helped many a motorist who had a flat tire or battery problems. (Photo Courtesy Bob Slaymaker)

them down the highway. While he wouldn't dare do this randomly, his closer friends fell victim.

The late Bill Ege (pronounced Eggy) from the small town of Garden Plains, Illinois, remembered that his first highway encounter with Arnie went something like this:

"My girl and I were on our way to the Saddle Club in Cordova [Illinois]. It was raining, but we were still doing close to 80. I look in the mirror and there's a new Olds gaining on me. It kept getting closer and closer. I couldn't believe it when I felt the bump of his front bumper as it tapped my back one. The speedometer jumped as he actually started pushing me. Either because I floored it or he backed off, I managed to pull away from him. Still, the race was on. That went on until the girl I was with told me how scared she was, and we both slowed down. It turned out Arnie was going to the same place, and we all had a hi-ho time that night."

A few others received the treatment and more with the same interests. Together, the car enthusiasts around Morrison formed the "Mississippi Modifieds." It was Arnie's first car club.

Army Days: Drafted and Going Through Procedures

The Korean War began on June 25, 1950, and within a month, US troops were in place. In 1951, the Universal Military Training and Service Act was passed. It was a revision of the conscription (draft) method used for recruitment since the Revolutionary War. It lowered the age of eligibility, which was set during World War II at 21 years old, and now required males to register at 18½.

Arnie was eligible and was drafted. He was ordered to report to Chicago to begin his two-year tour of duty. He was first administered a battery of tests to determine his skill set. His scores were high enough that the US Army determined that he should go to Fort Sill in Lawton, Oklahoma, the home of the field artillery. His official start date as an E-1 (private) for basic training was September 18, 1951.

After only four weeks of basic training, and because the demand for soldiers in South Korea was so great, Arnie was sent to Japan for his Advanced Individual Training (AIT).

After another high score on the second army skills test, this one called the Military Occupational Specialty (MOS), Arnie decided that the medical field was where he'd like to be trained. The training

One last shot before boarding the plane for Japan. Arnie was all smiles, on top of the world, and ready for departure out of Fort Sill, Oklahoma.

Part of the primitive accommodations high on the hilltop known as Mt. Papasan. Papasan was a Chinese Communist Forces (CCF) stronghold just outside where the heaviest fighting took place. It was northeast of the area described as the "Iron Triangle."

The gang's all here. Arnie and some of the guys in his unit enjoy a little down time. Looking at the dress, it's thankfully not wintertime.

I found it funny that this photo was in less-than-perfect condition. Did jealousy come into play a few years after it was first taken? Evelyn joked that Arnie was all dolled up for a date with his girlfriend, Lois. They went together for several years. Arnie even let her use his car while he was overseas. He got his "Dear John" letter while in Korea.

Arnie and Dale Harvey (right) knew each other before army life. Harvey was from Morrison, Illinois. They went through all the steps together, ending up at the same base in Korea.

in 1951 was nowhere near what today's soldiers go through. In 1951, the training merely covered very basic first-aid procedures, again only lasting four weeks.

As is often typical during wartime, the army decided that Arnie was needed in a different area, and he was given his assignment as a 1576. Translated into English, he was a forward observer (FO) for the field artillery. His job from high atop his foxhole on what was known as "Mt. Papasan" was to provide grid coordinates to the artillery battery's fire direction control (FDC), directing it where to fire the artillery rounds. Consequently, the FOs definitely had a high level of danger. There was even some danger from our own troops' short rounds, which were shells that didn't go as far as they were supposed to.

Seeing this picture reminded me of an old army cadence that goes, "You're in the army now, You're not behind the plow, You're diggin' a ditch, You son of a . . . You're in the army now!"

Helping with Arnie's Never-Ending Passion

While there were certainly quiet days, at times battles lasted hours. During the lulls in the fighting and while he was off duty, Arnie relaxed by poring over the car magazines of the day. Arnie told it this way:

"We didn't have much to do other than watch for enemy movement, so I'd asked my mother to find and send over as many hot rod- or motor-type magazines as she could. A lot of time sitting there in that bunker in Korea was spent sifting through all the [pause] reading and rereading all the hot rod and motor magazines that my mother used to send me."

On June 23, 1953, Corporal Beswick was released from his active tour of duty, a mere month and two days before the armistice was signed between the warring countries. After Arnie returned to the United States, he was assigned to Fort Riley, Kansas, in preparation to be honorably discharged from military service. Upon returning to his home in Morrison, he was transferred to the Army Reserve out of Sterling, Illinois.

Returning Home and the Next New Car

As Arnie's time in the US Army was coming to an end, he decided it was time for a new car. Like he'd done with his '50, Arnie researched what the hot ticket would be. It was still an Oldsmobile. The numbers were impressive, as the cars had won 10 of 19 NASCAR events in 1950 and 20 out of 41 in 1952. Another major factor in his choice of cars for 1953 was the fact that during that year's Daytona Beach Speedweek, a half-dozen new, specially prepared Oldsmobiles completely dominated the flying-mile competition.

While still stationed at Fort Riley, Kansas, Arnie ordered a new '53. Like he had done with his '50, Arnie went to McEleny Motors in Clinton, Iowa. However, this time he ordered the upgraded Super 88, again with a Hydra-matic transmission. The displacement hadn't changed since the Rocket V-8s were introduced. In 1952, Oldsmobile added a 4-barrel carburetor, increasing the advertised horsepower from 130 to 160 in 1952, and 165 for 1953. One thing that didn't change for Arnie was the color, which was dark blue. The company

Arnie was always proud of his cars, and the 1953 Oldsmobile was no exception. Once again, the car wasn't without all the options, including the fender skirts that matched the roof and the full wheel covers instead of just hubcaps.

called it *Serge Blue* in 1949 and 1950; in 1953 it was called *Baltic Blue*.

Corporal Beswick went on leave and went home to trade in the '50 and take delivery of the new car. After he did so and was on his way back to the base, driving through Kansas, another vehicle pulled out in front of him. The collision was unavoidable. Luckily, the car was still drivable, and Arnie took it to the local Oldsmobile dealer to have it fixed. Thankfully, an army buddy was able to get him back to base so that Arnie didn't go AWOL. The '53 was fixed by the time Beswick was honorably discharged, and he returned home to rule the highways with the new car.

A New Girlfriend

When his two-year army stint was complete in early summer of 1953, Arnie returned home to the farm. Work was always waiting there. However, he needed extra income to help make the payments on his car. During the winter months and slow times on the farm, Arnie worked at Bennett Box Company in Clinton, Iowa. His job was to deliver the raw materials to the various work stations. Working there at one of the stations was a very cute young woman named Evelyn Balk. She asked if Arnie ever went roller skating, to which he replied, "Yes."

That night, Evelyn, accompanied by her roommate at that time, drove her father's 1953 Oldsmobile to the rink. True to his word, Arnie, an avid skater at the time, was there.

Knowing Arnie, he was probably the fastest thing on skates as well as in a car, especially when a string of skaters whipped him (roller derby style) at Mach speed to the point of his inability to make the corner at the other end of the rink. That night, he made it a point to ask this gorgeous girl for a skate or two.

They both left the skating rink about the same time. Arnie, being an observant car-hawk, noticed that the car Evelyn was driving was the same make and model as his. Arnie followed her home. There's conjecture about whether the sparkle in Arnie's eye was from Evelyn or that Oldsmobile. When asked, Evelyn laughed and said, "The Olds." Arnie smiled and said, "Both."

Evelyn had been warned by her roommate and knew of Arnie's widespread reputation as a fast driver. She admitted to really stepping the *go* pedal down on her dad's Oldsmobile to the extreme on that particular night. Evelyn was driving so fast that her roommate was not only worried about her driving but also the headlights behind them!

Arnie fondly remembered, "Her roommate calmed down when she found out [that] it was me in the mirror. We chatted a little upon our arrival at their apartment.

"After that, as I made my rounds, keeping the raw lumber supplied to the various stations, I would frequently look her way through the mill, and catch her looking my way more than once. That definitely made me stop at her station more often than the rest to make sure she was well stocked with wood to make her quota. It was at that point that I also decided I had better check this out further."

Drag Racing for the Mississippi Modified Club

Already by 1953, the quarter mile had been the established distance for a drag race. This was due to the precedent set by the California-based races and events like Half Day, Illinois. Additionally, airports that were used had long enough runways to safely run a car for 1,320 feet. There were no strips yet in the Midwest, as Half Day closed after the fall of 1953. The performance enthusiasts needed a place to race.

Bill Ege explained how the club members fixed this problem.

"Bob Slaymaker and I decided we needed a quarter mile somewhere close to home," he said. "We went up on Route 84, just south of Fulton, Illinois, where US30 intersects. We measured off a quarter mile, and we'd brought paint with us to mark the start and finish lines. Arnie and all the rest of us used it quite a bit. We'd go there at night, especially after we'd made carburetor or other engine changes.

"The only problem was that Bob and I weren't too smart. We'd laid it out on a Sunday morning. Needless to say, all of our Dutch neighbor farmers were headed to Fulton for church. The word and wonder went around. They wondered what Ege and Slaymaker were doing, walking up and down the highway on a Sunday morning."

RACING SHOWROOM STOCK

While the Mississippi Modifieds from Clinton, Iowa, and Fulton and Morrison, Illinois, and other car clubs from surrounding communities undoubtedly raced on quiet highways, there were no safe places to race, let alone freedom from occasional dealings with the law. That was until Arnie and all the other performance enthusiasts heard about what is known as the first nationally advertised drag race.

This is one of the flyers for Half Day Speedway. (Photo Courtesy Ken Forster Jr., reproracingposters.com)

Organized Drag Racing Comes to the Midwest

The Half Day Drags took place on a 1/2-mile-long strip of concrete located on an abandoned airstrip 40 miles north of Chicago. It had been an outlying satellite airfield used by nearby Glenview Naval Air Station during World War II. It was called Allendale Field or Libertyville Airport. All reports list 1952 and 1953 as the years of operation.

The Founders

It was none other than the three Granatelli Brothers who started it all. Joe was the oldest, Andy was the middle child, and Vince was the youngest.

Their story began in the Chicago metro area when they purchased a Texaco station and renamed it "Andy's Super Service."

After a burglary, in which thieves stole every last thing out of their building, they had to start over. Instead of just selling gas and doing repairs on regular passenger cars, they renamed their company Grancor and devoted their attention to selling high-performance items, such as superchargers and building Fordillacs, which were made by stuffing the new Cadillac V-8s into 1949 and 1950 Fords.

Andy was the promoter of the three, and Half Day Drags was his brainchild. He thought if they had a place to test their goods and the cars that they'd helped build, their business would grow. Consequently, he leased the abandoned strip from the government.

Based on the popularity of these races, their business grew. When the races opened and word got out, racers and spectators clogged up every surrounding road. It was so busy that it was necessary to run the cars four wide to ensure that everyone got their time trials in.

A Sponsor and Rules to Race By

The Granatelli brothers did business with Arnold Maremont. Maremont Automotive Products put up the money for trophies and cash purses. If you won your class, you had a choice of a $25 savings bond (purchased for $18.75) or a trophy. The Maremont Company purchased the timing equipment, and some key people who will be mentioned later came up with the rules and regulations for this event.

The Automobile Timing Association of America (ATAA) was founded as part of its public relations campaign. The ATAA became the sanctioning body in the Midwest and Eastern states. The safety regulations and competition classes suggested by the ATAA were similar to those of the NHRA, which was founded in 1951.

Arnie Remembers

In the mid-1990s, Arnie had this to say about racing at Half Day:

"The first actual sanctioned drag race that I actually got involved in was when I went to Half Day, Illinois, with my Oldsmobile," he said. "They only had a class for stock cars and a class for modified [hot rods], a class for dragster- and roadster-type things. Motorcycles had their own class too. As I remember, there were only a total of like six classes that raced."

Arnie continued, "Now, I had my little Olds running quite well, and Oldsmobile was pretty much on the top of the heap for performance cars those years. Combined with that, I probably read the

The Mississippi Modified club members gathered around Arnie's '53 after taking off the front bumper to get rid of weight. Half Day's ATAA rules allowed this.

Arnie's Oldsmobile is in the staging lanes. He was just one of many who found this first outlet for the need for speed.

Arnie is getting ready to make a pass. These first nationally advertised drag races obviously weren't only popular with racers, as is evident from all of the spectators lining the strip.

flagman better than the next guy. Anyway, my first race I managed to come home with a first-place trophy.

"That sparked my fire even more with playing with cars and just turned me on when it came to getting out there and just competing against the next guy."

The significance of Half Day was tremendous. It spurred the opening of dedicated racetracks that soon sprouted up.

1954–1955: Years of New Things, Including Another New Car

The year 1954 began with another new Oldsmobile for Arnie. The cubic-inch displacement had been raised from 303 to 324. The 1954 models were 2 inches longer, but more importantly to Arnie, the advertised horsepower jumped to 185 with a 4-barrel carburetor. There was a big departure in color from dark blue, as this new car was white with a green roof and quarter panels. It immediately received the Beswick tuning improvements to keep his reputation of dominating the roads and highways alive.

Married Life Begins

Arnie and Evelyn were married on July 1, 1954. They went to Kansas on their honeymoon and vis-

This is Arnie and Evelyn's wedding picture. You have to admit—Arnie's tie is pretty cool.

The cute couple next to the 1954 Oldsmobile are dating. Arnie's Oldsmobile had two different paint schemes. Like this photo shows, it was white with green quarter panels and roof at first. Later, Arnie had the car repainted and reversed the two colors.

The wedding party (from left to right) was Arnie's brother Jim, Arnie, Evelyn, and Evelyn's sister Lois. The photo looks like it was taken at the farm.

ited several of Arnie's army buddies whom he served with in Korea. Evelyn continued to work at Bennett Box until it closed.

One of Arnie and Evelyn's first apartments was a small three-room place in Morrison, Illinois. Perhaps "small" does not describe it well enough—it was necessary to go through the bedroom to get to the kitchen. They only tolerated this for three or four months before moving to Fulton, Evelyn's hometown.

After Bennett Box, Evelyn found a job at the Dutch Boy truck stop in Fulton as a bookkeeper and part-time waitress. A positive aspect of taking this job was the availability of an apartment directly above her place of work. Arnie and Evelyn took advantage of the opportunity.

The World Series of Drag Racing Is Born

As summer gave way to fall, news of a big upcoming drag race spread. While promotion began only shortly before the event itself, ESPN's Bret Kepner mentioned newspapers and niche magazines, such as *Honk* and *Rodding and Restyling*, that told about the upcoming World Series of Drag Racing. While newspaper ads were also purchased, it was almost too little, too late.

Arnie explained the event's importance to him.

"In late 1954, we started hearing about this big race down in Lawrenceville [Illinois]. The more I learned about it, the more I knew I had to be there. It was my whole life late that year. No matter what it took, I was going to participate."

Dave Jamison, another participant of that first

Arnie at 24 years old stands next to his pride and joy with his class C/Stock and number on the window. (Photo Courtesy Beswick Archive, Courtesy Bob Slaymaker)

Arnie's '54 at the starting line of the first World Series. A good tailwind always helps the elapsed times. (Photo Courtesy Beswick Archive, Courtesy Bob Slaymaker)

Arnie leaves the line at the historic race. (Photo Courtesy Beswick Archive, Courtesy Bob Slaymaker)

I'm not sure if time slips were given to each individual driver, but the chalkboard kept the racers updated with performances. Notice that Arnie's number is not posted here. (Photo Courtesy Beswick Archive, Courtesy Bob Slaymaker)

Thought to be Jim Verdon's supercharged dragster in the foreground, Arnie's car sits in the background. (Photo Courtesy Beswick Archive, Courtesy Bob Slaymaker)

The first Green Monster appeared in 1952. It was a three-wheeled dragster powered by an Oldsmobile 6-cylinder engine and painted with leftover green tractor paint. Named the first time out, the announcer, Ed Piasczik (Paskey), more or less joked, "Okay folks, here it comes, The Green Monster." It stuck to all Arfons's creations. This car, built in 1953, was Green Monster 2. It was 20 feet long. Notice Arnie's car sandwiched in between two others. (Photo Courtesy Beswick Archive, Courtesy Bob Slaymaker)

Fred Lorenzen later went on to achieve fame in the NASCAR world. Arnie was a big fan. Here's his Fordillac at that first World Series. (Photo Courtesy Beswick Archive, Courtesy Bob Slaymaker)

The trophies are all lined up on display. Judging from the way the tablecloth is billowing, this picture must have been shot the same day as the one on page 21 with the flag straight out. (Photo Courtesy Beswick Archive, Courtesy Bob Slaymaker)

World Series, said, "I got a phone call from a friend who lived in Rockford. He asked if I was going down to this big race they were having in Lawrenceville. I told him I hadn't heard about it. When he told me that Art Arfons was going to be there, I knew I had to get down there."

Arnold Maremont, the Chicago manufacturer who helped bankroll the Half Day Drags, promoted this first two-day race. Held on October 1 and 2, it was sponsored and governed by the ATAA. The main organizer was Jim Lamona. A 1/2-mile-long taxi apron was used on George Field, the airport at Lawrenceville. That particular location was selected because of its long, smooth concrete surfaces. Despite the lateness of the publicity, the race attracted about 350 competitors and 7,000 spectators. After it was over, the event reportedly received widespread newspaper coverage.

Art Arfons took top honors with his *Green Monster II*. He was clocked at 132.35 mph and claimed the Maremont Speed Trophy and a $1,000 scholarship. Another Illinois driver, Fred Lorenzen, went on to achieve NASCAR fame.

Arnie did well and went on to win the SC Class in his Oldsmobile with a speed of 83.33 mph.

Strips Open Closer to Home

One of the more unique drag strips that was within reach of Arnie was in Seneca, Illinois. The Illinois Valley Idlers car club sponsored 1/8-mile drag races here. They used the paved streets of a surplus World War II shipyard housing development. The demolished houses didn't matter to them, but the abandoned concrete street sure did. A short season took place in 1954 and a full season followed in 1955. While it lasted, it was a popular place for spectators and drivers, routinely drawing more than 150 cars.

Although it was farther away, there was also a makeshift 1/8-mile strip in Ipava, Illinois, that was within driving distance for Arnie.

When it first opened in 1954, one of the first purpose-built drag strips in the area (as well as in the whole state of Illinois) was in Oswego. The problem during that first year of existence was that it wasn't paved.

1955 and More Firsts

On January 13, Arnie and Evelyn become parents when their first daughter, Arnette Gail, was

Arnie and another racer leaves the line, presumably at the first NHRA Nationals. (Photo Colorization by Dean Fait)

born. Kids can change daily life forever, and it did, especially for Evelyn.

On March 4, 1955, the very first issue of *Drag News* was released. Since most of the organized racing was taking place in Southern California, it made sense that the magazine was published there. This newspaper would come to be known as the racers' Bible.

Page 1 of the July 22 issue (number 10) ran a story promoting the second annual running of the World Series under the headline "ATAA World Series – Aug. 17-21." It went on to say that more than 500 hot-rodders from coast to coast were expected to compete for awards in speed, engineering, and styling. The article announced that there were more than 25 different classifications, which were determined by the weight of the car and cubic-inch displacement. One change for the 1955 event was that instead of using a taxiway, a mile-long runway would be utilized.

"The availability this year of a 5,200-foot unobstructed runway will enable us to accommodate safely the fastest hot rods now being built," said ATAA director Bob Wolfson.

Arnie wouldn't have missed this race for the world, and once again, he won his class.

The Start of a Family in a New House

Another first happened when Arnie's father, Raymond, decided to build a house for his son and daughter-in-law on the family property. This would be their home for many years. Along with the rent-free house, Arnie's father paid him $100 a month to work on the farm.

The First NHRA Nationals

Drag News didn't even report the upcoming event in time, so word spread from different sources. After the fact, reporters bragged about the first NHRA Nationals in the September 30 edition. Other periodicals undoubtedly told of the very first event that was to be held at the end of September. The dates were from September 29 to October 2.

About 1,000 participants in more than 30 classes were expected with extra incentive from Detroit automotive manufacturers. Chevrolet, Dodge, Plymouth, Nash, Mercury, Chrysler and Desoto offered new complete engines to the cars setting the fastest time that ran with their powerplants. The article said that merchandise and trophies in excess of $10,000 had been donated.

The next biweekly issue of *Drag News* published on September 14 told about the weather and the surface issues. Rain stopped all the racing late on Saturday afternoon and completely for Sunday. Apparently, the runway surface was a lot rougher than expected and "the same concrete surface afforded starting traction heretofore unheard of. Drivers quickly changed their techniques in getting off the line in an effort to keep the various drivetrain components together. There was a lot of carnage in the way of rear ends, transmissions, and even engines." One dip was so bad that a racer named Calvin Rice actually went completely airborne. Officials suspended activities that afternoon and evening and brought in a paving crew to fix the huge dip.

Lo and behold, the very first name of the winners on page 8 is Arnold Beswick. His 1954 Oldsmobile had taken Class B honors with a speed of exactly 80 mph. It was the perfect way to end the year!

Closer to home, property had been purchased for a track and very early construction had begun just 20 minutes from the Beswick farm.

Class champions were honored in Great Bend's auditorium on Saturday night prior to the rainout of Sunday's final runs. Arnie is fifth from the right in the back row.

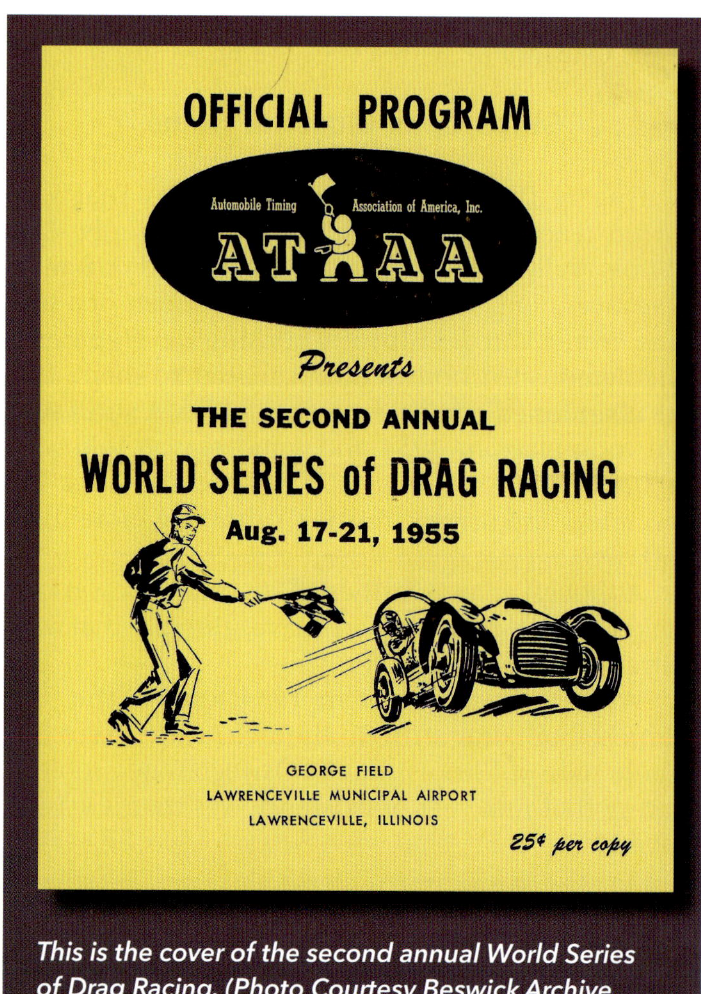

This is the cover of the second annual World Series of Drag Racing. (Photo Courtesy Beswick Archive, Courtesy Bob Slaymaker)

1956–1957 and a Switch in Car Companies

As the pages of the calendar turned and the weather began warming up, Arnie started hearing about the next hot ticket. Surprisingly, it wasn't with Oldsmobile anymore. Hudsons had taken away a lot of the dominance on the NASCAR tracks. The more he read, the more he believed that Dodge was the way to go.

Dodge had developed a special car, built for the roundy-rounders. One hundred of these special Coronets, called the D-500-1, were built to comply with circle-track rules. Not only was the engine a hemispherical-head version, the 315-ci powerplant came with a unique full-race camshaft, lifters, and pushrods; two 4-barrel carburetors; a dual-point ignition system; and pistons. Listed at 9.25:1 for the compression ratio, the D-500-1 was factory rated at a whopping 285 bhp.

There were other special things about the cars that didn't matter to

This Dodge advertisement was designed by Jim Wangers. He later became well-known in Pontiac circles, working closely with them during his time with the McManus, John & Adams ad agency. Wangers stated in his book, Glory Days, that this ad was a significant breakthrough because it used the "car talk" of the new generation of enthusiasts. The agency's copywriters were difficult to persuade.

The only thing that outwardly showed that it was a special car was these emblems, which were on both the hood and trunk.

In front of Arnie and Evelyn's brand-new house is the brand-new D-500-1. As he liked to do, the car was ordered loaded with options, including wheel covers and not just hubcaps. Another option readily found in the day was the white-wall tires.

Arnie. For example, it had stiffer springs and shocks as well as brakes that were also used on the police packaged vehicles.

Arnie went to the local Dodge dealer, Schuler Motors, which recently closed, and together with Eddie, the dealership owner, they figured out how to order one of these special cars.

The late Fred Coopman was a longtime friend and often crew chief for Arnie. He remembered the car vividly, as he was an owner later on.

"That car was one of the first Super Stockers to go over 100 mph in the quarter mile," he said. "It was very fast. But there again, it seemed like it was breaking something all the time. The minute you had one problem solved, something else would break, but it did run! The beauty part of it was that it was a Hemi and had a short stroke like a Chevy. It had those Hemi heads on it that breathed better than the human body!"

Spencer Knox, a lifelong friend of Arnie's, talked about the maintenance that the Dodge needed.

"One of my first trips to the drag strip was in 1956 when Arnie had the Dodge and the Oldsmobile. We were going to Oswego this particular Sunday. Evelyn drove the Oldsmobile, while Arnold was in the Dodge. We got about 5 miles or so away from the track and Arnold pulled off the side of the road under some shade trees. I wondered if something was broken, but all he was doing was setting the valves. He'd probably set them four or five times at home but here we were doing it again."

The car was unbeatable if it didn't break, which as Arnie remembered too, it often did. The worst, yet most memorable time was traveling down to Lawrenceville for the World Series. The race was held from August 22 to 26, now boasting that 1,000 hot-rodders would be there.

"We towed the Dodge down behind the Olds," Arnie explained. "During a time-trial session, I managed to break the Dodge's transmission. In those days, we didn't have any spare parts, so I was out of the running. I went and asked the officials if I could enter my Olds. They told me it was too late to enter another car, but that I could take the entry from the Dodge and put the Olds in its place. That's what I did. By now, the Olds had been moved down in class, I think it was in C Stock. But luck was with me and I won my class again, running with my 1954 Oldsmobile."

According to the following year's World Series program, Arnie's official speed was 89.463 mph.

A New Track Close to Home

In 1955, the drag strip just outside of Oswego, Illinois, had been paved, and Arnie went there when time allowed. It was just under 100 miles away, and back then there was no interstate highway to shorten travel time.

There were always chores to do on the farm, and for the most part, that was Arnie's job. Arnie's father thought that racing was foolish and hated that his son did it, so Arnie often just didn't tell him where he was going.

Spencer explained the problems of racing and farming.

"We'd get home from Oswego at about 9:30 or 10 p.m.," he said. "Arnold still had to do his chores. I didn't like to get involved too often, as it was kind of tough finding a black cow in the middle of the night with a flashlight. Of course, it'd be 11 p.m. when chores were finally finished. Then Arnold's father would always wonder why there wasn't much milk when he milked them at 8 a.m. the next morning."

Quad City Dragway

Arnie was ecstatic when construction was completed and Quad City Dragway opened on Labor Day weekend in 1956. The new quarter-mile strip was only 15 to 20 minutes away from the farm. It

The Dodge experienced transmission problems at the 1956 World Series in Lawrenceville. The rules required the removal of hubcaps or wheel covers.

One More Try with Dodge

Arnie's 1954 Oldsmobile is out in front of a newer Chevrolet at Quad City Dragway. (Photo Courtesy Grey Villet, Colorization by Dean Fait)

Despite the breakage issues, the D-500-1 was so potent that Arnie decided to give Dodge another try in 1957. Dodge appeared to have the most powerful car when it took a 354-ci Hemi engine out of the 300B and stuffed it into a Club Coupe. Arnie went back to Schuler Motors, and together they placed an order for a 1957 Dodge D-501.

Lee Smith, a Quad City native who later went on to have success racing Mopars, bought the car shortly after Arnie sold it to another party. Lee kept it the longest, finally selling it in early 2019. This is what Lee had to say about it:

"The '57 D-501 was another rare specialty car just like the '56, but it had more things special about it," he said. "There was the Chrysler engine with the dual quads, a Chrysler close-ratio 3-speed transmission, which you could hardly shift, heavy-duty suspension, Chrysler brakes, and other things the black car didn't have. I remember seeing it run. It turned low 14s, which was fast for the day. The announcers at the track all went wild about the car since it was so loud."

now meant that he could keep his dad happy and still feed the need for speed. It was there that he met others with the same passion, forming many friendships and sometimes rivalries that would last a lifetime.

The new drag strip was created by Bob and Don Bartel, from Moline, Illinois, a Moline police officer named Keith Cordell, and a somewhat silent partner named Kenny Moore from the Quad Cities. In the late summer of 1955, the group bought land from a farmer a few miles north of the tiny town of Cordova, Illinois. Most of the work was done in the first part of 1956. It was reported that $60,000 was spent in total to put in the roughly 4,000-foot strip, along with everything else needed to race. The name, Quad City Dragway, was used to show proximity to the greater metropolitan area that consisted of Davenport and Bettendorf on the Iowa side of the Mississippi River and Rock Island and Moline on the Illinois side.

In the spring of 2019, Bob Bartel's wife, Dawn, remembered Arnie like it was yesterday.

"Right from the start, Arnie was always there," she said. "He almost never missed a weekend, even when he didn't really have enough money to enter, he still raced. It was everything to him."

Against his father's advice, Arnie went ahead and "frivolously" lettered the car. This photo was taken in front of Schuler Motors with the owner, Eddie, and that year's trophies piled on the car.

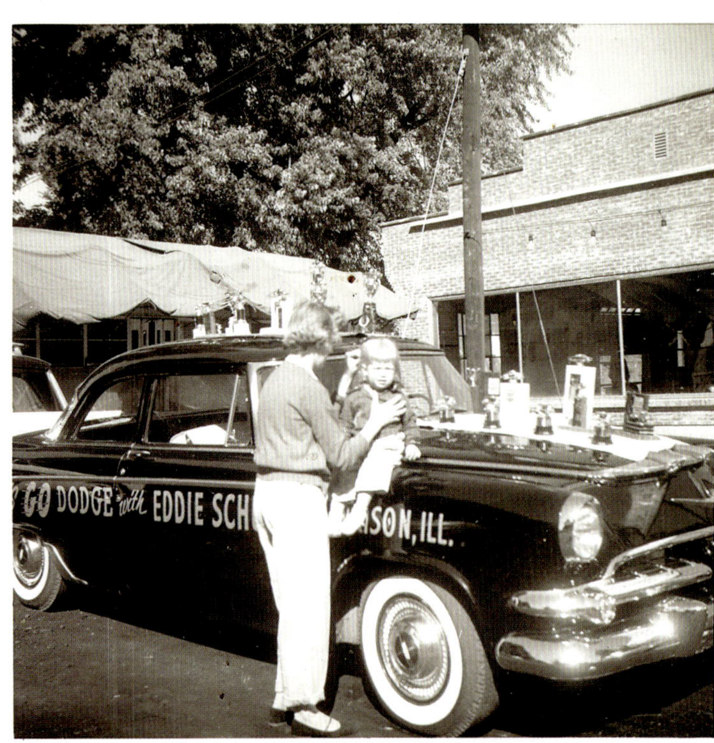

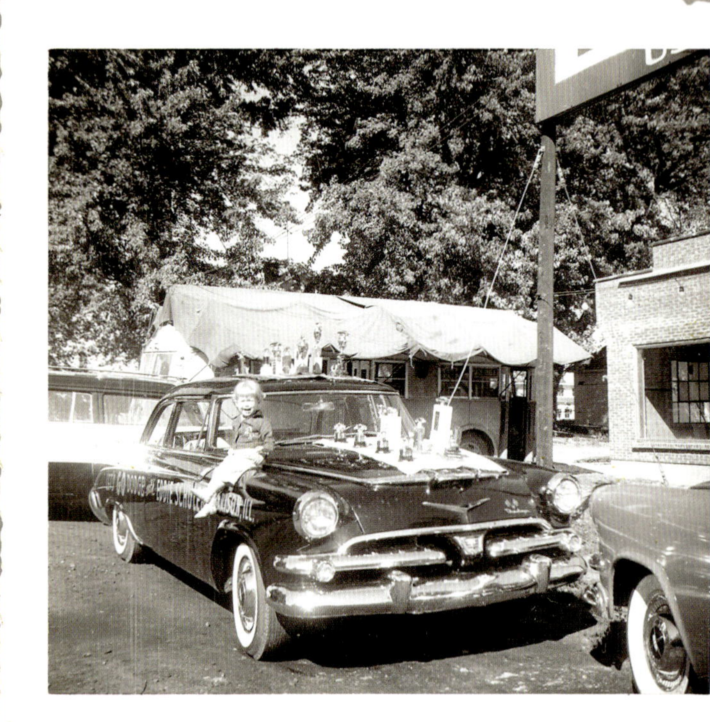

During the same photo shoot, Evelyn set the 21-month-old Arnette on the car. She wasn't happy about it at all!

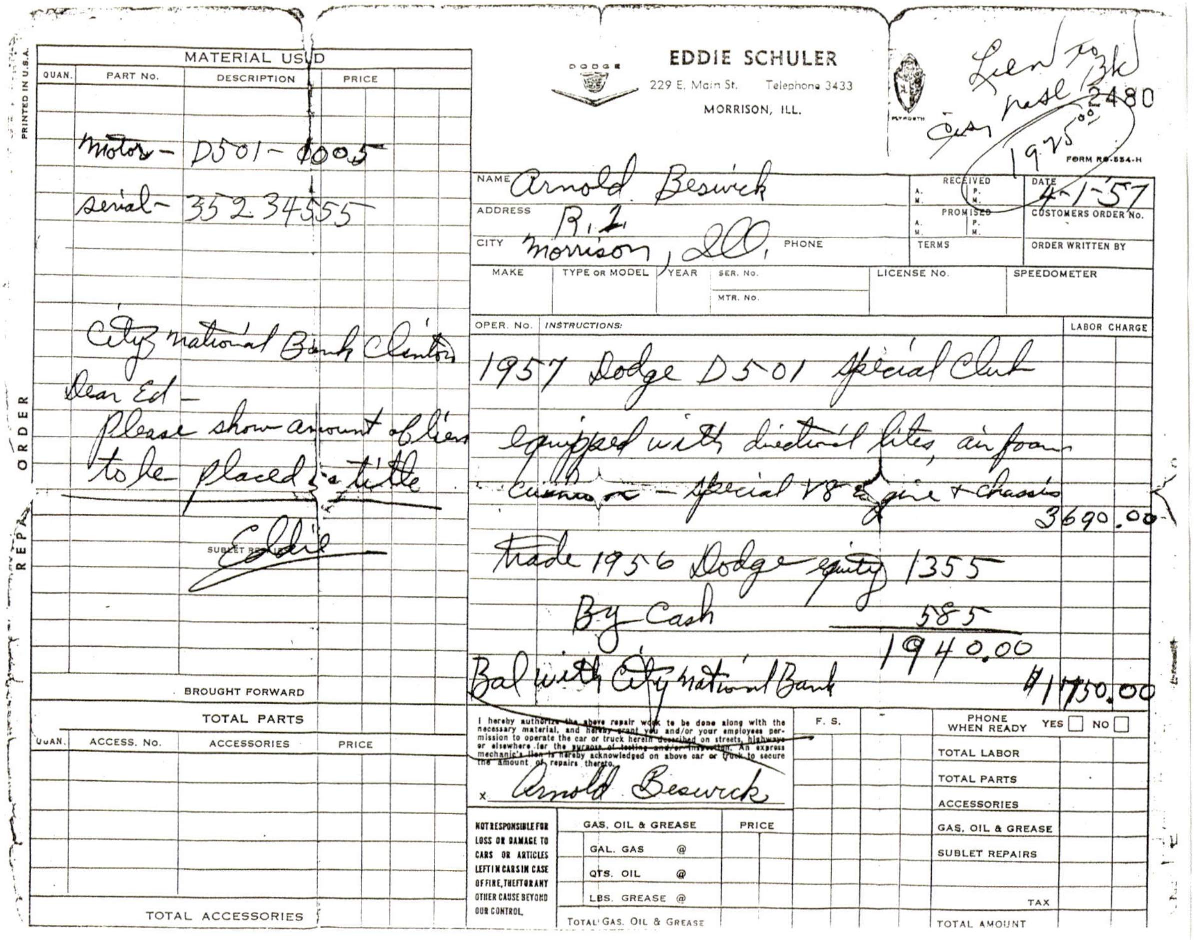

EDDIE SCHULER
229 E. Main St. Telephone 3433
MORRISON, ILL.

Lien to Bk
Gas need 2480
1925.00

FORM R6-554-H

NAME Arnold Beswick
ADDRESS R. 1
CITY Morrison, Ill.
PHONE
DATE 4-1-57
RECEIVED
PROMISED
TERMS
CUSTOMERS ORDER No.
ORDER WRITTEN BY
MAKE | TYPE or MODEL | YEAR | SER. No. | MTR. No. | LICENSE No. | SPEEDOMETER

MATERIAL USED
QUAN. | PART No. | DESCRIPTION | PRICE

motor – D501 – 1005
serial – 35234555

City national Bank Clinton
Dear Ed –
Please show amount of lien to be placed on title
Eddie

SUBLET REPAIRS

OPER. No. | INSTRUCTIONS: | LABOR CHARGE

1957 Dodge D501 Special Club
equipped with directional lites, air foam cushions – special V8 engine + chassis — 3690.00
trade 1956 Dodge equity 1355
By Cash 585
1940.00
Bal with City national Bank $1750.00

BROUGHT FORWARD
TOTAL PARTS

I hereby authorize the above repair work to be done along with the necessary material, and hereby grant you and/or your employees permission to operate the car or truck herein described on streets, highways or elsewhere for the purpose of testing and/or inspection. An express mechanic's lien is hereby acknowledged on above car or truck to secure the amount of repairs thereto.
X Arnold Beswick

F. S.
PHONE WHEN READY YES ☐ NO ☐

QUAN. | ACCESS. No. | ACCESSORIES | PRICE

TOTAL ACCESSORIES

NOT RESPONSIBLE FOR LOSS OR DAMAGE TO CARS OR ARTICLES LEFT IN CARS IN CASE OF FIRE, THEFT OR ANY OTHER CAUSE BEYOND OUR CONTROL.

GAS, OIL & GREASE | PRICE
GAL. GAS @
QTS. OIL @
LBS. GREASE @
TOTAL GAS, OIL & GREASE

TOTAL LABOR
TOTAL PARTS
ACCESSORIES
GAS, OIL & GREASE
SUBLET REPAIRS
TAX
TOTAL AMOUNT

PRINTED IN U.S.A.

The D-501 was an expensive car. A new Corvette was $600 less. Even after all these years, Arnie's signature hasn't changed much.

Lee Smith owned the D-501 at the time this photo was taken in 1996.

The powerful Hemi had unique air cleaners.

This is your view when sitting down low behind the wheel.

This was the only aspect that made the D-501 stand out with the hood closed. Lee said that Arnie didn't want to advertise what the car really was, so he took the emblem off. When he got the car, he had a hard time finding the correct emblem due to their rarity.

The World Series Moves to Quad City Dragway

Bob Bartel's involvement with drag racing didn't just begin with the building of one of the early purpose-built drag strips in Illinois. According to two sources, Bret Kepner and Dave Jamison, it was Bartel and Jim Lamona who had a hand in coming up with the rules for the ATAA in 1953 at Half Day. Bob was instrumental in coming up with the Lawrenceville location for the first three years of the Series.

Unfortunately, in 1957, Lawrenceville couldn't be used. The sanctioning body's insurance company wanted guardrails along the sides of the surface used for racing. The city refused to pay for this expensive addition. Consequently, while it took some convincing and some repaving, Bartel brought the World Series to Quad City Dragway that year.

Second Verse, Same as the First

The story was the same as the previous year when Arnie's new car, the D-501, broke. Arnie again had to take the entry from the Dodge and put the Oldsmobile in its place. Still, the results were the same, and the trusty 3-year-old Oldsmobile proved to be just that.

Arnie took home a class win, and this time the car was in S/C (C Stock). He won the eliminations with a speed of 81.59 mph with a best speed of 88.06 and elapsed time of 16.15. Arnie would not buy another Dodge for 1958.

Already in 1956, Pontiac (under new leadership from Bunkie Knudsen) was trying to gain sales in the youth market. People like Arnie were exactly the target audience.

Despite the problems, both Dodges won races, as is evident here.

1958 and Something Better

It was blatantly obvious, even to a blind man, that Dodge would not be the way to go in the immediate future. The Dodges were performers, that was for certain, but they were meant for a different arena. Arnie had learned that a car designed to run 500 miles wide open would use different parts than a car that was only designed to go a quarter of a mile as quickly as possible.

The D-500-1 had been fine, but Arnie was dissatisfied and disappointed with the current 1957 Dodge with its beefy frame, big Chrysler brakes, and suspension. After all, as has been said, "Brakes don't make a car go any faster."

Consequently, Arnie put extra effort into finding something better for the upcoming season. He knew about Pontiac's increase in performance levels for 1957. Already more than a few of the NASCAR drivers had switched to the once-stodgy company.

Arnie read articles and talked with people about the flying-mile competition on Daytona Beach. Apparently, even a regular Joe could run on the sand there to get flying-mile results and times for street cars. There were other performance tests done on public roads with even more common folk, such as housewife Vicky Wood, that also were very encouraging. Undoubtedly, Arnie daydreamed or hoped (even if it took a miracle) that he would get a chance to run wide open on that stretch of sand or around one of those Southern tracks.

Arnie drove the short distance to the closest local Pontiac dealer, which was located in Prophetstown, Illinois. He talked to the owner about

The Automobile Manufacturers Association (AMA) banned promotion of racing or anything to do with it. That prompted ads like this, where housewife Vicky Wood does the safe passing test in a Pontiac.

How could Arnie not be happy that he'd ordered a new Chieftain when ads like this were created?

The original sales invoice (reproduced below) shows a RETAIL INSTALLMENT CONTRACT from Associates, filled out by Arnold W. Beswick of RFD-1, Morrison, Illinois, to purchase from Murphy Pontiac Cadillac of Prophetstown, Illinois, a new 1958 Pontiac 2-door, serial number P7585-25C5. Total Bona Fide Cash Price $3174.25. Trade-in: 1950 Olds 4dr — $625.00. Cash $299.25. Total Down Payment $924.25. Difference between Items 1 and 2: $2250.00. Finance charge and insurance premiums $574.47. Coverages applicable for 36 months. Time Balance $2824.42. Time Sale Price $3749.17. 36 monthly installments of $78.47 and a final installment, beginning on May 10, 1958. Stamped JUN 20 1958 ASSOCIATES.

The original sales invoice shows the $625 that Arnie was given for his Oldsmobile and the $300 cash that he'd scraped up to put down as a deposit as well. That left a balance of $2,250 to be paid over the next three years. His first installment of $78.47 was due on May 10. (Photo Courtesy Beswick Archive)

ordering a new car. He had heard about Pontiac's increase in motor size for 1958. Bigger than Pontiac's 1957 offering of a 347-ci mill, Arnie wanted the code 395A option. That meant a 370-ci 330-hp engine.

Initially the dealership couldn't help. After repeated stops in December, it finally produced the forms, and Arnie was finally given the chance to order the car of his dreams.

Arnie picked out his obvious motor, transmission, and rear gear choices. To his dismay, the best manual transmission was no better than the general public could get: a three on the tree column-shifted 3-speed. In 1958, Safe-T-Track (Posi-Traction) was offered for the first time on a Pontiac. Arnie checked that box.

Arnie was like a kid at Christmas. He visited or called the dealership often to check on the progress, especially when he saw magazine articles touting the Pontiac's performance capabilities. Normally, a car took about six weeks to build. One can be reasonably sure that the special axle hindered progress, as did the 395A motor. That was the case for Arnie, as six weeks turned into more than three months.

It's Finally Here!

On Saturday, April 19, he received the call that his car was in. He dropped everything and excitedly drove a 1950 Oldsmobile to the dealership as a trade-in. The deposit had come from his regular wages and from helping neighbors bale hay, as well as other part-time and winter work. Considering that Arnie's wages back then working for his father were only $100 a month, it was a lot of money for him. Thankfully, Evelyn's jobs helped with expenses.

As soon as he picked up the new car, he was happy as a lark and quickly drove to Moline, Illinois, to gloat to a friend from the drag strip, Fred Coopman, and break it in. Into the wee hours of the morning, Fred and Arnie took turns putting on what, hopefully, were enough miles to break in the car before Sunday's race day at the strip.

Taking It to Cordova

The *Quad City Times* report for the track showed the impressive results for his brand-new Super/Stock entry. After Arnie tuned the car, added better rubber, and played with the suspension, the car got down to the 14.8-second range. In an arena where a hundredth of a second (or even less) makes a difference, everything counts.

QUAD CITY DRAG STRIP
Cordova, Illinois
Results of April 20 — *1958*

Class	Name	Engine	Time	E.T.
DRAGSTER				
D/A	Hawley-Olson,	Fl Chrys	118.42	11.60
OPEN GAS				
O/A	Bowles-Dhammers,	Olds	116.88	11.82
O/B	Mohr-Deggendorf,	Olds	112.00	12.14
COUPE & SEDAN				
C/A	Jerry Lyon,	Olds	95.12	14.88
C/B	Charles Chad,	Chev	98.00	13.97
C/C	Ed Carleton,	57 Chev	88.23	15.04
C/D	Ken Cordts,	Chev	82.56	16.66
C/E	Marsh Hesler,	Ford	79.01	17.15
MODIFIED COUPES & ROADSTERS				
G/B	Bill Wirges,	Pontiac	101.00	13.27
B/B	Loren Spencer,	Chev	100.00	14.26
FLATHEAD CLASS				
F/CC	Frank Teeple,	Ford	85.90	16.26
STOCK CARS				
S/S	Arnie Beswick,	58 Pontiac	96.00	15.01
S/A	Bob Warner,	57 Chev	90.00	15.16
S/B	Glen Wicks,	57 Chev	87.00	15.97
S/C	Dale Scalf,	55 Ford	81.20	17.05
S/D	Rich Genovese,	53 Olds	71.42	17.90
S/E	Bill Asplund,	50 Olds	75.00	17.96
S/F	Tom Herbert,	49 Ford	70.58	19.33
STOCK—AUTOMATIC				
S/SA	Larry Johnson,	58 Olds	88.23	15.93
S/AA	Denny Lyon,	57 Olds	84.00	16.48
SPORTS CARS				
X/A	Stella Booth,	57 Corvette	93.75	15.20
X/B	Bob Crane,	55 Bird	84.11	16.52
X/C	Mike Henderson	58 Fl-vette	95.74	14.79
X/D	Jerry Lyon,	54 Jaguar	90.00	17.63
MOTORCYCLES				
B	Bob Crawford,	Harley 45	75.00	16.23
C	Bob Berlin,	Harley	—	—
D	Roger Relman,	Harley XLR	101.90	13.24
TOP ELIMINATOR				
	Bowles-Dhammers,	Olds	116.88	11.82
TOP TIME				
	Olson-Hawley,	Fl Chrys	118.42	11.60
TOP E.T.				
	Olson-Hawley,	Fl Chrys	118.42	11.60

The original clipping from the paper shows that with little break-in and on stock street tires, the Chieftain ran a 15.01 ET at exactly 96 mph. The next stock class down S/A (A Stock) ran only 90 mph, and Arnie's top speed was faster than almost every one of the Coupe and Sedan classes, except for the B class. Since changes in the Gas classes were allowed, they were all faster as well.

The '58 is at the track. The Chieftain is still in the stock class for the year. It's presumed to be Gordy Matson's '56 Chevrolet behind the Pontiac.

Becoming a veteran like her older sister, Arnette, Paula sits on the fender of the Chieftain at Cordova.

Dealing with Dissatisfaction

After a few weeks, Arnie grew tired of the 1-2-3 shifts, as linkage would frequently bind up from the hard and fast motions needed to keep power to the ground at all times. He determined that with a higher ratio, he might be able to eliminate the shift from second to third.

It is important to remember that Arnie had experience with his own higher-geared Oldsmobiles by now, and he frequently drove other people's cars down the strip as well. The only problem was finding a rear center section that had a better ratio and would still fit.

Coincidently, Arnie's folks owned a 1957 Oldsmobile. Arnie knew that Oldsmobile and Pontiac used the same center section that housed the gears. It took only a quick peek underneath their car to see that the differentials looked very similar or even identical, yet Arnie knew that the Oldsmobile had a ratio of 3.64:1. Luck was with him, as it was even equipped with Safe-T-Track!

Uh Oh!

Arnie, Fred Coopman, and another friend from the track, Gordy Matson, waited one Saturday night until they were sure that Arnie's parents were asleep. Sometime way past midnight, they quietly pushed his parents' Oldsmobile from their garage to Arnie and Evelyn's little house located a mere half a block or so away. They proceeded, merely using bumper jacks, to switch the cars' center sections.

Fred added the oil and pushed himself out from under the car, and unfortunately, that little nudge was more than the jacks could handle. They leaned to one side and gave way, sending the car crashing to the concrete floor and into the side of the garage door opening.

As the confines of Arnie's little one-car garage were tight, the rear passenger door now had a huge dent. Arnie seemed doomed to face his father's wrath and was panic stricken as they got the car back up off the cement and finished the task at hand. They had to try to fix the door, at least to minimize the depth of the dent.

So, as time grew short (the sun was coming up soon), they pulled the door panel off and pushed and punched as much of the dent out as they could. Even before the roosters started crowing, they pushed the Oldsmobile back up to its original parking space in his parents' garage. Then, they went back to finish the installation of the rear end in Arnie's Chieftain.

Later that morning, as Arnie headed to the drag strip, Raymond and Marie Beswick opened their garage door and headed to church like they normally did. When they returned to their car after the service, Marie saw the dent. She couldn't believe that someone in their church was so careless in the parking lot to bump into their car and not leave a note or anything.

Meanwhile, at the drag strip, despite the fact that the swap actually slowed his ET, the newspapers reported that over time his speed went up. Arnie had indeed completely eliminated the 2-3 shift, and from that standpoint, his win consistency was much better. The proof was in the press, as his name showed up week after week in the newspaper for winning the S/S class.

His thought process had been correct in that the engine's RPM would be fine without the slightest concern about floating the valves. Arnie learned a valuable lesson. While his track dominance continued, he knew that it wouldn't be done with the '58 in stock trim.

Racing a Second Car

Another fellow racer, whom Arnie had made friends with, was Moline resident Gordy Matson. Gordy owned a black-and-white '56 Chevrolet and, according to the former track owner and founder of the Cordova track, Bob Bartel, it was *very* competitive. He had a major hindrance in the car in that he was handicapped with a withered right arm and leg that made it very hard for him to shift at all, let alone quickly. Bob said that watching the car race from ground level was scary because Gordy would lean down to change gears and completely disappear from sight.

In early May at the Quad City Dragstrip, Gordy showed up with his car and pitted close to Arnie. The reason was because there were some recent changes to the car, including a Corvette floor-shifted 4-speed transmission. Gordy asked Arnie to drive for him.

Still All Stock, Yeah Right!

Our buddy, Lee Smith, famous for his Mopar connection, was one of the Quad City Dragway's first tech inspectors. He recounted what happened one particular day when Gordy and Arnie came through.

"They came up and ran the car through tech," he said. "I quickly looked it over, making sure that everything looked all right and safe. Other than a fender cover or a blanket in the middle of the front seat, there was nothing unusual. I didn't think anything of it and, as in previous weeks, wrote the stock class number on the window.

"The car was very fast in those days, and we all wondered if Gordy was cheating. That day, I found out for sure that they were. I remember hearing the car go down the strip and counting not two but three shifts. Apparently, under the blanket that I failed to look under, they had a newly installed 4-speed

Looking mighty proud of his ride, Arnie stops for a snapshot. (Photo Courtesy Beswick Archive)

transmission. Practical joke or not, that was the last time that Gordy ever tried to enter his car into a stock class. From that day forward, it went into D/G (D-Gas) with Arnie continuing to drive, even winning the World Series with it."

Since Arnie's car was in the Stock class and Gordy's car was in the Gas class, it was possible for Arnie to drive both cars during every weekend's races. This combination got both the names of Gordy and Arnie in the newspapers as winners for many weeks to follow. Perhaps of more importance, their names also appeared in the *Rods Illustrated* Gallery of Champions for the year. Arnie had broken the D/G coupe record by three hundredths of a second as well.

Arnie's name also appeared on the previous page of *Rods Illustrated* in the S/S (Super Stock) class with his 1958 Chieftain and a speed of 100.55 mph, beating the previous year's record of 98.11 mph.

Family Life and Other Jobs During the Slow Times

While it still was no bed of roses, life was pretty good for Arnie and Evelyn as 1959 opened. The couple had been married for 5½ years now and had two of the cutest daughters one could imagine: Arnette and Paula.

Arnie gained national attention as various car magazines printed his achievements for the world to see. They exalted Arnie by reporting that his Pontiac Chieftain had set records in the S/S class at racetracks the previous year. It was reported that he'd also raised the bar in the D/G class, breaking records using Gordy Matson's Chevrolet. Most of these accomplishments were noted at one of the biggest drag races in the country: the World Series of Drag Racing.

In these early days, the drag strips closed earlier in the year than in modern times. Cordova's Quad City Dragway closed shortly after the late-August running of the World Series. The other area tracks all did the same in mid-September, despite any "Indian Summer" tendencies in the weather.

So, while life was good, there was no racing for Arnie. To help supplement income for his growing family, Arnie found winter jobs in his early married days. Among them were jobs at Bennett Box, the Sterling/Rock Falls bowling alley (working as a pinsetter), and General Electric, the big local industrial plant.

Arnie worked at the GE plant for a few winters until his supervisors figured out that he would quit in the spring with the extra farm duties that his

The growing family is shown in the late 1950s after the second daughter, Paula, was born.

father required of him. It was also true that he fully intended to participate in the racing scene. By 1959, General Electric was wise to his ways and wouldn't hire him anymore. Fortunately, Evelyn committed herself to work full time, and the company hired her at about the same time. Ever the rock, Evelyn worked there until her retirement, 30-plus years later.

Another New Car?

Wintertime is when racers in the upper Midwest work on their cars. Consequently, it was during these cold months that Arnie was having machine work done to freshen up the '58's cylinder heads. That required a visit to one of his favorite shops: Abraham's Machine Service in Davenport, Iowa, which is still in business today.

While Arnie was at Abraham's Machine Service, he ran into a fellow racer who worked as a service manager for Langwith Pontiac/Cadillac, a dealership less than a mile away from the shop. During small talk, it was mentioned that if Arnie was ever looking for a new car, the Warren Langwith Pontiac dealership was *the* place to try first.

While he really wasn't seriously looking to buy a new car, the seed was planted. After mulling it over, it started to make sense. If it did happen though, Langwith or any dealership would have to really sharpen its pencil in order to sell him a car.

Reasoning and Justifying

As days passed, the idea consumed more of Arnie's thoughts until his mind was in overdrive thinking about the possibilities. First and foremost was the fact that if he got another car, he could then modify the '58 to fit into one of the Gas classes. He loathed and despised everything about driving the three on the tree, especially after experiencing Gordy's floor-shifted 4-speed car. Still, he knew that if he made these changes to the 1958 Chieftain, there would be consequences.

The biggest problem was that the modifications would mean the car would no longer be eligible for any Stock classes. Secondly, it would no longer be desirable for public roads, as another rear-end swap was among the changes. Arnie would have to change it back to its original 4.30:1 gear ratio, maximizing the potential of the 4-speed. That also meant he would have to make a tow bar for it, but that couldn't be too hard. He'd seen a few of them at the track already, and they looked pretty simple to fabricate.

Another reason to buy a new car was that there were advertised improvements to the 1959 over the 1958 model year. The most important improvement was that the 1959s had a larger displacement. The 370-ci engine was bumped up to a 389. There were also reports that the 1959 models had a better shift linkage.

If he had a new '59, not only could he race the Chieftain in the Gas class but also the Catalina could run in the S/S class. It all seemed too good to be true. The more research he did on the '59s, the more he had to have one. As more information was released, it looked like the only downside was a little increased weight of the car. Since his eagerness had grown by leaps and bounds and he was optimistic about all the posi-

tive aspects, Arnie didn't think the extra weight was a major concern.

Besides all of the positive aspects that he considered, he also figured that if he bought a new car, Evelyn now could ride in style to work (except on race days, naturally). After a quick conversation with her, she agreed that yes, she would like a new car. His mind was made up. A consultation with his bank was next. The bank told him that it would lend him the money, providing the purchase price was in line with the appraised value of the National Automobile Dealers Association (NADA) book of the day.

Talking with the Dealership

The next step was a trip to the dealership. Arnie took the mechanic/service manager's advice and went in to talk with Langwith. As Arnie recalled, Langwith was not just hungry—it was starving for new business, especially in the performance realm.

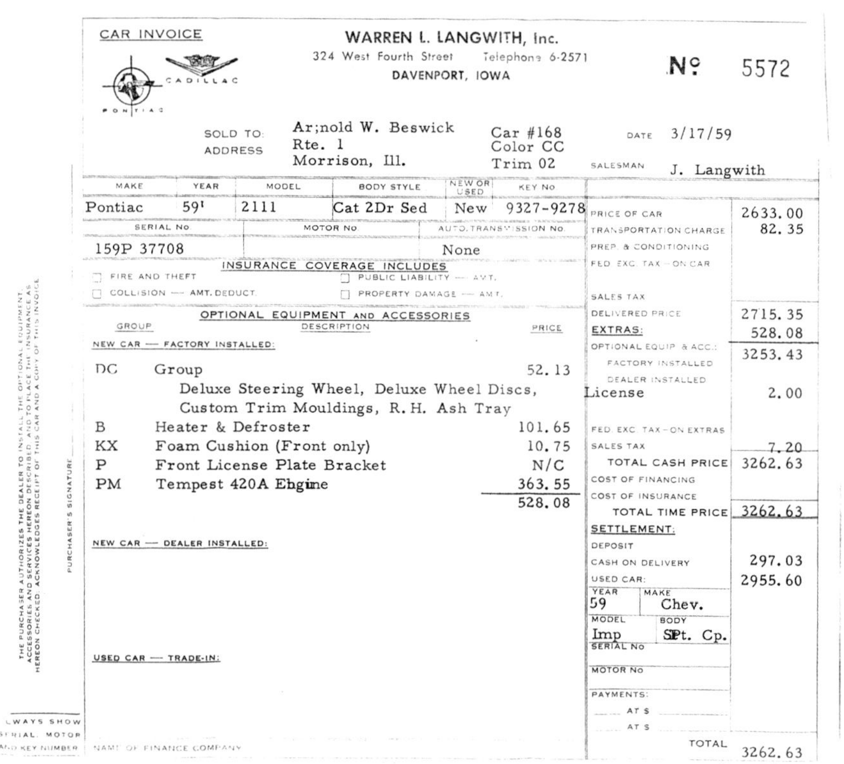

Here's the sales invoice for the '59. One of the more interesting options was the right-hand ashtray. It was because Evelyn was a smoker back then. A more perplexing entry on this invoice was the 1959 Impala sport coupe that Arnie appeared to have traded in on the Pontiac. Arnie had no such car to trade in; it would have been a car that was less than a couple of months old. Apparently, one reason it was recorded this way was because John was trying to save Arnie some tax money. In this case, it was almost $70. Writing it as they did also ensured that it was within the banker's guidelines for the appraised loan value.

His contact had told him that John was the man to see at the dealership. Warren, the owner, was an older, careful, perhaps stodgy gentleman who would rather make an easy sale on a four-door Catalina or Star Chief to his aged crowd than get into an unproven kids' market.

Warren probably reasoned like my own grandfather, the small-town Chevrolet-Pontiac dealer, did with a scowl, "After all, kids don't have any money." However, his more youthful nephew, John, did not share this mentality. As a result, when Arnie came in to Langwith, John sat down with him. Together, they put in the order for his new car.

On March 17, Arnie's car arrived at the dealership. After it had been inspected, Arnie was called and told that his car was ready to be picked up. Most items on Arnie's sales invoice were pretty straightforward.

No Better than the 1958

As the 1959 racing season progressed, it seemed that while the 1958 Chieftain excelled at making headlines, the new Catalina received little mention. Almost like the red-headed stepchild, it seemed des-tined for obscurity, getting little or no attention at the track by photographers or sports writers. Was it because of the car's extra 250 pounds or the fact that Arnie completely concentrated on making his Chieftain the fastest car at the local tracks?

Mostly, it was due to the fact that the initial excitement and self-justification of the new car didn't materialize, as Arnie had believed the publications'

This photo of Arnie's '59 came from the second owner right after that person had been married. The whole car was full of graffiti that had to be cleaned up. (Photo Courtesy Harlan Tiesman)

. . . BUT ON THE ROADS!

While it might not have made the biggest splash on the drag strips, it certainly earned respect on the highways, as Spencer Knox would attest. Spencer was a few years younger than Arnie but played a major part in keeping the Beswick cars winning at the tracks in the mid-1960s. Due to family money and the fact that his uncle was the local dealer, Spencer always had the best cars that Chrysler Corporation had to offer. His ride of choice at this particular time was the Plymouth Fury, and more often than not, he had a convertible.

It was a gorgeous spring morning on Easter Sunday, and Spencer headed west toward home on Route 30. As chance would have it, Arnie's new Catalina pulled out of the church lot and onto the highway just a few blocks ahead of him, heading in the same direction. Marie Beswick (Arnie's mother) was a Sunday school teacher at the church and, of course, being Easter, the whole family was there for the special service that day.

Spencer squinted a little, leaned into the wheel, and smiled and nodded with determination as he saw Arnie's new Catalina pull out. He would take his revenge for the losses to Arnie at the drag strip. Spencer kept his distance through town, so he wouldn't alert Arnie of his intention, but as Arnie made the slight left turn onto Garden Plain Road and left the city limits, Spencer mashed his foot to the floor.

"Victory is mine," Spencer thought as the big Mopar mill came to life and the speedometer climbed rapidly.

Whether it was the Beswick girls standing in the back seat who saw him first and started jumping around, screaming, "He's coming, Daddy," or Arnie himself who saw the speed that Spencer was gathering in the mirror, something made Arnie aware of the quickly approaching Plymouth. Spencer got almost alongside of the Catalina and had pulled out to pass, but his victory was denied because by that time, Arnie had his foot to the floor as well. Evelyn, concerned about safety, told him that he had proved his point and not to do anything stupid.

Spencer recounted, "Arnie left me so fast, I thought my car had shut off at first."

This is a side view from the same place as the first. (Photo Courtesy Harlan Tiesman)

hype on the new car. The reports had told of better shift linkage, yet he didn't find any evidence of it. He broke the same parts early in the season that he had on his 1958 Chieftain. Plain and simple, the 1959 Catalina wasn't what Arnie had hoped for in a race car.

Shortcomings Don't Matter on the '59

By the time the first robin in the spring of 1959 had been spotted, Arnie had been getting used to his new Catalina. Even on the roads and highways, he discovered the obvious weak points of racing the car. The shift linkage was no better and performed just as poorly as his 1958 Chieftain's did, despite advertised improvements. Then there was the weight. In his excitement about the new car, Arnie had overlooked just how much 250 pounds actually weighs. He would pay for it. That factor was making itself crystal clear as the area tracks opened up.

Still, these factors paled in comparison to his original main goal, and brooding over such details wouldn't help win races. There was no time to dwell on such insignificant things for the most important transformation because the new season could now be realized.

Since the Chieftain needed to be worked on, it got the garage, a privilege the Catalina would never see. With another car for Evelyn to drive to work, the Chieftain

was now due to get some parts that would not just give a snarl to the competition, it would give them all a vicious bite!

Making Changes

First and very foremost was the replacement of the "junk" three-on-the-tree, column-shifted stock transmission. That meant replacing it with a Corvette floor-mounted 4-speed. Initially, one couldn't be located. Then, at the Oswego Drag Strip, Arnie met Billy Harris.

Billy was a salesman for the famous Nickey Chevrolet in Chicago. When asked about getting a 4-speed, he confidently told Arnie that obtaining one was no problem. He was true to his word and delivered a BorgWarner T-10 transmission with the correct 4-speed shift linkage. Arnie's smile during delivery and installation was made bigger by the price that he'd paid. Either because of a warranty issue or dealer discount pricing, Arnie remembers getting the transmission cheaper than Gordy did and saving a bit of money.

With the new transmission's gear ratios came the need for lower rear gears. A 4.11:1, 4.30:1, or such would be optimum again. Coincidentally, Arnie knew from previous experience just where such an axle could be found. Once again, the late-night swap with his parents' Oldsmobile was repeated. This time it went without incident, and Arnie had his old 4.30 gears back again.

Arnie realized within the first couple of passes at Quad City Dragway that because of the gear change,

Arnie stands next to the '58 and looks down the track at Quad City Dragway in 1960. Not much modification had been done to the car yet. (Photo Colorization by Dean Fait)

the valves had a tendency to float ever so slightly at the top end of the track. However, it wasn't long into the 1959 season that Arnie fixed that problem by ordering and installing an Iskenderian E2 camshaft for the '58. The E2 was a mild camshaft, actually very close to stock specs on the *hotter* cars of the day. It was mild enough that ATAA and NHRA allowed it even in the stock classes.

The complete cam kit came with all the necessary parts. Arnie immediately installed the cam itself along with the solid lifters. Since he didn't have access to a spring compressor and couldn't afford the time lost to take off the heads to send them to a shop that did, Arnie ran without the Isky springs for the 1959 year. Consequently, performance wasn't up to speed.

More Engine and Exhaust Work

Since the World Series of Drag Racing was the race of all races in those days that rivaled the attendance, payouts, and prestige of the NHRA Nationals, Arnie wanted to proudly show how much of a vicious bite his Chieftain actually had. He painted flames on the hood.

Arnie didn't want to oppose his father's iron-fisted mentality about racing or cars with crazy paint schemes, so for that year's event, a friend painted the hood in Tempera water colors. After the race, a garden hose quickly removed all traces of any wild behavior, regarding the flamed hood.

Over the winter between 1959 and 1960, the Chieftain had the top half of the motor taken apart and sent to a machine shop to install the heavy-duty

The first flame job still had the stock grille. The eggcrate grille from Pontiac wasn't all that good looking. It's no wonder that Arnie went with the tube grille.

The girls grew up at the drag strips. There were always other kids to play with. Arnette was about 7 here; Paula, 6. (Photo Courtesy Evelyn Beswick)

springs and the rest of the parts from the Isky E2 cam package. That really brought the motor to life, as times are recorded for the 1960 season at Cordova in the 13.30s.

Of course, other factors came into play. Tires helped, as racing slicks started to become available and were allowed. Headers were also allowed in the Gas classes, although the rules mandated full exhaust. Arnie's '58 was thought to be one of the first late-model doorslammers in the Midwest to have a set of headers custom built for it. His were built by Bill Wirges (pronounced Whir-jess) from the Sterling/Rock Falls area.

Classification and Optimizing the Potential

Cubic inch to weight was how racing associations determined which cars fell into each class. The lighter a car was with more cubic inches put it into the top Gas classes, and tech always included a weigh-in. Arnie's Chieftain came in right on the border between C and D classes.

Thanks to stiff competition in C/G, Arnie tried staying in D/G, but often the tech department's scales dictated otherwise, and they put him in C/G. Unfortunately, the Pontiac was heavier than his competition in this class. The easiest fix to that problem was to drop the front bumper off. That helped immensely because the assembly weighed 100 pounds, including the brackets.

Complete with the tube grille, flames, and lettering, the '58 is in the staging lanes at Quad City Dragway. Home movies showed the correct colors for the letterman's jacket on the passenger. Bob Bartel issued these jackets to points champions at each year's end. (Photo Colorization by Dean Fait)

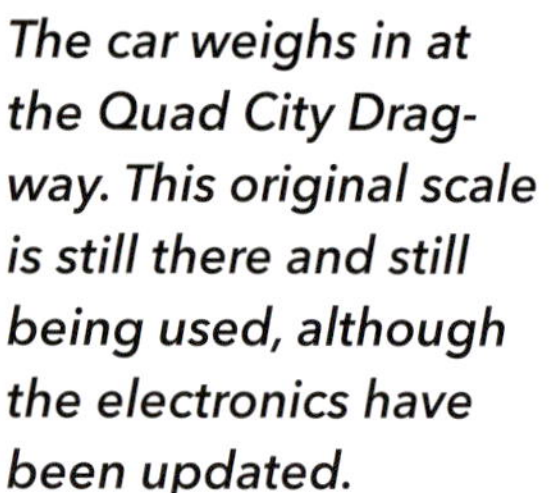

The car weighs in at the Quad City Dragway. This original scale is still there and still being used, although the electronics have been updated.

Arnie waves to the family from Quad City Dragway's return road on his way back to the pits.

The final change was more for aesthetics than weight because the '58's stock grille looked rather ugly without the bumper in place. A tube grille fixed that, adding a cleaner look to the car. Later, permanent flames and lettering adorned the car. It now told the competition that Arnie was ready to do some serious business with the Chieftain. History recorded it to be true.

As the 1960 and 1961 seasons unfolded, Arnie kept the car around for one more chance in the winner's circle if time allowed, but that was only for Cordova and the close-to-home tracks. Usually, this meant a busy day, and as home movies showed, sometimes it required the help of friends to flat tow the car to the track.

Evelyn Joins the Fun

The 1958 Chieftain was often used for powder-puff races. Several of the Midwest, and specifically Chicagoland, tracks began incorporating them into their programs. These programs allowed women to become involved to increase the overall appeal of the sport. They were occasionally scheduled and sometimes happened impromptu. Evelyn almost always entered that part of the competition and did well, using her husband's car and his coaching. Occasionally, there was even the use of other people's cars.

"Despite the fact that they [powder-puff races] didn't happen that often up there, I remember Great Lakes Dragaway in Union Grove, Wisconsin," Evelyn said. "They had a Le Mans start. That's where you run to your car, start it, and then race down the track. I was a lot faster on my feet back then."

The fact was that she was heading down the track while most of her competition was trying to start their cars. Drag racing for Evelyn ended during the 1960 season when the clutch exploded in the 1958 Chieftain at about half or three-quarter track.

"The pressure plate and some of the clutch parts came right up through the floorboard and then the cowl, just missing the windshield and my right foot," she said. "While I didn't get hurt, I remember hearing the announcer say over the loudspeaker, 'Don't worry about the car, Arnie. See if your wife is all right.'"

Arnie remembered the incident like it was yesterday.

"I was standing on the starting line at the time the clutch blew up." he said. "As is sometimes the case with track announcers, they report on just what they perceive at the moment in time. Jim Sweet was the announcer back then, and the comment was definitely made to get a laugh. I didn't take it that way.

"I was able to catch a ride from someone in a pickup truck that was also sitting close by the tower. When we reached the car, Evelyn was obviously shaking from the intensity of the explosion. The first thing I asked upon opening her door was, 'Are

NEW OWNERS FOR THE 1958 CHIEFTAIN

The 1958 Chieftain sat almost untouched for the 1962 racing season. As the end of that year's racing neared, Arnie was approached by Jimmy and Nita Burton. They wanted to buy the Chieftain.

The Burtons were a couple from the South whom Arnie met when he started S/S racing in the Southern states. Jimmy was just as much of an avid racer as Arnie. They had become such good friends that Arnie would stay at their house when he traveled near Atlanta, Georgia.

The longest day for the Burtons started with Jimmy driving up to Morrison, Illinois, with Nita by his side, towing the trade-in behind them. Without even spending the night at the Beswick's, Jimmy then towed the '58 straight to the event and entered it into the competition.

The Last Trip

After a full day of racing, the Burtons again hooked up the tow bar and headed for home. Jim was dead tired, so he decided to ride in the Chieftain, which was being towed, catching a few seconds of sleep while Nita drove.

Nita was almost completely without towing experience, and on a downhill slope mid-route, the Chieftain began sashaying back and forth, controlling her instead of the other way around. Finally, the '58's wild momentum caused her to jackknife the two vehicles, going off the road, rolling both.

While Nita wasn't seriously injured, Jimmy suffered chest and abdominal injuries from the sudden impact with the steering wheel. He was never the same physically afterward, and the accident shortened his life by

Four views of the Chieftain show extensive damage. No wonder Jimmy was never the same afterward.

several years. The '58 was even less lucky, not even making it home in one piece. It was never repaired.

If songwriter Neil Young is correct in that "It's better to burn out than fade away," then the 1958 Chieftain certainly went out the right way. The car has since been lost, undoubtedly crushed, as it was a total loss. Although, Arnie heard rumors for a few years as to where parts, such as the engine and transmission, went.

you alright?' While a little dazed, she finally admitted that she was. I then proceeded to check out the car, as I'd never seen this happen before."

A Career Change

As the seasons changed from fall to winter in 1959, Arnie added another job experience to his resume. While farm duties were still required of him, he finally landed the job of his dreams as an auto mechanic.

Arnie began working at the newly opened Pontiac dealership in Clinton, Iowa. Undoubtedly the dealership owner, Lee Morrison, knew beforehand that any job that Arnie held took a distant second place behind racing, especially for a big race to be held that year in Florida.

Ordering a New 1960

Initially, no one at Pontiac Motor Division would guarantee that the floor-mounted 4-speed transmission would be available for 1960. However, after some time, they gave every indication that it could be ordered with confidence.

Time was short, as a first-year race approached in Daytona Beach, so Arnie was told that he needed to get in touch with Bob Emrick to order his car. Bob was in charge of customer relations at Pontiac Motor Division. Arnie called him, and they went through the order form together. Bob was probably puzzled when Arnie did not want the performance axle ratio installed. Arnie had his reasons, so Bob checked the box for a 3.64:1.

Pontiac marketing was offering another new option, so Emrick checked the box for the eight-lug wheel option. What wasn't to like here? Not only did they have a new fresh look but they were also 80 pounds lighter than the old traditional steel wheels!

The Mad Dash Preparing for Florida

Arnie's car showed up on January 29. Since the Speedweek competition began on February 7, time was incredibly short. Preparation began immediately and proceeded nonstop.

Arnie used his trailer, now lettered with Quad City Dragway, for all the things that he would need along with timing equipment and other necessary items for codirectors Bob Bartel and Ed Otto. Besides the equipment, the trailer was pretty much stuffed full of Arnie's spare parts. With less than a week before the race started, it was a mad scramble to get everything done.

Andy Perry, a longtime friend of Arnie's, said, "As I came over to throw my suitcases in the car, I remember that Arnie had a whole bunch of engine parts in the trailer, including another transmission and the rear-end center section—not to mention the set of mounted cheater slicks. All of us were excited about the upcoming week of racing."

Setup at the Track and Solutions to Issues

Having changed the rear-end gears to better suit the needs on the strip, Arnie's car was as ready as could be. On Monday afternoon, they rolled out to the Flagler Beach Airport in Bunnell, Florida, to set up their pit spots.

Flagler Beach Airport was an airstrip built along the border of the United States during World War II. Long since abandoned, it made for a perfect drag

This is the promotional flyer for the drag racing festivities in Daytona for 1960. (Photo Courtesy Ken Forster Jr., reproracingposters.com)

This sign greeted participants of the one and only joint venture to this point: the NHRA/NASCAR Winter Nationals event.

and other track-operating equipment was also easily solved by using a city transit–type bus. It was lettered with the event and sponsor logos, as well as the hosting organizations.

Everybody's Here

Hot Rod magazine reported that the best racers from at least 20 states were at this event to compete. Years later, Bartel confirmed this, adding that everybody who was anybody in racing was at this first-ever cosponsored NASCAR–NHRA Winter Nationals drag event. While that mostly meant racers, the list of attendees included reps from the car companies as well as drag strip owners and promoters from a lot of the Southern states.

As the first night of competition began, Arnie thought his biggest competition would be the driver of another brand-new 1960 Pontiac: Ronnie Sox. That was not the case, as Ronnie had installed too high of a gear in his borrowed Pontiac and it was topped out at 1,000 feet. Consequently, the first nights of racing went well for Arnie. He tore up the competition, at one point running against the 1959 NHRA Nationals winner, Harold Ramsey.

That first night of racing, Arnie took Harold by a good car length and a half but noticed that the valves were floating at the top end of the quarter mile and between power shifts. The following night, Arnie ran against Harold again, narrowly beating him by a fender at best. Once again, the floating valves were the main problem.

strip, despite the fact that there weren't any buildings close to the runway that had electricity for the timing equipment. Generators were used to provide power.

As for the lighting, two huge searchlights solved that problem. They were pointed down track to provide visibility. Bartel got the idea from Dave Jamison, who had run night races at an eighth-mile strip about 10 miles south of Rock Falls, Illinois, on Route 88 (now Illinois 40).

The issue of where to put the trophies, timing equipment,

After the first night of competition, Arnie and Billy Wagner had their picture taken for winning, showing off their trophies. The wagon in the background is thought to be Bob and Dawn Bartel's car.

Arnie's 1960 Ventura is in the far lane racing an unknown 1959 Chevrolet.

The Final Night

Arnie fixed his floating valve problem on Wednesday by using a trick that he had figured out on the '58. The trick was to double-nut the rockers. After that, things went smoothly for the rest of the week. Arnie's winning streak meant that the last night's race once again pitted him against Ramsey.

Reportedly, this was probably the most coveted and contested spot at the meet. The field was loaded with super-tuned new-model stockers in all classes, many of which had come down to compete in Daytona's beach trials as well as the nightly drags.

The flag for the final race came down and both cars were off with the entire Quad City contingency watching. Not far from the Beswick supporters was Thelma Ramsey, who was rooting for her husband. Anticipation grew as everyone watched to see who would cross the finish line first. It was Arnie.

A cheer went up from the Arnie camp, the loudest of which came from Andy Perry. As he was excitedly hooting and hollering, Thelma Ramsey walked over and slapped him for showing too much delight.

It was probably after Arnie won the second or third night that either Harold or his firecracker of a wife, Thelma (using Harold's name), protested Arnie. Despite the window sticker still displayed on Arnie's car, they couldn't believe that Beswick's new Ventura had come equipped with the 4-speed transmission. The transmission issue was so controversial it went all the way to Bill France's office. It literally took a telegram directly from Pontiac to finally quiet all the protests. And there were many, considering that all the cash awards were withheld, pending the outcome of the protest.

Here, Arnie's up against another unknown '57 Chevy. (Photo Colorization by Dean Fait)

Andy was stunned by this, but without thinking or hesitating, he immediately slapped her back. That, of course, shocked her and the rest of the onlookers. Andy was given the title of "woman beater" from the band of travelers for the entire trip home.

Still on a High from Daytona

Arnie and Larry Johnson, as the Morrison Pontiac newspaper ad from early March 1960 showed, were on a high like none other . . . and for good reason. Arnie had defeated the best drag racers in the nation.

The first NHRA/NASCAR Winternationals was like nothing in which Arnie had ever competed. He didn't know it at the time, but this single event put him on the racing map, making him a household name that was known to track promoters across the nation. It also gave him work as a drag racer for the rest of his life. The calls started coming in within a month after the event or sooner.

Fellow drag racing friend and foe "Dyno" Don Nicholson had the same good fortune the following year after the first West Coast NHRA Winternationals in Pomona, California. It was the same pivotal moment in time that all professional athletes encounter.

As the weather warmed up and the racing season began in the Midwest, Arnie readied his cars for the year. The first thing that he felt should be done was to bring the 1960 Ventura back to the way it

This is the final night's final run between Arnie and Harold. Notice that Arnie switched wheels and tires in the back, as the eight-lugs are gone.

OVERALL WINNERS
MEET RESULTS

Class & Entry		Engine	MPH	E.T.
A/G	Shirl Greer, Kingsport, Tenn.	Chevy	105.07	13.01
B/G	Perry Browning Jr., Jacksonville, Fla.	Chevy	99.33	13.37
D/G	Allen Waitsman, Miami, Fla.	'57 Chevy	89.55	N.T.
E/G	George Weiler, Birdsboro, Pa.	'59 Chevy	89.14	15.49
A/GS	Ollie Olsen, W. Palm Bch., Fla.	Bln. Chevy	131.00	12.04
C/GS	John Gellner, Parma, Ohio	'59 Chevy	113.63	13.53
A/SR	Cranston & Cathgart, Trenton, N.J.	Olds	118.27	11.02
A/A	Swenson & Kayohye, Milltown, N.J.	Buick	106.30	12.59
B/A	Richard Lee, Ft. Lauderdale, Fla.	Chevy	103.09	13.05
B/A	John Horn, Jacksonville, Fla.	Olds	102.15	13.03
C/A	H. B. Clements, Jacksonville, Fla.	'60 Anglia	61.94	20.91
A/R	Roy Lowe, Atlanta, Ga.	'53 Chrys.	134.12	11.43
B/R	Dave Whalen, Hollywood, Fla.	'59 Chevy	114.78	12.00
C/R	Dick Goodsell, Daytona, Fla.	'48 Ford	84.19	N.T.
B/C	W. R. Rayall, Henderson, N.C.	'57 Chevy	111.00	12.90
A/M	Joe Jacona, Chester, Pa.	'59 Buick	136.98	10.26
B/D	Lewis Carden, Birmingham, Ala.	F.I. Chevy	141.95	9.55
C/D	Dave Johnson, Atlanta, Ga.	Chevy	127.47	11.10
D/D	Hail & Hyder, Dade City, Fla.	'48 Ford	90.36	14.45
AM/SP	Kenneth Sitton, Waskom, Texas	'57 Bocar	114.79	12.44
F/SP	Jerry Hanes, Beecher, Ill.	Triumph TR-3	N.T.	N.T.
G/SP	R. D. Griffin, Lansing, Mich.	'60 Corvair	71.72	18.42
I/SP	Ed Zeller, Bunnell, Fla.	Triumph TR-3	N.T.	N.T.
S/S	Arnold Beswick, Morrison, Ill.	'60 Pontiac	93.55	N.T
A/S	R. D. Griffin, Lansing, Mich.	'59 Chevy	91.03	15.83
B/S	David Redwine, Longwood, Fla.	'60 Chevy	88.21	16.73
D/S	Robert Morris, Owensboro, Ky.	'54 Ford	78.46	17.49
E/S	Charles Seabrook, Alloway, N.J.	'53 Stude	77.00	19.00
F/S	Harold Danton, Prince Fred., Md.	'50 Ford	72.52	19.02
S/S/A	Grayson McClure, Murray, Ky.	'60 Dart	94.35	14.92
A/S/A	Jim Kurzen, Akron, Ohio	'60 Pontiac	93.45	15.35
B/S/A	Harley Morse, Eustis, Fla.	'57 Chevy	85.55	16.58
C/S/A	Rolf Hardt, Corydon, Pa.	'55 Chevy	83.98	17.82
D/S/A	Wm. McGreedy, Toms River, N.J.	'59 Olds	72.98	18.79
TOP ELIMINATOR				
B/D	Lewis Carden, Birmingham, Ala.			9.55
MIDDLE ELIMINATOR				
A/A	Swenson & Kayohye, Milltown, N.J.			12.59
LITTLE ELIMINATOR				
B/G	Perry Browning, Jacksonville, Fla.			13.37
STOCK ELIMINATOR				
S/S	Arnold Beswick, Morrison, Ill.			N.T.

1960 NASCAR CHAMPION

Pictured here is Arnie Beswick, mechanic and Larry Johnson, salesman, employees of Lee Morrison Pontiac, Clinton, Iowa, with their trophys and winning 1960 Pontiac automobiles.

1960 PONTIAC Eliminated over 100 competitors, representing all areas of the U. S. A. and every make of automobile . . .

We of LEE MORRISON PONTIAC are very proud of the accomplishments of the 1960 PONTIAC and these two drivers. We invite the public to see these cars and test drive the proven BEST PERFORMING CARS OF 1960.

Morrison Pontiac was proud of the fact that Arnie and Larry had won all those races. Here's the big newspaper advertisement, purchased by Lee Morrison and likely published in the Clinton Herald. The attitude of "Race on Sunday, Sell on Monday" was already becoming a slogan and words to live by for dealerships.

The published race results show Arnie's name highlighted in yellow.

was originally delivered, putting the transmission and rear gears back to the factory stock configuration. He then put the borrowed parts from the 1958 Chieftain back where they belonged. Had the extra performance parts been available within Arnie's finances, he definitely wouldn't have changed it back.

Arnie's reason for doing this was not so much complacency with the '60. He was never one to be lulled into that. It was that the Gas classes were getting a lot of attention, especially on late-model cars.

Money began being offered in 1960 instead of just a trophy. If there was a payout, Arnie was there. If no track offered money, there was always the camaraderie of the close friends who attended Cordova's Quad City Dragway each and every Sunday. Arnie treasured this almost as much (if not more) than the gamble of an unfamiliar track, although the allure and possible financial gain usually won out.

The Super Duty Parts

It was previously a consensus that Arnie's Super Duty package arrived in the trunk of the Ventura when he took delivery. After lengthy discussions about this

with knowledgeable Pontiac people, it was learned that these special parts (consisting of heads, valve springs, solid lifters, and the McKellar #7 cam) were shipped to Arnie midsummer. This only occurred after repeated calls to Frank Barnard.

Frank was in charge of distribution of the Super Duty packages as they became available in Pontiac's inventory. Additionally, all the NASCAR orders for the parts were filled first. While this might be a surprise, NASCAR was getting all of the manufacturers' attention because drag racing had not yet emerged as a viable way to sell cars. Plain and simple, a drag racer (no matter who he was) had to wait until all the NASCAR orders were filled. Arnie had to wait as well, so he did.

It is a commonly known fact that these Super Duty parts raised the advertised horsepower from 348 to 363. Even in factory stock form, the 1960 Ventura was a formidable weapon on the road and drag strips, especially in the hands of someone who knew engines and what it took to make a Pontiac motor perform to its maximum potential.

Arnie needed the extra insurance that the Super Duty package provided because the late-August World Series and the US Nationals in Detroit, which was slated for the following weekend, was approaching.

A pretty impressive collection of trophies is shown after Daytona. If I'm not mistaken, this photo was taken on the banks of the Mississippi River on the levee in Clinton, Iowa.

On any given Sunday, the '60 wouldn't have had the Morrison Pontiac banner. That was saved for big races with many spectators.

Arnie arrives home after dark still with the Ultra Stock (U/S) class and number on the window.

Pontiac Motor Division (PMD) shipped the parts out three to four weeks before the World Series, which provided plenty of time to install them and perform the adequate testing, tuning, and tweaking that was necessary before big events.

World Series of Drag Racing

Despite extra responsibilities on the farm as the summer wound down, there was no way that Arnie would miss the seventh-annual World Series of Drag Racing. Arnie was ready, as the previous week's newspaper showed. A *Drag News* column called the "Standard 1320" mirrored the *Moline Dispatch* and showed the '60 in the U/S (Ultra Stock) class running at 13.9 at 101.124 mph.

With everything done that Arnie could think of doing in the C/G class, the '58 now ran a 13.52 elapsed time at 103 mph. Consequently, that year he made hay (as is a farmer's motto) while the sun was shining—not only on the farm but also at Quad City Dragway.

Paul Carlson, a sports writer for the *Moline Dispatch* reported, "After last [Friday] night's coronation ceremonies, Arnie Beswick of Morrison, a regular winner at Quad-City Drag Strip, won top stock eliminator honors in his 1960 Pontiac Ventura. Beswick was clocked at 100.897 mph in 14.17 seconds in the final elimination run."

The icing on the cake was that he also took C/G honors with an amazing best run of 13.32 at 105.75 mph, dropping two-tenths of a second off the previous week's best time. This two-tenths drop from the previous week was more than likely due to the extra track surface preparation done during the World Series event.

NHRA Nationals

As elated as Arnie was over his World Series win, there was still a burning desire to be at the NHRA Nationals, which was at Detroit the following week on Labor Day weekend. However, there were too many farm obligations, and there was no way that he could get away.

It might have been different if the event was nearby. This wasn't just a matter of a weekend trip because Arnie would have needed to arrive by Tuesday and stay the whole week. As he read the reports on the event, he undoubtedly wondered what could have been. Jim Wangers went on to win the S/S class that year with a 14.14 ET at 102.4 mph in a similarly

The car is ready for the World Series: the Super Duty parts were installed, and the banner was displayed. (Photo Courtesy Gary Munson)

prepared 1960 S/D Pontiac. Arnie's best at the Series was a 13.9.

Bob Bartel kept the track open later that year, as results were printed for October 9. The cooler autumn air helped Arnie's 1960 Ventura run a 14.02 at 102 mph and his C/G '58 backed up the World Series run with a 13.34 at 105 mph.

I'm sure Arnie was glad that Palmer Lazarus was now out of his class and placed in B/GS (S standing for supercharged). Palmer's Chevrolet was reported with an 11.98 ET at a (misprinted) 161.62 mph (121 mph would be more accurate). This was due to the addition of a supercharger to the car.

All in all, 1960 had been a great year. He finally received what he asked for in a four on the floor, he won a very prestigious race in Daytona, he met some of his NASCAR idols, and he recorded a class win at the seventh-annual World Series of Drag Racing. How could life be any better?

The final round at the 1960 US Nationals in Detroit, where Jim Wangers won. (Photo Courtesy Jim Wangers)

CHAPTER 3

THE SUPER STOCK ERA

Arnie poses at the 1962 World Series. The big tent in the background was set up by Bob Bartel for a multitude of reasons. Meals were served under it, and tech services could be offered there as well in case of rain.

There had been a change of ownership at the Clinton, Iowa, Pontiac dealership where Arnie worked as a mechanic during the winter months. Lee Morrison faced health issues and had been bought out by none other than Arnie's friend and fellow Daytona racer Larry Johnson.

Arnie ordered his 1961 Ventura with some worry that it would not be delivered in time for the start of Daytona. Even though the event had been pushed back a week (February 20–26), there was still not much time. The '61 was to have almost exactly the same options as his '60, including the Bristol Blue paint option, 348-hp 425A motor, 4-speed transmission, and eight-lug wheels. The Super Duty parts were again available for the 1961 model year. These included the better-flowing, higher-compression heads; McKellar #8 cam; solid lifters; and 1.65:1 rockers. This time, they would be in the trunk.

The 1960 racing season had ended. The brown paper covering all of the dealership showroom windows, including the one in Clinton, Iowa, was pulled down. Coffee and donuts were served to prospective buyers, and they were introduced to the new 1961 Pontiacs.

The Second Year for Florida

Wally Parks had gone west to Pomona. The NHRA wouldn't be associated with the Speedweek races for 1961.

Arnie never considered California over Florida for even a second. There were a multitude of reasons, but the distance was obviously the biggest. Another was that he was a big circle track and NASCAR fan, and in Florida he would be in the company of those stars. Once the new Ventura arrived, barely in time for Daytona, it was the same frantic pace as in 1960.

A Who's Who List for the Second Year

Arnie knew the competition would be stiff. Unfortunately, he lacked the time to immediately install the Super Duty parts. He settled for just switching rear ends before the first night's races to the performance 4.30:1 ratio.

The competition for 1961 not only consisted of the familiar names that he'd met the year before but also newcomers. Ronnie Sox was back as well as Harold Ramsey, who switched from Chevy to Pontiac. Other notables included the Platt brothers (Hubert and Huston) and many names known specifically to the South, such as Ronnie Butler, Billy West, and Gene Hinsen.

Junior Johnson was the engine builder of several of the 409s that showed up. They were supposedly going to kick everyone's butt. The Wood Brothers, another famous name in NASCAR racing, had engines in several Ford entries. More entries showed up as each night of racing progressed.

While Arnie knew after the first night that he would need the extra performance from the S/D package, he still managed to win the first night. While Arnie's lightning-fast reflexes and driving skills can't be overlooked, he was also aided by how almost all of the racers were also doing new car tune-ups. He was also thankful that not all the big names were able to make it that first night. That was not the case for the rest of the week though, as attendance skyrocketed.

Optimizing the Pontiac's Potential

On the second day, Arnie installed the Super Duty heads, cam, and rockers. Even though Pontiac recommended that the block be chamfered, Arnie didn't want to risk getting any filings in the cylinders. The heads were installed without performing the chamfering process. Now, with the S/D parts installed, Arnie immediately noticed that the motor had a more-throaty sound due to the higher compression of the heads. The car ran great, but other problems developed at the end of that second night.

The first problem was a loss of oil pressure—at idle, no pressure showed at all. Even when the engine was revved above 2,500 rpm, there was still only 15 to 20 pounds of pressure. Rather than risk hurting the new car's engine, Arnie needed to address the oil pressure problem.

A Unique Engine Hoist

Fixing the oil pump wasn't an easy task, especially in the motel parking lot. One of the main hurdles was lifting the engine high enough to get the oil pan off or lowering it far enough to get it out of the way for access to the oil pump. Obviously, Arnie did not have an engine hoist with him. However, the solution was nothing short of genius.

The guys quickly scoured the lot and surrounding area for a way to help lift the engine. When they found a long, wooden light pole, it all clicked. The pole was positioned to run across the top of the fenders, and a chain was run over the top of the pole and bolted to the front and back of the motor like a normal cherry picker.

Once the oil pump was accessible, the problem was quickly found. A check ball that relieves

Three friends on each end of a nearby light pole provided the lift that Arnie needed to lower the back of the pan far enough to access the oil pump.

oil pressure from getting too high during high RPM was stuck open. Apparently, that was due to an ever-so-small piece of debris inside the engine, which was then picked up by the oil pump, possibly when the Super Duty parts had been installed.

Arnie went back for the remainder of Speedweek with a lot more confidence in his powerful Pontiac. It didn't disappoint, as Arnie once again faced racer after racer, continually getting the wins each and every time. While the West Coast contingent of racers probably weren't there, the best from the South, East, and Midwest were there in large numbers.

Protested Again!

As was the case during the 1960 event, Arnie had protest problems. After Arnie's win on the third night, he was protested for nonproduction cylinder heads and both manifolds. At this point, he was told that his previous three nights of wins would not count unless he could come up with proof that all the Super Duty parts were legal and added on the assembly line.

Once again, Pontiac sent a Western Union telegram with the proof that Arnie needed to reinstate his wins. That piece of paper also allowed him to remain in competition for the remaining nights. With the documentation in hand, Arnie found the head tech official and explained the dilemma about his disqualification problems. Arnie's worries were all for naught, as the official apologized to Arnie for all the extra work they had put him through.

That fourth night, Arnie pulled into the tech inspection line. Strangely, not one official showed up, and the inspector for that night merely put the class number on his window without saying so much as boo. His extra efforts and worry, it seemed, had been for nothing.

His Worst Engine Fears Realized

Everything went smoothly for the remainder of the week. That is until the last run of the last night. As Arnie passed through the finish line, a loud thud erupted from the engine compartment. Then, smoke billowed from the bottom and back of the car.

While elated over the week's wins, Arnie knew he was in serious trouble. The harsh reality was that he was 1,300 miles from home with a car that basically didn't run. His father's admonitions of "How are you going to afford to fix your car when

Bob Bartel and Arnie pose for a photo at the awards ceremony after racing concluded. Who would have guessed how huge these events were?

This hood full of trophies was merely from Arnie's races in Florida. Judging from the lack of leaves on the tree, Evelyn probably took this picture when Arnie was back home in Morrison.

it breaks" were as clear as a church bell on Easter Sunday morning, continually ringing in his mind.

Arnie tossed and turned that night, worrying about what he was going to do. How he was going to get home? Would he have to "eat crow" and face other possible repercussions from his father?

The next morning, still somewhat unsure and distraught about what to do, Arnie used his ticket to the Daytona 500 race and grabbed his 8-mm camera. Instead of heading to the grandstands like most people did, he instead headed straight to the pits. Besides capturing some up-close action that included Linda Vaughn doing the twist with Fireball Roberts and Richard Petty waving hello, he hoped to find someone who could help with his engine problem.

Arnie knew better than to bother Henry "Smokey" Yunick while he was at work during the race, but that still didn't stop him from talking to some of Smokey's other crew people. Arnie was told, "Oh, you need to find Bob Emrick," by someone who knew some of the Pontiac management chain. Arnie found Bob without too much difficulty and explained the situation. Bob heard the plea and told him that he should go see Smokey on Monday, when he wasn't immersed with his crew chief responsibilities in the 500-mile race.

Monday morning came with a glimmer of hope, and the motor was torn down. Sure enough, one piston was broken. Not only was it broken but it was completely shattered. The connecting rod and wrist pin remained, moving freely up and down and side to side inside the cylinder wall, scratching and scoring it beyond belief. Starting the car all those extra times hadn't been such a good idea. Now, it also looked like the block either had to be replaced or at least the one cylinder had to be bored, honed, or possibly sleeved.

Scolded by Smokey

Thanks to Bob Emrick's talk with Smokey, Arnie was able to have Smokey pay attention to his dilemma. The fact that one of Smokey's cars (Marvin Panch driving a 1960 Pontiac) had won the race on Sunday certainly helped him to be in a better mood.

When Arnie told Smokey that he was still running the stock rods and pistons, Smokey barked, "What the hell is wrong with your head? Why are you still running them wimpy-ass things? Those damn cast pistons and rods were designed to be used in production street motors, and they're no good when you start putting on those Super Duty parts. How that motor ever lasted the whole week of competition is hard for me to comprehend. You certainly must have had your favorite lucky charm in your pocket."

Arnie didn't let the demeanor of the man with the cowboy hat dissuade him from getting what he came for. Sadly, Smokey didn't have any of the right parts that Arnie could use. Before Arnie could hang his head in despair, Smokey told him about his employee named Vernon Blank.

Marvin Panch explained, "Smokey supplied the body parts and the engine, but the mechanics were on their own. They weren't even paid for their labor."

A Solution with No Cost

Vernon Blank was into the flying mile and economy run–type competition, where all the parts in the whole car had to be stone-cold production stock. This sounded like what Arnie needed, and he went to see Vernon.

The engine Arnie found at Vernon's was a smorgasbord of parts, including a 4-bolt-main block with rods, pistons, and the crank still intact. It was the exact ticket that Arnie was looking for. The short-block was loaded into the back of Arnie's friend's (Billy Harris) pickup truck. On the way back to the motel, Arnie realized just how lucky he had been and commented about the lucky charm that Smokey spoke of. It had just done another good deed for him. Billy agreed and remarked that it sure appeared that way.

Again, with the help and muscle of friends and several man hours, Arnie was back on the road, heading for his next destination.

Match Racing Begins

With the Ventura fixed, Arnie and the others headed to Yellow River, Georgia. Arnie met Shug Campbell and other Southern track owners, including Bobby Starr, owner/manager of Piedmont Dragstrip in Piedmont, North Carolina, the year before in Daytona. These track owners figured out that money would bring in the big names. If a handful of racers were paid at least $200 in appearance money for a Super Stock shootout, it meant that those racers would show up. When the big-name racers showed up, the owners knew that the fans would flock to their tracks to witness the racing excitement.

Yellow River Dragstrip was located between the Atlanta-area cities of Covington and Conyers, and it was owned and managed by Shug Campbell. The drag strip was typical of the vast majority of Southern strips at the time, merely a small line of pavement running through a hollow of trees. It wasn't just the Southern tracks that were sometimes literally two lines of pavement just wide enough for a car to drive down. The Piedmont facility lanes were separated by a 5- to 10-foot section of grass or dirt. The fact that Yellow River offered virtually no safety measures or fan protection led to its demise before the decade ended.

Yellow River consisted of small dirt banks with a single strand of thick number-9 wire stretched between posts to keep the fans (at least in theory) approximately 20 feet from the track surface. While the heavy wire lined both sides of the entire length of the strip, fans could lean hard against it, taking all of the slack out of a section. It was like stretching it. If enough fans pushed hard enough, they could practically reach out and touch the cars as they blasted by.

The determination of first, second, and other finishers was not without its drawn-out procedures, and the best promoters, such as Campbell and Starr, learned to use the drama to their advantage, keeping the fans glued to their seats a lot longer. The way it worked was that once the first-place winner was determined, that car would sit out while the complete class would run again to determine the second-place winner. Once the winner and runner-up were decided, these two cars were then paired up against each other to crown the event's Super Stock Class Champ.

In 1960, $200 was a lot of money to drag racers like Arnie. The year before, he had traveled down to Piedmont for the promise of $200, and sometimes when he won, he was awarded an additional $300. After winning one of these early races, he thought himself to be the richest man in the world, at least in drag racing.

After running at Yellow River, Arnie hitched a ride back to Illinois, leaving the '61 with friends in the Atlanta, Georgia, area to have a tow bar installed. Towing the car would eliminate the need to change rear gears from track use to highway use.

Barefoot Bobby

A few weeks later, Arnie returned to pick up the car. From there, he headed to his next stop at Piedmont, North Carolina. Arnie had been booked in by the track owner/manager, "Barefoot" Bobby Starr.

Like Shug Campbell, Barefoot Bobby was a colorful character; his nickname was due to the fact that he often ran around barefoot. He was proud of the fact, and often, when inviting racers in for special events, made mention that his facility could best be described as "cow pasture racing at its best."

Arnie wrote the following on the back of this photo: "This picture was taken after I won top Stock Eliminator honors at the NASCAR Winter National drags in 1961."

Bobby was a virtual rubber ball of energy, bouncing from place to place on the facility. Whether that was a normal characteristic for him or a lack of qualified help at the various track positions, Arnie didn't know.

Bobby's announcer was qualified, that was for sure. Whether he learned it on his own or Bobby filled him in, the announcer knew all the accolades, downfalls, recent ETs, and gossip about the big-name competitors. They seemed to know and tell all to the throngs that showed up at the track that day.

Arnie won more than his fair share of races at this special North Carolina track. After winning what he could of the prize money, Arnie and the friends who stuck with him for the tour, headed for home. Spring was just around the corner. It wouldn't be long before planting season began.

The First Match Race at Home

One of the first events in northern Illinois for the 1961 season was a best-of-five match race at the dragstrip in Oswego, Illinois. Arnie's reputation already made him legendary around home. There was another racer out of Argo, Illinois, a Chicago suburb, who was a consistent winner at Oswego Dragway with his Fords. His name was Don Gust.

The announcer and special-event director at the track for this event was Ron Leek, a man who went

on to be the track owner of Rockford Dragway. Ron had hyped the match between the two for months, printing hundreds of flyers and distributing them anywhere that a performance enthusiast might see one. By voice or print, Arnie was hailed as "King of the Super Stocks" and as "never losing on his home track of the Quad City Dragway." Ron and the signs proclaimed the same of Gust, saying that he never lost at Oswego, his home track.

A newspaper article from around the time of this event gave Don Gust credit for winning that first best-of-five matchup with his new 390-ci 401-hp Galaxie Starliner. Yet it was a comparison of apples and oranges. While Arnie's motor was completely stock, Gary Dyer, a man who would be mentioned in many aspects of drag racing in the years to come, had massaged the Ford with a full blueprint of the cylinder heads and block. Gary and his brother Glenn recalled Don Gust's black Ford. Glenn quickly remembered that one of the advantages that Gary gave to the Starliner was a specially tuned set of hand-fabricated exhaust headers and unique collectors.

Both cars would be torn down after the race to ensure that they were indeed legal and neither owner was cheating. Consequently, very little could be done to dramatically increase power and speed, but there were still tricks. There were always tricks. Gary confessed with a sly smile that when they'd reworked the Ford, a way to increase compression was to leave the head gaskets off, effectively making the combustion chamber smaller.

Most engine builders question if it was even possible to seal the combustion chamber without having excessive water and compression leaks. It's interesting to note that, even to this day, Arnie thinks that Dyer had connections to get much thinner gaskets than what were stock. That, along with the blueprinting, is how extra compression and additional horsepower was gained.

As it went down that day, Arnie won round one, but he broke second gear in round two, giving Gust the win for that round, as well as the next two. Arnie tried various launching and driving techniques during these passes, but the Ford was strong enough that Arnie absolutely needed second gear for a victory.

Before the last run, a spectator who was a mutual friend of both Arnie and Gust approached the absolutely frustrated Arnie with a solution. He had a GM transmission that would work in Arnie's car. Arnie's competitive nature dictated his decision, as he was desperate to get at least the last-round win. He readily agreed, and they installed the good transmission in place of his broken one.

Adding insult to the injury of losing this first best-of-five match race to Gust was the fact that Leek attached the "Farmer" handle to Arnie's name while announcing. He did it every time he was talking about the Gust/Beswick match race over the track microphone. Knowing Ron's style of announcing, the phrase surely came with a strategic pause between the two words. Leek probably meant no ill will from the handle he attached to Arnie's name. He admitted later that he just figured that anyone who lived less than 10 miles from the Iowa border had to be a farmer.

Leek was also new to the game in his role as a track announcer. He was going to do everything he could to get and keep the crowd's attention, and he had aspirations, hoping that the track owner would hire him on a full-time basis to promote more races.

Arnie didn't see it that way. In those days, especially in his mind, farmers were often considered as lowly second-class citizens at best. It was Arnie's opinion that Leek had labeled him as a poorly dressed hillbilly hick (which he probably resembled, wearing his work or farm clothes). If the clothes characterized the man, then how could a mere farmer ever have a chance against the engine-savvy Dyer?

The more Leek used "the Farmer" to describe Arnie that day, the more Arnie growled and the angrier he became, especially after a mere Ford had gotten the better of him in the quarter mile. It didn't matter that he hadn't won on account of a very good reason—major parts breakage. Arnie just did not want any part of the word *farmer* attached to his name.

Let's Try This Again

The rematch had a much different outcome. As one fan remembered it, Arnie defeated Gust soundly, winning three straight. However, Gust complained that the only reason Arnie won was due to the extra horsepower of the Super Duty Pontiac. Arnie suggested to the fancy-pants boy that maybe it was just problems with the driver.

Gust snapped back. "Okay, smart-ass, let me drive your damn Pontiac, and you take my Ford."

As the Beswick/Gust match race was one of the features for the day, there was a large crowd gathered around the two racers from the start of the day until the end. A lot of fans heard the verbal jousting between the two.

The crowd grew excited about this twist and really wanted to see this happen. As anticipation began to build, one eager fan prodded, "Come on, Beswick! Show him how it's done and what a farmer is really made of!"

Arnie realized that he wasn't going to get out of this one without making the switch, and finally, albeit somewhat reluctantly, he agreed. It wasn't long before Arnie was instructing Gust, explaining to him starting-line RPM as well as the shift points of how he drove his Pontiac. In the spirit of sportsmanship and fair competition, Gust did the same for Arnie with his Ford.

While the original day's main feature was their best-of-five match race, news about the driver swap spread like wildfire at the track. Naturally, word got to Leek. When Arnie and Gust pulled to the line for this spectacular race, Leek used the public address (PA) system to make sure that not only every spectator was lining the fence along the track but the other racers were too. This was unheard of and was too good to be true. Nobody was going to miss this.

Arnie knew that the race would be close. It was. Yet, the outcome was the same and the Farmer won the race, driving the competition's car! As the cars crossed the finish line, Arnie let out a big sigh of relief that was followed by the feelings of joy and jubilation from the win. Even he hadn't been completely sure that he could pull off a win, especially driving someone else's car. Some of Arnie's closer friends found amusement in the whole situation, and for months they teased Arnie, asking him when he was going to get rid of that slowpoke Pontiac and get a fast Ford.

The Farmer nickname stuck. He is still known by that moniker today, and like it or not, it had a big part in creating a certain image for Arnie in the not-too-distant future.

Naming the Car

Shortly after the first go-round with Gust, Arnie decided that he needed to get his car permanently lettered. It was no longer just a fad among racers. Arnie had seen more and more full-time race cars adorned with names, sponsors, and other information. His father's conservative thinking about writing, flames, or wild paint had to be overruled by the current trends that were developing in drag racing.

Arnie had the perfect name. In conversation, someone told him that he sure was passionate about his Pontiac. It was like a light switch had suddenly been turned on. Arnie told his friend and boss, Larry Johnson, about it. Larry now owned the Clinton-based Pontiac dealership. Johnson loved it too and said that if he could also use the name on his car, he would pay to have both cars lettered. Larry could write the whole thing off as an advertisement expense. Arnie agreed, and both cars were taken to local sign painter John Hanson, who worked his magic.

When Arnie went to pick up his car, he wasn't happy with the result. If a person in the stands glanced quickly at the car, it looked like Larry Johnson owned both cars because Arnie's name appeared in a rather small font on the roof, while Larry's was bigger and appeared on the doors. To a child or someone extremely short standing close to the car, Arnie's name would be completely out of sight. Arnie put up with the eternal question of who actually owned the car. While Larry was willing to have it redone, more than likely due to busy schedules, that never happened.

The icing on the cake for Arnie was the fact that Larry's wife, Darlene, did not like the name at all. To her, the word *passionate* was dirty and vulgar. As far as she was concerned and in roughly her words, profanity or swear words might as well be used on the quarter panel. It couldn't be any

These photos were taken in 1996 after the fresh restoration by the owner, Alan Ranz of Polo, Illinois. He'd only seen photos the way that Larry originally lettered it. The sign painter merely followed the original photos, in a sense, lettering it wrong.

worse. The controversy all added to Arnie's delight, especially when Larry admitted that he was forced to sleep on the couch for several nights because Darlene accused him of being guiltier than Arnie. After all, it was Larry who had taken both cars to the sign painter and given him instructions on what to put on the cars.

Unquestionably Legal in the Stock Classes

The 1961 race season was shaping up. The shoot-outs down South and the match race with Don Gust had been a huge success, despite Arnie's new "Farmer" nickname. Arnie's car was completely legal, still using merely the stock Pontiac rods and pistons borrowed from the block that was picked up from Vernon Blank's garage in Daytona.

Upon teardowns, everyone was amazed to see that no machine work had been done at all. Even the 0.060 allowable overbore and bringing the cylinder heads down to factory specs hadn't been done. Arnie bragged about the fact that his motor was untouched at the rematch with Gust so much so that he (or more likely the fun-loving Andy Perry) hastily applied masking tape letters to his car that read, "100% legal." Gust couldn't say the same, as teardowns even revealed porting and polishing on his Ford.

Arnie's name was seen winning the U/S (Ultra Stock) class in *Drag News* almost every week of the whole year. This drag racer's Bible, as the paper was often labeled, reported for the week of May 21 that Arnie went beyond the U/S win to capture Stock Eliminator for that week's event. While stock eliminator honors didn't happen every week, bracket-style rules were beginning to be implemented. Competitors to Arnie were given a 20-foot head start at first. Arnie's dominance increased this to even greater distances.

There was more good news for Arnie's racing career when Raymond (Arnie's father) finally realized that (1) Arnie wasn't frivolous with his cars and they weren't breaking as Arnie's father had predicted, or if they did, the cost of fixing them was negligible, and 2) he was bringing home good money, more than farming paid. For the first time in his career, Arnie no longer had to rely on his measly farm wages to pay his repair bills.

These two facts, aided by influential talks by Arnie and his mother, were good enough reason for Raymond to hire extra help on the farm. This gave Arnie more freedom to pursue his racing goals and travels. Even though he was still opposed, Raymond bit his lip and let Arnie use a more permanent paint for the car's lettering scheme. It was explained to Raymond that by bringing attention to the car, it was "Race on Sunday, Sell on Monday."

A Publicity Stunt Leads to a Royal Stomp

Darlene Johnson had simmered down enough that she was now speaking to Larry and wasn't having him sleep on the couch. After some more thought and talks between the husband and wife, they began to formulate a plan. What if a challenge was sent to Royal Oak Pontiac in Michigan, the much-ballyhooed dealership that had the self-proclaimed fiercest Pontiacs in the country?

As fate would have it, the challenge wasn't necessarily because Royal Oak Pontiac's cars were whipping up on all the competition at the racetracks. It was because their main driver, Jim Wangers, happened to work for the Pontiac ad agency. He seemed to have free run to continually blow his horn on how great the Royal Pontiac race cars were.

A challenge seemed like a good idea to both Larry and Darlene, as Royal Pontiac was getting a lot more ink than Johnson Pontiac, located in the small town of Clinton, Iowa. They thought it might help boost sales of either cars or parts at their dealership. Another plus was that it might give them notoriety or fame in the race publications of the day, a goal to which Larry aspired. They ran the idea by Arnie and Bob Bartel.

Arnie loved the idea because he also wanted to see how awesome the highly touted Royal cars really were. This would give Arnie the chance to beat Jim Wangers, who won the NHRA Nationals the year before. Bob Bartel naturally loved the idea because it was an opportunity to sell more admission tickets and spice up his weekly race program. Bob contacted the Royal Oak dealership for a best-of-five match race, and the race was previewed in an issue or two of *Drag News* before the event took place.

Royal Pontiac had two cars: the 4-speed and an automatic. While it definitely would be Arnie taking on Jim Wangers in the battle of the manually shifted S/D Ponchos, Bartel found a unique way of qualifying the other car to race against Royal's automatic car. On the weekend of July 23, Bartel let the winning Pontiac with an automatic

transmission face Dick Jesse, driving the Royal automatic race machine.

The late Paul Carlson was a Quad City–based writer for the *Moline Dispatch*. Paul was also the person responsible for most of the highlight stories that were sent to *Drag News*. He told how Billy Wagner, a regular at Cordova and Daytona traveler, got the honor.

Paul wrote, "Billy Wagner, Rock Falls, in his 1960 Pontiac proved to be the quickest automatic transmission auto of the day. Wagner turned 14.93 seconds and 97.82 mph to win the honor of competing next Sunday, July 30, against Royal Pontiac from Detroit."

He went on, "This big dealer from the Detroit area sponsors four of the fastest stock autos in the country."

Paul went on to list the accolades of both Beswick and Wangers. The stage was set.

Arnie's home movies show the two Royal race cars hooked up to tow bars behind two brand-new bubble-top Venturas, just after entering the confines of Quad City Dragway. While Royal's race cars were white with red stripes down the middle, the tow cars were the exact opposite, painted bright red with single white stripes down the center of the hood, top, and trunk lids. Footage of a very confident Jim Wangers, who was smiling, laughing, and strutting for the camera follows that of an equally jovial attitude from his Michigan-based teammates, Dick Jesse and the rest of the traveling crew. That was all short lived, however.

Race Time

Jim Wangers has repeatedly and freely admitted that he's never beaten Arnie in a drag race, and the

Jim Wangers's 1961 Ventura sits in front of the automatic car in the staging lanes. (Photo Courtesy Jim Wangers)

Cordova footage shows that he was probably one of the slower U/S cars that Arnie raced all season. Ben Brown, a weekly commentary writer for *Drag News* summed it up this way:

"Several weeks past at Cordova, Arnie match raced Royal Oak Pontiac, and the rumor is that Arnie shut 'em down so bad that you had to give up trying to count the car lengths between the two Pontiacs (when they went through the 1/4-mile finish line)."

Paul Carlson's article referred to "small town" Beswick beating up on "big city" Royal Pontiac at Quad City Dragway. He mentioned the crowd of 3,800 spectators and 285 participants who were on hand to witness the finest races along with the two match races that day.

"CORDOVA, ILL., July 30 – Undefeated!!" Carlson continued. "Once again, Arnie Beswick met and beat another highly touted Ultra Stocker. Unbeatable! The people here and elsewhere that have seen Arnie run, firmly believe that there is no faster stock machine in the country. ROYAL PONTIAC, Detroit, was matched against Arnie in a three out of five race. Both cars are 1961 Ultra Stock 368 HP Pontiacs. BESWICK turned 105.99, 13.54; 107.14, 13.45; and 106.88, 13.62 against ROYAL'S 104.65, 14.18; 103.44, 14.35; and 105.12, 14.02 in the three match races.

"In the automatic transmission division, Bill[y] Wagner, Rock Falls, driving a 1960 Pontiac, had like success in shutting down the Royal Pontiac. Bill went Ultra Stock with his car just two weeks ago. Prior to that, he was running in C/SA (C-Stock Automatic). His hard work paid off as he won three in a row with 104.62, 14.41; 101.12, 14.42; and 102.85 in 14.29.

"It looks like the home of the "BIG HOT INDIANS" has changed from ROYAL PONTIAC, Detroit, to JOHNSON MOTORS, Clinton. Larry Johnson is the sponsor of two of the runningest Pontiacs in the country today."

Looking at the speeds and times of Wagner, there was no doubt that Billy received a little help from the Farmer, as his ETs dropped over a half second from the previous week's qualifying session and his top speed increased by as much as 5 mph as well. Arnie explained that he indeed helped Billy simply by changing his stock cylinder heads and cam to a set of 1961 S/D heads and a McKellar #7 cam.

While the Royal group limped home with long faces, it was a win for all on the home team. In the late August issue of *Drag News*, Ben Brown gave Larry Johnson a big plug and wrote about the *Passionate Ponchos* of Arnie, Bill Wagner, and Don Bennett. He also mentioned that all of the high-performance parts you might need could be purchased through Johnson Pontiac.

As gratifying as it was to show the world the location of the Pontiac racing headquarters, the allure of Southern money was too much to pass up. On August 5 and 6, Arnie was booked into Greensboro, North Carolina, for another shoot-out. The payout was $400. More importantly, this was one of the first times that he met a future friend and one of the fiercest competitors that he would ever know. His name is as well known as Arnie's, that of Dyno Don Nicholson.

All in all, it was shaping up for a good year, but controversy was just around the corner.

Engine Work

As soon as Arnie arrived home from his trip to Greensboro, North Carolina, it was time to prepare for the World Series and one of the biggest races of the year: the NHRA US Nationals.

Competition at the World Series was always tough. Trips to Daytona had taught Arnie that the cream of the racing crop from coast to coast always appeared at the US Nationals, which was in Indianapolis for the first year. He would need his car to be in top tune to hold his own against hundreds of competitors.

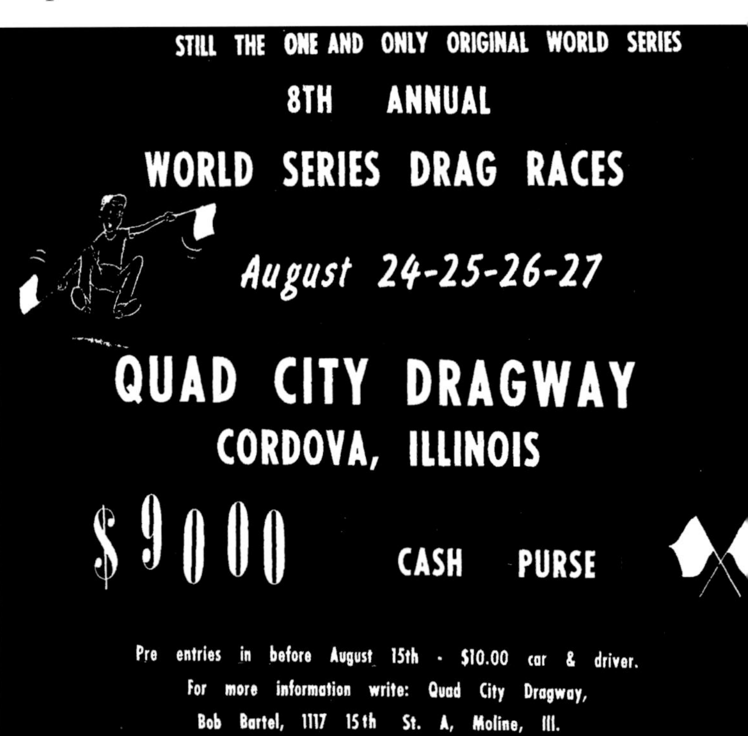

This ad, taken out in Drag News *in mid-July, promotes the upcoming 1961 World Series of Drag Racing.*

421 S/D

Unbeknownst to Arnie, Pontiac had just released the 421-ci Super Duty engines. Arnie received his during the week of the World Series. There was one major reason that he didn't make the switch from his 389 to the bigger mill for the US Nationals, and that was due to machine work with Ray Nichels. Had Arnie known about the 421 engines that were released in July and August, he never would have bored, balanced, and blueprinted the block of the 389. Unfortunately for him, Pontiac kept the release of the 421 S/D motors as one of the best-kept secrets of the decade (at least until that date).

The most important factor that influenced Arnie to stay with the 389 was the sermon from Smokey Yunick about the unreliable cast rods and pistons in the 389's stock motor. The comments made by this knowledgeable man came back to haunt Arnie time and time again. Consequently, he decided that it was a necessary evil to have a professional short-block built that would include the optional forged aluminum pistons and forged steel rods. Despite the cost factor, he was now confident that the bottom end was much more bullet-proof than one that consisted of stock cast parts. Since overboring the motor by 0.060 was allowed, he would have that done as well.

Pontiac was using Ray Nichels a lot and recommended him to put Arnie's short-block together. Arnie's trips to Daytona again came into play. While he may not have actually shook hands with Ray, Arnie knew who he was. The credentials were certainly there, and even with the discounted labor rate, Arnie bit the roughly $1,500 bullet and ordered a short-block, complete with Pontiac Super Duty–type forged pistons and rods.

The difference in power was instantly noticeable. Prior to the new block, most of the runs for Arnie's *Passionate Poncho* were in the 13.50 to 13.60s

The most important factor caption follows the form below.

1961 WORLD SERIES OF DRAG RACING
QUAD CITY DRAGWAY
CORDOVA, ILLINOIS
AUGUST 24 THRU 27
$9615.00 CASH AWARDS

24 Stock Classes		$40.00	$960.00	2 Competition Coupe Sedan	A/C	250.00	
6 Stock Sports		$40.00	240.00	2 Modified Roadster	B/C	150.00	400.00
3 Modified Sports	AX	75.00			A/M	250.00	
	BX	65.00			B/M	150.00	400.00
	CX	50.00	190.00	4 Gas Single Engine Dragsters	A/D	300.00	
3 Sportsmans		50.00	150.00		B/D	250.00	
6 Gas Coupe Sedan		75.00	450.00		C/D	200.00	
3 Gas Coupe Sedan Supercharged		100.00	300.00		D/D	100.00	850.00
3 Street Roadster		75.00	225.00	2 Gas Dragsters Dual Engine	AA/D	300.00	
3 Altered Coupe Sedan Gas		100.00	300.00	And Or Supercharged	BB/D	200.00	500.00
2 Altered Coupe Sedan Fuel A/AF		200.00		2 Fuel Dragsters	A/FD	500.00	
	B/AF	100.00	300.00		B/FD	250.00	750.00
2 Roadster		100.00	200.00				$6215.00

Eliminator	Award
Top Eliminator Of Meet-	500.00
Top Eliminator Fuel	400.00
Top Eliminator Gas	400.00
Middle Eliminator	200.00
Junior Eliminator	150.00
Little Eliminator	300.00
Top Stock Eliminator	100.00

Top Speed Fuel	100.00	Second Fastest Fuel	50.00
Low Elapsed Time Fuel	100.00	Second Lowest Elapsed Time Fuel	50.00
Top Speed Gas	100.00	Second Fastest Gas	50.00
Low Elapsed Time Gas	100.00	Second Lowest Elapsed Time Gas	50.00

Top Speed Friday, Day Up To 5:00	50.00	Top Speed Saturday, Night,	
Top Speed Friday, Nite, 7:30 To 11:00	50.00	7:30 To 11:00	100.00
Top Speed Saturday, Day Up To 5:00	50.00		2900.00

$$$ ADD THEM UP, FELLOWS, TOTAL $9,115.00 $$$
$$Worth Of Merchandise Awards In Every Class
Plus Fully Engraved Trophies ** Speed & Eliminator
In All Classes & Brackets Proclaiming That You Met
The Best & Won!!

Send entry to; Bob Bortel   1117 15th St 'A'   Moline, Illinois . Phone 764 - 0574

NAME _______ AGE ____ PRESENT OCCUPATION _______
FULL ADDRESS _______
DRIVERS NAME _______ AGE ____
FULL ADDRESS _______
Car Description   (Please send recent photo if available) _______
Does car have a permanent number on it? If so, list it _______
Does car have official name? If so, list it _______
Body, Year & Make _______ Chassis, Year & Make _______
Engine, Year & Make _______ Cubic Inches _______ Total car weight _______ CLASS _______
Best speed to date _______ E.T. _______ Where Recorded _______ FUEL _______ GAS _______
If stock, please answer following;
Year & Make _______ Body Style _______ Advertised H.P. _______
Prepaid entries on or before August 20th ...... Car & Driver $10.00 for entire meet
Entries after August 20th ... Car and Driver ... $15.00 for entire meet
Crew members must register with car, $6.00 each for entire meet
Entry Fee Enclosed _______ Crew Members Fees Enclosed _______
CREW MEMBERS
NAME _______ ADDRESS _______ AGE _______
NAME _______ ADDRESS _______ AGE _______
NAME _______ ADDRESS _______ AGE _______
Each prepaid entry will receive receipt and rule book.

BONUS!! If Any Machine Takes Top Speed Friday, Friday Night, Saturday, Sat. Night, Class Eliminator, Top Speed Of The Meet, Low Elapsed Time Of The Meet, And Top Eliminator Of Meet, Quad City Dragway Will Add $500.00 To His Take Home Pay.

Here is an early registration form for the World Series. Back then, instead of sending it to the track, you just sent it to Bob and Dawn's home. His old phone number is listed.

at 102 to 103 mph. *Drag News* reported the Farmer's elapsed times in Indy at 13.41 at 106.78 mph.

Heading to Indianapolis for the Big Go

After winning his class for the eighth year, Arnie was off to Indianapolis. The NHRA Nationals, always on Labor Day weekend, follows the World Series by a week. While the eighth-annual World Series was less than 20 miles away from Arnie and offered decent money for a class win or better, the seventh-annual

NHRA Nationals were established by a national organization with a large staff that ran all aspects of promotions and marketing and organized race event operations. So, NHRA events offered far more cash and contingency prizes than the single-track owner of the World Series could raise. A brand-new Thunderbird was offered by the Hurst-Campbell Corporation in 1961 for the Competition winner in points. There was also a brand-new 1961 Pontiac Catalina sport coupe from George Hurst's company for the Stock winner. This car was set up for drag racing by Royal Pontiac.

Tech opened for inspection early Thursday morning, so Arnie had just a few days to pack up before leaving for Indianapolis so he could arrive when the technical inspection gates opened. If present trends follow tradition, it was late Wednesday night when Arnie and fellow travelers checked in to their hotel rooms in Indianapolis.

Unforeseen Mechanical Issues

Before going to the track the next morning, Arnie (along with Jim Andrews and other crewmembers) had breakfast at a restaurant that was close to the track. It was a popular race crowd hangout and a place where you could learn more about what was going to happen later that week than any other place. In conversation with one of the California tech inspectors, Arnie learned that the stock axle shafts in the type of rear end that was in his car had a habit of breaking from the kind of pressure that the S/D motor and the added traction of the race surfaces at the bigger events was putting on them.

Once Arnie was inside the confines of the track and before going through tech, he decided to check the axles in his car for any signs of spline twisting. He needed to find out if they possibly should be replaced. The car was put up on stands, and the wheels and the bearing caps were removed.

The axles would not budge with the tools Arnie had available. Serious problems called for serious measures. Arnie decided that extra force was needed and that a pickup truck pulling on the axle would certainly be enough power to pull out the possibly twisted axle shaft. Jim and the boys backed one up to the side of the car that they were working on and wrapped a chain around the car's axle shaft. This should certainly provide the necessary force to do the job, but Arnie also had to think about how the axle was such a stubborn component and that the truck might pull the *Poncho* off the jack stands

before the shaft came loose. That was easily fixed by finding another truck and fastening another chain from this vehicle to the frame of the Ventura.

Now, with the '61 sandwiched between the two vehicles and the chains secured, the first truck was put in gear to pull out the obstinate part. As the old pickup moved away, the chains went tight, and a little throttle was applied. All of a sudden, the truck moved away quickly from the *Passionate Poncho*, and a loud bang was heard. They couldn't believe it. The chain broke and snapped back, putting dents in the quarter panel of the race car. How infuriating!

Arnie was temporarily at a loss, being unable to devise a way to remove the axles. Time was a factor, as the tech lines were getting longer, and Arnie needed to get in line to complete his inspection. The axles would have to wait until a heavy-duty axle puller was found and the operation could be reattempted.

A Big Win That Maybe Shouldn't Have Been

As eliminations progressed, Arnie went round after round, making it to the final run in Super Stock. There, he faced none other than Mickey Thompson. Both cars staged. The flag man leaped into the air, and the two Pontiacs had great starts with every fan on his or her feet. Ben Brown summarized it this way:

"At the finish line . . . Unbelievable! The Morrison farm boy from Illinois crosses first to take the win with a 13.53 ET at 107.27 mph."

Arnie is pictured here talking to the media after winning the S/S class on Saturday. He's being presented with the Sturdevant Auto Golden Torque Wrench for being the mechanic on his winning car. The prize was sponsored by parent company, New Britain Machine Company. Arnie still has the torque wrench.

Arnie was on an adrenaline high like no other. He just defeated one of the biggest names at this national event. Not only that, but Thompson was also one of the major sponsors. Once back at the pits, it was inferred that Arnie was not supposed to win. The facts were starting to sink in. It appeared to be a political race here, one where the lowly second-class peasant farmer should never take away a win from the California-based crowned prince.

Sunday was hot and muggy, but it was a day off for Arnie. The schedule called for Stock and Modified roadsters, dragsters, sports cars, Gas class entries, and supercharged vehicles. The street roadsters and the altered cars were also to run eliminations.

So, Arnie had the opportunity to enjoy watching the races and talk to people. His main concern was the stubborn axles that refused to come out. Even on Saturday, he had started talking with anyone he thought might have a puller. He even talked with the people from Royal about it, and they told Arnie that they had a heavy-duty axle puller at the dealership in Michigan. After Indy, Arnie was going east for scheduled races and Royal Oak Pontiac was not very far out of the way, so he could give the tool a try. However, he would be in debt to the very race team that he soundly defeated less than a month before.

Going for the Biggest Win

Monday's weather was perfect, and now it was time to find out who would be Top Eliminator, Middle Eliminator, Little Eliminator, Street Eliminator, and No. 1 Stock Eliminator. The No. 1 Stock Eliminator title was last on the schedule, but it was the next step for Arnie.

When he crossed the finish line, it was with the win over Hayden Proffitt, thanks to a missed shift

There are no less than four photos of this final run-off between Don and Arnie, taken from various angles. The view that appeared in Hot Rod magazine looked down from the tower. (Photo Courtesy Bob D'Olivo, Colorization by Dean Fait)

This is the same race from a different angle. The signatures are real! (Water Color Painting by Dean Fait)

by Hayden. Arnie had a 13.41 ET at 106.78 mph.

After this, it was time for Stock Eliminator Overall. A racer didn't necessarily need to be a class winner to be in these final races—the racer merely had to be one of the 50 fastest cars in the S/S or OS/S classes on the property that weekend.

The final round was between the Nicholson Chevrolet and the Beswick Pontiac. Both Don and Arnie agreed that the Stock Eliminator overall winner would run a best-of-three grudge race.

While a best-of-three at a national event seems highly unlikely, Ben Brown said, "At the flag, both Arnie and Don came out of the hole even up, but on the top end it was the big 409 Chev of Nicholson across the line first at 13.37 sec. 108.69 mph."

The Tear Down

While out of the running for Stock Eliminator honors on Monday, Arnie had still won the S/S class on Saturday, so that meant that a teardown was required. It was late in the day already when an official jumped in the car with Arnie (and all of the other winners) to make sure nothing was changed on the car.

All racers and their chaperons headed for the big single-story building where the vehicles were torn down. Arnie parked next to Nicholson with Lloyd Cox on his other side. The intake manifold and one head must be removed during inspection. Arnie picked the driver-side head to pull. The car was so hot that Arnie could hardly touch anything. Lloyd

even suggested that Arnie should wait for the motor to cool off, but the Farmer was eager to get on the road as soon as possible.

The lead tech man for this meet and all national events was in his second year of working for NHRA. It was none other than Bill "Farmer" Dismuke. Bill received his "Farmer" nickname because he drove a vegetable truck for Farmer Brown Produce Company in the early 1950s.

Arnie remembered him clearly, and he found Bill to be one of the most arrogant men that he'd ever met. Arnie's opinion was that his head tech position let him exploit his power at the expense of both innocent and seasoned racers who weren't considered to be NHRA favorites. Of course, it was only confidence from Bill's point of view. Bill knew he had the power to make or break a racer when it came to legalities. In that garage, he held the power.

Under watchful official eyes, each racer began to tear down. Since Arnie was one of the first ones to have his hand up, indicating that his intake and head were off, his car was one of the first that Bill inspected. Without looking at much else, he stuck his micrometer inside the cylinder farthest back, pulled it up to see, and almost too quickly stated, "You're done!"

"What?" Arnie said in disbelief. "What are you talking about?"

"You're over by a thousandth and a half," Bill sneered as he moved to the next racer whose hand was in the air.

"That's impossible!" Arnie said to his back.

Arnie moved to face Bill again, protesting that there was no way that he was overbore.

Bill wouldn't listen as Arnie continued to protest the call. Bill, moving from car to car, eventually disqualified the Nicholson car, citing carburetor and valve spring issues. Don was also livid, but not as much as Arnie. Don admitted that to me on the phone before he passed away.

Arnie found someone in the shop who had a micrometer and took the time to measure carefully. It was right where it should be. He knew it was. He hadn't spent all that money getting a professional block built to have it be overbored.

Let's take a breath and step aside here to review the evidence. The bore number is 0.0015 inch. To understand how thick that is, here's a comparison: a sheet of normal typing paper, even the thin bond (not the heavy card stock) measures 3/1000ths (0.003), and that is twice as thick as the infraction amount.

Lloyd Cox was shocked about the treatment that Arnie received. "You just got screwed!" He said, shaking his head, "F——ed with a capitol *F.*"

Again, Arnie approached Bill to show his results to the insensitive tech man. No sooner had Arnie started talking than he was cut off.

"Listen," Bill snapped, "you're out! Don't ask me to come back and recheck it. It's not going to happen!"

Arnie remembered that Indy car racer Roger Ward was on the property. Arnie succeeded in getting one of his experts to look at the motor. Roger's shop technician found Arnie's car to be the legal bore size. Arnie again pressed Bill to reconsider.

This time, the official virtually exploded in anger. "Get out of my face!" he yelled. "And don't come back!"

It was crystal clear that even though it was wrong, the NHRA's position and decision would never be changed. The NHRA had really left a sour taste in the Arnie's mouth.

According to Jim Andrews, there was some mystery regarding the whereabouts of the trophy for Super Stock. When the newly crowned winner came looking for it, it had somehow disappeared.

Closing out the 1961 Season

Despite his anger, disappointment, and resentment toward the politically motivated NHRA organization, Arnie was approached about match races. This was due to the fact that other track owners witnessed the cream of the drag racing crop battling it out at the US Nationals.

One such person was Gilbert Kohn, who owned Motor City Dragway in New Baltimore, Michigan, as well as a few other tracks. The other track that booked Arnie was York US30. They both made Arnie and Don offers. The Pennsylvania track added Dave Strickler to the list for that year-end match race.

The prospect of earning some match race money had its appeal to any driver, so Arnie pointed the car northeast to Detroit. There was also the extra motivation to go there instead of home, as the words of the Royal Pontiac employees came back to him. That stubborn axle would be no match for the heavy-duty puller that was waiting just for Arnie.

Jim Andrews remembered their stop at the Royal Oak dealership.

"When their axle puller was used, it came out like it had almost no resistance at all," he said. "We couldn't believe how easy that tool made it look."

When the old axles were removed, it was clear that they were on their way to breaking. The splines were already showing signs of twisting.

Even though they were the fiercest of competitors on the track, off the track Don Nicholson and Arnie were developing a friendship. It was somewhat guarded at first. At the time, Don called California home, and any opportunity to match race or appear at a track in the Midwest was beneficial—win or lose. Arnie knew that if track owners would put up money for Don, they'd put up money for him.

Quad Cities Showdown

With that in mind, Arnie called Bob Bartel about the possibility of a match race at Quad City Dragway between Don and Arnie. Bob liked the idea and began working immediately to promote the race. Time was short before the end of the season, and October 1 was the date selected.

After various appearances and a lot of rain, the weekend of October 1 finally arrived. The reporter for *Drag News* magazine told it this way:

"During the morning, Arnie Beswick, tuning up for the big match race with Don Nicholson, Pasadena, California, turned 12.93 seconds and 111.11 mph. The effort resulted in a blown piston. Beswick returned home, put his 421-ci Pontiac engine together, and returned to run the match. On the first run, Beswick was the winner at 110.42 and 13.05. Next time around, Arnie blew his 4-speed transmission and Don Nicholson roared through the lights, turning 110.43 mph and 12.85 seconds. There is no doubt about it, Don Nicholson owns the 'runningest' Chevrolet in the country. This left Don the winner of the match between the two hottest stockers in the country."

Arnie and Jim Andrews remembered a very different story about the day, thanks to some activity that occurred a few weeks earlier. Like the other prominent racers of the day, Pontiac had sent Arnie one of the Super Duty 421 engines. Since Arnie had paid a lot of money to Ray Nichels to balance, blueprint, and otherwise enhance his 389, Arnie elected to put the 421 engine into the car of Jim Andrews, his good friend and fellow Pontiac owner.

According to Arnie, the "blown piston" was really a wing nut that fell down the carburetor when the air cleaner was removed. Arnie was not about to risk hurting that expensive motor. The decision was made, despite some verbal protests from Don, to substitute Jim Andrews's 421-ci car in this special best-of-five match race.

While street and highway testing had been performed, this was the first time that anyone had taken Jim's 421 car down the quarter-mile track. There were big smiles on the Pontiac people at Cordova's Quad City Dragway that day, while frowns and more complaints were heard from Dyno Don and his Stovebolt people. While the outcome was as reported and Don headed home with a little more traveling money, it was because of this day that Andrews now had his own 12-second time slip with his red 1961 Ventura.

Pontiac's Hood Scoop

As the 1961 season ended, there was the day-to-day job that Arnie needed to be at to support himself, his family, and his racing career. Besides the family farm duties, the money he made working for Johnson Pontiac helped support Arnie's racing addiction. A split between Arnie and Johnson Pontiac was on the near horizon. (There's more on the Beswick/Johnson split later.)

One day, Arnie and fellow racer Don Bennett were enjoying the lunch hour at Johnson Pontiac. As expected from two racers, their talk was about how to improve their chances of winning. Both knew all too well that it was always nice to have even the slightest edge.

Burpee Seed Company had a distribution center just across the street from the back of the dealership. Mail order was everything to them, so both

big and small trucks came and went constantly. Don's attention was suddenly grabbed by three Ford Super Duty trucks that were being used to haul mail. Atop each of their hoods was a scoop that faced the windshield.

"There's what we need," Don said, "a scoop like that."

"Yeah, that'd be nice," Arnie agreed, knowing how it would help bring colder outside air in versus the hot air that was under the hood. He'd seen scoops in Indy.

"Why don't we do it?" Don wondered aloud.

"Well, it would need a part number obviously," Arnie countered, "or else the tracks won't let you use it in the Stock classes."

"Sure, so call Frank [Barnard with Pontiac]," Don replied.

"Why not . . .?" Arnie said. He nodded and got up to go to the phone.

Frank most likely laughed at Arnie's cleverness as he relayed the request. He told Arnie that he'd get it done and that within a few days they'd have a part number. Arnie's next call was to the Ford dealership in town to order one of those scoops. Coincidently, by the time there was a scoop in hand, Arnie had an official letter from Pontiac with the part number on it. He kept it handy to silence any tech inspectors, racers, or track owners.

Next came the installation. Don Bennett chuckled as he told about this process.

This photo showing the hood scoop was taken just before Arnie sold the car. Notice the Taber name on the door and no more Johnson Pontiac or Larry Johnson on the upper door, indicating the split between the two.

While it looks like Arnie's name is still on the roof, all references to Johnson Pontiac are gone from the car. Taber, out of Atlanta, Georgia, is on the door in this race with Phil Bonner's brand-new 1962 Ford Galaxie. It's easy to tell from the crowd, including those in the trees, that this is at Yellow River either in late 1961 or very early 1962.

"Arnie took an electric [jig]saw and just started cutting," he said. "As I remember, he wasn't too careful either from the way it looked. He just zapped a hole in that nice hood, and we put it on there. Of course, while the Ford trucks had it facing the windshield, we turned it around to face the front.

"The first time we took it to the track," Don continued, "[Bob] Bartel, well, he didn't say too much, but he was amazed how fast we had come up with a part number for it."

While Quad City Dragway let Arnie slide with the scoop, there were a few tracks that positively would not allow him to stay in the S/S class with the scoop on. It only took one time arguing at great length with a track official to figure out that he needed to order another hood. He painted the second hood blue to match so that he had one untouched without a scoop.

1962: Pontiac Steps It Up Like the Other Brands

The performance race escalated for 1962, and Pontiac upped its game with the Super Duty program. Just like the others, the first 421 that Arnie received in 1961 was a race-only engine, hand-built in a special factory tool room. They were estimated to have between 373 and 405 bhp. They all came with four-bolt mains, forged rods and crank, solid lifters, and twin Carter 500-cfm 4-barrel carburetors perched on top of an aluminum intake manifold. Then, there were the exhaust manifolds.

The units boasted separate bolt-on collectors that contained cutouts to bypass the 2.25-inch dual-exhaust system and low-restriction mufflers. The engines also received a specific harmonic bal-

ancer, oil pan, and fuel and oil pump. While the 1962 S/D 421s were officially rated at 405 bhp, it's been stated that the real output was closer to 460.

An NHRA rule change for 1962 stated that engines and body parts for the Stock classes must be production pieces. The other sanctioning organizations adapted the same rules. This meant that there would be a limited run of them. It also meant that if there were possible gains in the weight department, it must come from the factory that way. Pontiac solved this problem by fitting its cars with aluminum front ends and bumpers.

No More Johnson Pontiac

Arnie's association with Johnson Pontiac ended late in 1961 for two reasons. The main reason was that, like all of his previous employers, Larry wasn't happy that Arnie had farming obligations during three of the four seasons and that if the phone rang for a race down South or out East, Arnie was there. Secondly, Arnie was still a little miffed about Larry's name being so prominent on the door while his was smaller and on the roof.

Consequently, Arnie placed his order for a new '62 through Seltzer in the Chicago metro area. He was adamant about the color. Even though the dark Ensign blue was close, he wanted the 1961 color of Bristol blue. This meant a longer delay in delivery, despite political games by Arnie. He thought that by buying not one but two of the fairly-hard-to-obtain 409 Chevrolets (one white and one red), it would speed up the process and show Pontiac that he wasn't necessarily loyal. It didn't work. Apparently, neither did the 409s. Consequently, it meant driving the year-old '61 for the first part of the year.

Trouble in Florida

The first stop, which had become a tradition, was in Daytona for Speedweek. The 1962 season did not start out well for Arnie, as politics again reared its ugly head.

According to an article called *Don's Department*, the writer told about the event. He wrote that it was the most unorganized event he'd ever attended. Competitors never knew which class they were running against, and several vehicles were so far out of class that it was "ridiculous."

Then, there was the protest period. Protests were supposed to be filed before eliminations, but the writer witnessed friends of the officials getting them in almost before racing was over for the night.

"That meant there was no time for the protested party to fix his mistake [if he was able] and gave others a decided advantage," the writer said.

Such was the case for Arnie, who was protested after the fifth night of racing. He had again won his class every night. The car had to be torn down in the presence of an official, but Arnie was told that they were too tired to tear down the car that night. It would be done the next day.

A friend stayed with the car during the night, and when Arnie showed up to get the car, there was no official. Arnie's mechanic told him that the official had said that he was to take the car to the pit area, basically giving the okay. Upon arriving at the pit area, the head official disqualified Arnie for bringing his car out of the impound area without the escort of an official.

Just like at Indy, Arnie could not get the head official to listen to him. It was even discovered that Arnie had come straight to the track from the impound area and not touched the car's engine. Arnie continued to state his case, all the way to Ed Otto, vice-president of NASCAR. Still, the head official would not change his mind, and all of Arnie's wins at Daytona in 1962 were stripped from him.

It turned out that the party who protested Arnie went on to win Top Stock Eliminator honors and was from the same town as the official.

Arnie Has No New Car That Works

Back home in the spring, Arnie was talked into selling the 1961 Ventura to Charlie Venable of the Atlanta, Georgia, area.

Arnie ordered a new 1962 Catalina, but he specifically wanted the previous year's color of Bristol blue. He was told that he would have to wait for lulls in the production schedule for that to happen. As a threat to Pontiac, Arnie bought two brand-new 409 Chevrolets: one white and one red. It was his way of telling Pontiac that he might not be as brand loyal as the company thought.

The red 409 was strictly for resale, but that still left the white one and his 1958 Chieftain to drive. *Drag News* reported a win at Cordova on April 15 in the C/G '58 with an ET of 13.02 at 106.38 mph. There was no win recorded for the Chevrolet in the April 21 issue of *Drag News,* and then the following week, it reported that the car had a spun bearing. Recently, Arnie denied that. He remembered that it sat at home due to the broken valvetrain parts for which the 409s were notorious.

The next recorded event was on May 6, when Arnie traveled south and *borrowed* his '61 to match race Nicholson during a shoot-out for no less than $1,000 at Yellow River, Georgia. From there, it was back up north driving, of all brands, a Dodge. Arnie's ability to tune a car became obvious. Over the next few weeks, his elapsed times in the 413 dropped from the low-13-second range all the way to the high 12s.

Notice the artsy "VA" logo on the lower front of the quarter panel. It stood for Venable Atkinson, the Atlanta, Georgia-based race team. Its name is also on the fender. The photo was taken in June 1962. (Photo Courtesy Joel Naprstek)

While in its heyday, it probably had plenty of exposure, but this is one of the only known photos of Roger Haan's 1962 413-ci Dodge Dart. Arnie's name is as bold as can be on the roof.

The Beach Boys sang about the mighty 413 Max Wedge Mopars in the song "Shut Down." The 413 Max Wedge engines were rated at a strong 410 hp and roughly 460 ft-lbs of torque.

The car was sponsored by Schuler Motors and Spencer's Automotive. Roger is in the car and Spencer is standing next to it. It would have been a strong runner in any man's hands. It was clocked at a 13.14 ET at 111 mph with Arnie wrenching on it. By reports, it was close to the track record of the day.

All Is Well Again

Finally, on June 24, the first reports of Arnie's new 1962 Catalina were published. The wait had been worth it, as not only was it painted in his preferred color but it also ran like a scalded cat!

The first reports had it in the high-12-second range—right out of the factory box. Arnie absolutely loved the car. Some 30-plus years later, he still bragged about how fast this powerful and potent *Poncho* was. He remembered how the car, even in some instances, won races without the benefit of all four gears. Occasionally, he'd lose second or third due to powershifting, the technique of not lifting your foot off the gas pedal between gear changes.

As the 1962 season passed, journalists gave Arnie a number of different nicknames. There were references to him as "King of the Stockers" and the "Flying Farmer." In one particular article from *Drag News*, Bob Bartel called him "Eliot Ness," as Arnie and the Catalina were pretty much untouchable.

Both Arnie and Bob confirmed that in those days, Arnie had become so dominant at Cordova that Bob literally gave Arnie the entry fee for other tracks to give other racers a chance for a win. I'm sure he was thankful when Arnie traveled down South or there was a bigger race in the area that pulled Arnie away.

ADVANTAGES FOR ARNIE

There were other reasons that Arnie won so much in his day besides the ability to tune a car. One of them was reflexes. Arnie's were second to none. In the early days of drag racing until the mid-1960s, a flagman was used to start the race. Before his class was called to the lanes, Arnie would intently study each flagman so that no sooner than the starter moved or even so much as twitched, he left the line.

Arnie had dealings through Anderson Pontiac in the mid-1960s, some of which were not entirely pleasant. It was the owner, Bill Knafel, who noticed how quick Arnie could be. Arnie was in his shop doing an engine swap when, from out of nowhere, a mouse ran across the floor. Arnie not only saw the rodent, he was actually fast enough to step on it!

The track surface was also very important to Arnie. One must remember that in the early days, there were no burnouts like we see today at every racetrack in the world. Plenty of Arnie's home movies show him cleaning off the launch pad with an article of clothing or towel to ensure that his lane was completely free of any dust or debris.

Don Bennett provided another example of Arnie's care for using the best available resources, that of tires.

"There was a Goodyear store in Clinton [Iowa]," he said. "Arnie somehow found out that some of the same size tires could be an 1/8 or 1/4 inch wider than others. We got permission to go upstairs to check the width of all the Double Eagle tires that Arnie was using."

Don continued, "In those days, the tires were all wrapped in paper. You'd bang 'em on the ground, breaking the paper loose so you could measure. Well, there were a lot of tires up there, anywhere from 40 to 60 of them as I recall. One by one, we checked them all, and Arnie picked out two that he wanted. When the shop owner came upstairs and saw that we'd broken the seal on all those tires. He got mad as hell, so uh, Arnie got chewed out for that."

This is an early photo of the '62 on the starting line at Cordova. By this time, Bartel had changed the name to Cordova Dragway. The dollar sign on the window meant that Arnie was running for the Bonanza.

The Catalina, complete with the little Seltzer nameplate, drew a crowd wherever it went. Arnie and Evelyn are in this photo, which was taken at Cordova.

Arnie and Evelyn pose in front of the car on the return road at Cordova. Again, notice the dollar sign next to Arnie's number.

MATCH RACE

Best 3 out of 5

ARNIE BESWICK

The King of the Super Stocks

Driving A 1962 Pontiac

113.93   -   12.83 E. T.

VS

ROGER HAAN

Eddie Schuler Special

1962 Dodge Automatic Transmission

112.50   -   12.89 E. T.

WED., JULY 4TH

OSWEGO DRAGWAY

1½ miles west of Oswego on Rt. 34

General Admission $1.50   Children 13 and under Free

This flyer promoted a race a mere two weeks after Arnie received the 1962 Catalina, taking on the very same Dodge he had just driven. Dave Jamison, a fellow racer and friend to the local Cordova people, told how Bob Bartel printed off hundreds of these and put them in his trunk. It was then Dave's job to distribute them wherever he thought would attract the most attention. He would cover a 75- to 100-mile radius around the track.

"I'd heard of Arnie but never met him," Harder said. "Brannan was killing everybody on the track at the time, but he was a guy I loved to hate due to his attitude and the impressive Ford he was driving. When Arnie put Brannan down three straight, I absolutely had to meet him. I shook Mr. Beswick's hand and we talked. He was as gracious then as he is today, listening to everything I had to say, including the invitation that if he ever needed a place to stay, he was welcome. It was the beginning of a long relationship that still exists."

In early August, Ben Brown mentioned in his "Mid-America Remarks" column in *Drag News* an upcoming match race on August 19 between Arnie and Dick Brannan at Oswego. He didn't get back to it until after the World Series, when Arnie once again was recorded as winning the Super Stock Bonanza.

In the September 1 issue, Ben stated, "Arnie Beswick sorta proved that even the best-running FoMoCo is no match for the best-running Pontiac. It's no secret that a goodly share of [the] race-going public would just as soon watch the battle royale among the Super Stocks as anything, and at Oswego, it was proven. Beswick had just returned from a two-week, three-race tour of the South, where he done the job on Nicholson at all three places.

"To stick my neck way out with another prediction, in my opinion, Arnie can put it on any stocker in the nation, three out of five, as long as they can race on a strip that both are none too familiar with. When you travel as much as Beswick does, it's rather difficult to get the maximum out of your car at any particular track. Give the opposition the same handicap, and 'the Farmer' will beat 'em every time."

Match Racing
the Nation's Best

During the summer of 1962, Arnie showed up at Martin, Michigan, to race Dick Brannan in a best-of-three race. Willie Harder, a non-Ford fan, was there to witness the event.

This is a Cordova shot that's been colorized from World Series time. (Photo Colorization by Dean Fait)

Sitting in the staging lanes at Cordova. Judging from the number of people, there's no doubt that it's during the World Series.

This is another shot from Cordova that's been colorized. This time, the Catalina is just pulling onto the starting line. (Photo Colorization by Dean Fait)

Arnie and "Dyno" Don Nicholson in May 1962. More than likely, this photo was taken while Arnie was between rounds of a match race down South.

Arnie stopped for a photo in front of Jimmy Burton's service station in Georgia. Arnie still has the four-door 1955 Oldsmobile that he's using here as the tow vehicle.

A Little Extra Insurance with Fringe Benefits

As the competition continued getting faster, Arnie saw the need to step up his game. There was also still Smokey Yunick's reminder that the stock parts weren't meant to last with the punishment to which Arnie was subjecting them. Once again, like he'd done in 1961, the '62 received the same short-block work from Ray Nichels.

It just so happened that *Custom Rodder* was doing an article on Nichels's shop when Arnie's car was there. The May 1963 issue went into great detail, explaining a lot of the neat tricks that Nichels did to the bottom half of the engine while telling how Arnie worked his magic on the top half and the rest of the car. Arnie's list of modifications included widening the inner rear fender wells to accommodate the widest possible tire, louvering the hood to let out hot air, using deep-groove pulleys to prevent the loss of belts, and cold-air ductwork for the carburetors.

An interesting little addition to the car was a chain and padlock to make sure that no one but Arnie opened the hood. The article mentioned a bad experience when someone tried to steal engine parts from the car when it was parked at a motel near Yellow River.

Another unusual addition was a heavy-duty rubber band looped around the clutch pedal and the steering column near the bottom of the dash.

This helped ensure that it snapped back up, making it possible to simply move his foot to the left, side-stepping the pedal instead of lifting it off. When combined with the reinforced clutch equalizer bar, Arnie admitted that it was a lot harder to push the clutch pedal in.

This photo shows Arnie displaying an M&H slick mounted on a steel wheel. It narrowly fit the wheel wells of the Catalina, even after modification of the car. Rosin had started to be used to help with traction by this time, ensuring even better elapsed times.

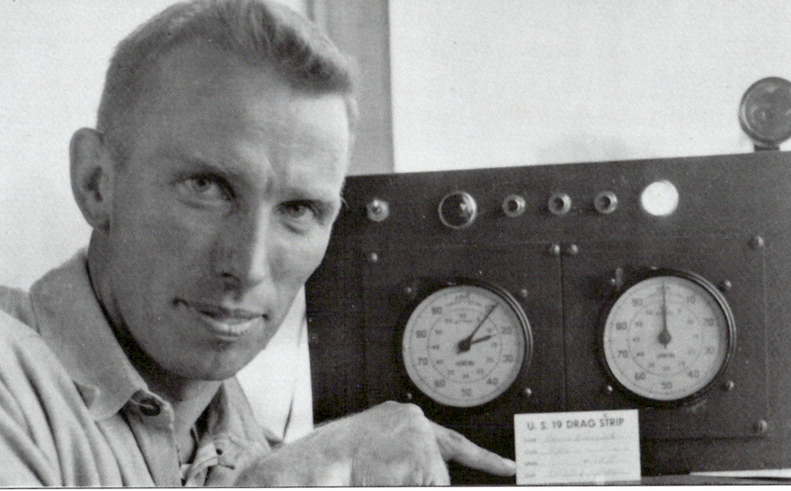

This photo has been used forever by Arnie as being associated with the Albany, Georgia, record-breaking passes.

One proud racer is pictured here in front of the time slip and clock. The caption on Arnie's 8x10 reads, "U.S. 19 Drag-way, Albany, Georgia, Sept. 23, 1962 – A new world record low E.T. of 12.11 backed with 12.12 by Arnie Beswick in Passionate Poncho 1962 SS/S Pontiac."

While Tim Frederick admits that this whole picture was only in his mind, this could have been the scene from many a Southern track. (Illustration by Tim Frederick)

The car was brought to life like nothing before with all of Arnie's little tricks, the factory Super Duty features, the punched-out engine, as well as the balancing and blueprinting. The results were instantly noted, as on September 23, Arnie set a track record of 12.11 ET at U.S. 19 Dragway in Albany, Georgia. As the Northern tracks closed for the season, 1962 was going out with a big bang!

1963 Begins with Sad News from GM

As the new 1963 models were released, the exponentially growing number of drag racing fans was becoming an obvious target for the Big Three. The adage "Race on Sunday, Sell on Monday" was never so true. It was all-out brand war frenzy, at least until January of the year, according to Fred Simmonds of Pontiac Motorsports fame. That was when General Motors, worried about being broken up due to antitrust issues, decided to live up to the 1957 American Manufacturers Association (AMA) racing ban.

While no one seemingly adhered to the mandate back in 1957, General Motors pulled out of each and every area of racing in 1963. That one act changed the shape of every single aspect of motorsports activity for years and affected Arnie on many different levels.

One of the first things that happened when the NASCAR teams all switched was the availability of the car haulers that Cotton Owens owned. There

was no way that Chrysler Corporation would let him be seen hauling his Dodge on a GMC truck. However, it was definitely a step up for the Farmer.

Specialty Vehicles of Epic Proportions

Try as we might, you or I could never get one of these cars without the credentials that Arnie or any other racer of the day had. Pontiac built 26 of the most radical cars it had ever produced to date on a production basis. While the first of these looked like a regular Catalina, they were far from that upon closer inspection, mostly from underneath.

Of those, 14 silver Super Duty 421-ci cars were put on a crash diet. Pontiac drilled some 150 holes in the frame to lighten up these special vehicles. As one would expect, they came with aluminum front ends, bumpers, and other drivetrain parts—not to mention, no body filler or sound insulation. That saved 100 pounds.

Additionally, they came with a Plexiglas windshield that was placed in the back seat to be dealer installed. As in 1962, the cars came with the lightweight header-like exhaust manifolds that had the warning to not subject them to wide-open throttle for more than 14 seconds. Because of all the holes in the frame, they quickly became known by the moniker that we all call them today: Swiss Cheese Catalinas.

The S/C Cats had their issues, thanks to all the missing framework. Any and all of the racers who took delivery had to reinforce them in critical areas. It was rumored that they couldn't even be transported without additional support added to the four wheels, otherwise damage would occur in transit.

Tempests

Pontiac's ultimate vehicle was the Tempest. The automaker took only six wagons and six coupes and stuffed its mighty 421 S/D engine (about 500 hp) into the midsized, already-lightweight cars. Aluminum front ends were expected, and that was indeed the case.

Then, a transaxle transmission was installed. While this technology was not entirely new, it was for the drag racing world. The 12 Cameo White Tempest wagons and LeMans coupes all had 4-speed automatic/manual

*The **Blue Goose** is lettered up and ready to travel. GM's ban in January 1963 made it possible for Arnie to step up to this improved method of hauling cars.*

transmissions. Simply put, a clutch was used to start moving. After that, the shift lever was bumped or pushed to the next gear without having to lift your foot off the *go* pedal.

No sooner than Arnie had heard about them, he placed his order through Seltzer Pontiac for a Catalina and a Tempest wagon. Not long after, he contacted Pontiac about getting one of the coupes. However, the ban was already in place, and the memo was distributed around GM corporate that there would be no further sales or even promotion of race-related activity.

You may have deduced from the description of the Tempest wagons, as well as the LeMans coupes, that they might be controversial. That was an understatement! It started no sooner than when Arnie showed up at the Spruce Creek Airport with the car for the Daytona Speedweek on February 16.

1963 Daytona Speedweek

Ben Brown was a respected writer for *Drag News* back in the day, and he was a fan of Arnie back then (and still is today). He reported that 313 competitors entered the Daytona race and that there were about 22,000 spectators. Bob Bartel ran the event. Ben refers to Bob as the "sun-tan kid."

Dave Jamison was one of the Quad City tech people helping the sun-tan kid. According to Ben, Arnie showed up in true Eliot Ness fashion with a car that was "unclassifiable."

"If you didn't already guess it, Arnie, the Farmer, Beswick towed in with the wildest thing Pontiac ever came off the assembly line with," Ben wrote. "This machine was so way out that no one in command knew where to put it!"

Dave remembered the event and had this to say:

These photos were taken at Arnie's favorite place of lodging: the Snow White Hotel. This is after some nightly wins at Daytona Beach. Notice that the Tempest and the truck are so new that they're not even lettered yet.

"I didn't know how many of those silver Catalinas they [Pontiac] made, but there were sure a lot of them there in Daytona. If they were that rare, probably all of them were there!

"There had been nothing from Pontiac about the Catalinas and especially about the little station wagons," Dave continued. "Luckily for Arnie and the other Pontiac drivers, John DeLorean himself was there to validate their new cars that year and stop the protests."

Ben Brown continued about the Daytona-based Winternational event:

"As the NASCAR digs had awards going to both Top Stock Stick and Automatic Elims., needless to say, the Flying Farmer literally sailed through the shiftless bunch. For the Grand Finale,

The Catalina didn't get to show off all the awards that it won at the NASCAR Winternationals until Arnie arrived back home in Morrison.

This photo is interesting from two standpoints. The first rather minor thing is that the Catalina had a license plate. The second and biggest item is the sponsorship lettering on the decklid. The sign painter spelled Spencer's name wrong. Both Arnie and Spencer were surely thrilled about that!

Arnie had hopes of sponsorship money and initially lettered the Catalina with Seltzer's name on the sides. This changed before the year's end.

Who'd have thought these cars would be so sought after in years to come. They were just race cars, tools of the trade. As they'd done in the past, Arnette and Paula sit on the aluminum fenders. The location is most likely Cordova Dragway.

management arranged a two-out-of-three money race between Beswick and Nicholson, who had won the stick elim., and the rosin kid from RR2, Morrison, Illinois, came through in two straight. When you can turn on like 11.96 and 12.02 the first time out, pal, who needs a speed stick!"

The Catalina was placed in the B/SS class. Wins were reported each and every night with that car as well.

As the 1963 season unfolded, there were reports of match races all over the Midwest and down South. Arnie performed as well or better than expected most of the time, taking on the best of the best of this nation's Super Stockers. When he was not on the road, there were wins on the home track of Cordova.

One of the biggest drag racing events in 1963 was in West Salem, Ohio, on the Fourth of July weekend: the *Drag News* Stock Car Invitational. It was the first time "the Drag Racer's Bible" had brought it east, being a California-based publication. In April, *Drag News* began promoting that year's event. Thanks to the big money and other prizes to be won, the event drew all the big names as well as those hoping to make one.

The cars are lettered and loaded onto the "freight train," ready to travel, more than likely to Ohio.

Here's the promotional flyer for the Drag News Stock Car Invitational.

The headline to the coverage submitted by Ben Brown read, "Beswick wins $2,500+ at D. N. Invitational." The story told how Arnie won with both the wagon and the Catalina and then, during teardowns, was found to be 100-percent legal.

The Golden Commando team put up $500 in protest money for each car and had to be mad as hell when Arnie got to keep that $1,000 as well. There was also close to $4,000 worth of merchandise awards that Arnie took home.

One of Arnie's favorite stories is from one of his best wins. It has been told a few different ways, one of which was with Dyno Don when he was still alive.

"I had to run against one of my fiercest competitors," Arnie said. "I think it was for the final run for the Top Stock Eliminator. We were about two-thirds or so down the track, and I was ahead by maybe a fender, when all of a sudden, my friend, Dyno, fell back pretty fast. I knew he must have missed a gear. Being the friendly rivals that we are, I decided to wave at him. Well, this apparently must have upset my friend because he opened the door, almost falling out of the car to give me the victory sign."

Taken in the pits at West Salem, Ohio, the wagon is ready to go. This time, the sign painter spelled Spencer's name right on the back of the car.

Arnie races the Golden Commandos at West Salem.

A happy tech official stands guard over the cars in the protest area waiting for teardown.

Here's the Catalina preparing to launch at the 1963 NHRA US Nationals in Indy. Since there was no hope of sponsorship money, you'll notice that the lettering had been changed. It would stay close to this configuration for the rest of its life.

Dyno Don finished telling the story in 1986, when he said at a nostalgia event, "Well, if he saw a victory sign, he was seeing double!"

Winning that event alone put Arnie at No. 4 on the *Drag News* Stock Eliminator list and in the top positions in the Stock classes of its Standard 1320 column that ran on page 2 in every issue. The Catalina stayed there well into 1964. This now-weekly periodical was indeed the racer's Bible, and challenges helped keep Arnie busy defending his position. Don Nicholson led the list at No. 1, and he was followed by "Akron" Arlen Vanke at No. 2 and Butch Leal at No. 3.

Match Racing in the Midwest

There wasn't a huge need for Arnie to travel all the way down South during the summer months. The Midwest match-race scene saw him racing Indiana's own Dick Brannan a lot over the summer. Report after report showed that Arnie's car rarely lost, and even when he did, it might have been one race out of the five that were run. Ben Brown mentioned Arnie taking three straight more than once.

This is a colorized version of the S/C Catalina taking on Dyno Don at the US Nationals. According to reports, the NHRA brought in a Native American, or in some cases a Canadian, to do an anti-rain dance. (Photo Colorization by Dean Fait)

This was the final round at Indy in A/FX for Arnie in the wagon as he raced against Bob Frederick. The Tempest has now been lettered to match the Catalina. According to Arnie's note, he was informed right away on the return road that he'd been disqualified.

After yet another win at the World Series of Drag Racing, Arnie headed to Indy for the US Nationals. After his disqualification in 1961, Arnie was told that he would not be allowed to compete in any of the NHRA's national events in 1962. Nicholson was more of "their boy" and didn't take it completely seriously, but Arnie did. That almost self-imposed ban kept him away for 1962.

However, there was big money to win in 1963, so he returned with high hopes, armed with plenty of ammunition. Still, the results were the same as in 1961. Since Arnie brought two cars and he was driving both, he needed help. Consequently, while he pulled one up, he received help with the other from a new and upcoming star, Don Gay. It was a strange rule, but Arnie was disqualified for having the car pulled forward in the lanes by someone else.

Summer turned into autumn, and articles appeared almost every week in *Drag News*, telling of win after win at almost every track around the Midwest. By now, because of their extreme low production numbers, the Tempests and LeMans coupes had been reclassified. Already, at the *Drag News* Stock Car Invitational, they were classed as A/FX.

Another Car in the Stable

As the '64s began showing up in the fall of 1963, Arnie felt that he needed more of an edge. He began making calls in earnest to Pontiac and Mickey Thompson about how he might obtain the LeMans coupe that was originally shipped to Mickey.

The coupe had originally been sent to Mickey that year in the middle of January. The minute that General Motors dropped the no-racing bombshell, Mickey did the same as almost all the other

Lettered almost immediately upon its arrival, the LeMans coupe is pictured here at Cordova.

racers and jumped ship away from General Motors. Henceforth, the S/D coupe had been parked for a good part of the 1963 season.

While Arnie wanted one originally during the first part of the year, the cost of the wagon and the Catalina was enough. Now, one of the reasons that he was persistent about it was the 200-pound weight savings that the coupes had. Since Pontiac Motor Division was no longer directly involved, Arnie sent the check to Mickey Thompson, spending more on the car than he did on the wagon because Mickey had supposedly made improvements to the car. Thanks to that transaction, Arnie was the only racer to own all three factory lightweight cars.

Three 1963s Is the Charm

The first report of the coupe being seen anywhere in the neighborhood was on October 6 at Cordova. Arnie remembered that it was a hot day when the car came in to Spencer Knox's shop, which was now home base for Beswick Enterprises.

The car arrived with several bumps and bruises on the sheet metal exterior, and the interior looked like it had already gone through several racing seasons.

Arnie is across from Gary Wagner on the left and Spencer Knox on the right. All are hard at work on one of the Tempests. The Beswick base of operations was Spencer Automotive, right in Morrison. (Photo Courtesy Bob Nelson)

It was obvious that the car had been treated with little respect while it was in Mickey's possession.

The transport driver who delivered the car even commented to Arnie that the motor backfired "real bad" as he started the car. He also commented, "It must have a full-race cam," because it would not idle, and he killed it several times as he attempted to unload it.

If the car actually showed up in early October, as Ben Brown mentioned, Arnie was scheduled to compete at a match race with none other than Dick Brannan that weekend with the Tempest wagon and Catalina. The match race didn't go exactly as Arnie planned. Dick Brannan had his new 1964 Ford Galaxie, complete with fiberglass parts to help reduce weight. For the first time, Brannan actually won this best-of-five race, as Arnie went red on the fifth race. By this time, Christmas trees started to become the universal method of starting a race. Like it or not, they didn't flinch or have individual characteristics, and there was no disputing them.

Spencer Knox talked about the LeMans in a somewhat sarcastic manner.

"In '63, when we ended up running three cars, we thought we had our hands full just running two," he said. "Then, one afternoon, this coupe shows up and Arnie tells us that we're running the third car. Gary and I were doing most of the maintenance work on the two, and we thought that's exactly what we needed—one more car."

While Arnie was up at Great Lakes Dragaway, Spencer Knox took the little coupe to Cordova for a quiet weekend of testing and tuning. Performance was disappointing to say the least. Spectators and commentator alike noticed a lot of smoke on that first public appearance. While some might have thought it was from the tires, it actually came from the exhaust blowing directly onto the tires. The little S/D coupe was in bad need of a lot of R&R: not rest and relaxation, remove and replace.

It didn't take long to discover why the engine smoked. The pistons came out of the cylinder bores with zero effort. It was deduced that someone had lost a fan belt in the car's early days and the engine had gotten excessively hot. Several of the rings were stuck in their respective grooves and the ones that weren't stuck had almost no tension.

Arnie, Spencer, and Gary Wagner completely went through the LeMans coupe. Once the little S/D coupe was put back together and put through a few debugging passes, the car took on a completely different personality.

Years later, Arnie talked to the late Paul Zazarine with *Pontiac Enthusiast* magazine about the LeMans. Paul quoted Arnie and wrote, "The competition just knew the coupe had to have more than 421 ci of Pontiac power, so it went through several protests and engine teardowns. It always came through with flying colors.

"Every racer dreams of giving their competition a whipping like that car gave. Seldom does it ever become a reality."

Fixing the bumps and bruises and lettering it up like the wagon and Catalina had to wait until it got home.

Challenging for No. 1

It was almost the end of the 1963 year that Arnie traveled south to Houston, Texas, to challenge Dyno Don for the number-1 position on the Mr. Stock Eliminator list on December 8. The event had been talked about several times in *Drag News*'s pages, and there was even a half-page advertisement promoting it.

After Arnie's coupe took the best-of-three win, that statement was proudly proclaimed on the front fenders of the car. Oddly enough, Don went on to win the event, taking three out of the five. The rules for *Drag News* were specific though. Challenges were two out of three, and Arnie's coupe won the second and third rounds to claim the title of number 1 on the list!

It wasn't long before Arnie was challenged. The very next weekend, on December 15, Ronnie Sox issued it in his brand-new Mercury Comet Caliente. Kinston, North Carolina, was the place for this showdown. Ben Brown joked that Sox didn't want to admit defeat and the best-of-three race turned into a best of seven. Arnie won it in four straight.

Financially, 1963 was the biggest year ever for Arnie. Racing had earned him more than $30,000. Not too bad for a farmer.

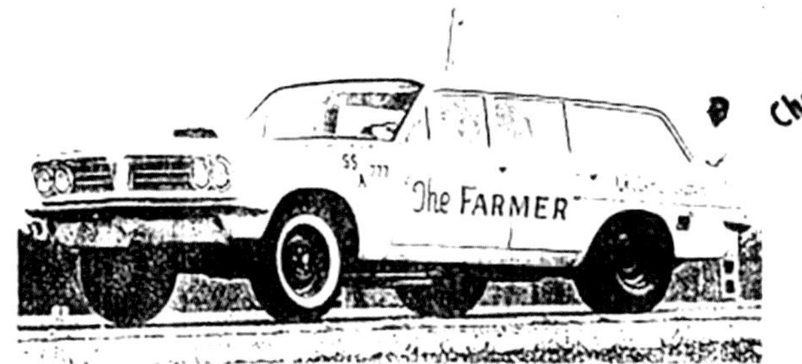

The promo flyer for what was going to happen in early December.

While not the best quality, this is the only image to date taken from Houston with Arnie challenging Don for the number-1 spot on the Mr. Eliminator list.

CHAPTER 4

THE AF/X YEARS

According to the January 25, 1964, issue of *Drag News,* Arnie had joined Bill Knafel's Anderson Pontiac team along with Arlen Vanke. A later issue confirmed this but changed the official date to February 1. Ben Brown's column explained that this meant Arnie would receive a new GTO and Catalina tow car.

The fleet of four was photographed by the old Morrison high school early in the year. (Photo Courtesy Bob Nelson)

While there was nothing special about the Catalina, mystery shrouded Arnie's GTO. The year 1964 was the first model year offering of what is considered to be the world's very first muscle car. In late 1963, John DeLorean went against GM's policy of putting big engines in little cars. He did so through a loophole that said that if the big 389s were optional, then they could be built and sold. Before General Motors realized what was going on, Pontiac had taken 5,000 orders for them, and GM consented and went ahead with the program.

Arnie's GTO was rather special. It was ordered specifically for racing and shipped to the dealership in Akron, Ohio. Jim Mattison, with Pontiac Historical Services, showed that it was a very plain car with almost no options. His printout shows a special code, indicating that it received preferential treatment. It was a white post coupe with a black interior, a Tri-Power 389, and a 4-speed transmission.

There was no radio or even a heater. Years later, it was mentioned that it seemed to be ultra-light for a factory body.

Arnie admitted that he ordered it without seam sealer or sound insulation. As he remembered, the car leaked like a sieve in the rain and was very prone to rattling. The item that made it extra cool and completely unique was an aluminum front end.

According to multiple sources at Pontiac, no car like this was ever built. That is true. So how did the aluminum hood and fenders come to fruition, especially after the racing ban that General Motors self-imposed in early 1963?

Aluminum Front Ends in 1964?

In late 1963, an agreement was made with Bill Knafel for the two cars. At that time, Arnie was on a first-name basis with many of the key people at Pontiac. His wins came with a cost, and he was in constant need of high-performance parts, especially for the temperamental Tempests.

One day, Arnie and one of his Pontiac engineering contacts were walking through an

Who needs a special background? Just find a quiet side street in Morrison and bring your ladder. The recently purchased LeMans coupe and the newly obtained GTO pose nicely.

An article was written for American Rodder magazine by Walt Alexander with a similar picture. It told that Arnie and Spencer Knox shared the driving, the maintenance chores, and the trophies that this 421 GTO gathered at drag strips all around the country. The car was still naturally aspirated with dual-quad carburetors and a 4-speed transmission. I'm rather sure this was taken just outside of Spencer's shop.

That same article mentioned that when Arnie moved out to go racing, he did so with an impressive array of Pontiac power. The only thing missing from this picture was the S/C Cat, although it's said to still be in the stable. Notice Arnie behind the wheel of the GTO because there weren't enough tow vehicles and trailers.

The original article explained how the exhaust headers were reworked to make room for the clutch linkage of the original 4-speed. The completed header is ready to go here. Arnie believed in long collector pipes when this photo was taken.

Evelyn, Arnie, Arnette, and Paula pose in front of the Tempest wagon and the high school. (Photo Courtesy Bob Nelson)

The "freight train" loaded with the crew posing is (left to right) Gary Wagner, Arnie, and Spencer Knox. The truck and cars have all been loaded and lettered. (Photo Courtesy Bob Nelson)

The Knafel Catalina pulled the trailer with the LeMans. (Photo Courtesy Bob Nelson)

off-the-beaten-path part of the Pontiac plant and happened to pass a row of about 25 or 30 aluminum 1964 LeMans front clips that had been shipped over from Fisher Body.

Arnie asked, "What's with those?"

"Oh," his contact said, "the bean counters found 'em, and we gotta crush them all."

When he found what he came for, Arnie coincidentally bumped into John DeLorean and asked, "Is my name on one of those front-end goodies?"

John's answer, as was always the case, was short and sweet. He didn't want to know anything about anything. With permission granted, Arnie basically smuggled one front clip out of the factory to use on the GTO.

While there were promises from Knafel about picking Arnie up with his airplane and taking him out on his yacht on his private lake, none of these things ever happened. Arnie wondered if Knafel really possessed any of these things because he never saw them. Arnie and Spencer Knox had to drive to the dealership to pick up the two vehicles.

Once at the dealership, Arnie was shocked to find that the GTO was minus the engine, as well as the hood and fenders. The Tri-Power-equipped 389 had already been pulled, thanks to Knafel's mechanics. That's what Arnie got for spilling the beans about finding the aluminum pieces and using his own engine.

While Arnie and Spencer both needed to drive a car back and had brought a tow bar for the GTO, the Knafel deal looked less favorable all the time. However, Arnie stayed true to his word, and Anderson Pontiac was lettered on the Tempests and GTO.

Daytona Speedweek

While the GTO stayed home for the first part of 1964, its first stop, as tradition dictated, was the Daytona Beach Speedweek competition. Promotional stories tell that the event that was scheduled for the week of February 15–22 and would be run under National Association of Drag Strips (NADS) rules. This was, according to ESPN's Bret Kepner, a heavy anti-NHRA set of rules written by Bob Bartel, "Broadway" Bob Metzler, and Ron Leek, using the somewhat gutsy acronym.

Arnie was not worried about classification because it was mentioned in the ads that the 1963 rules would be used. That would become an issue for 1964 because Arnie's cars were not new and the NHRA had no classification for his Tempests.

There was more than $20,000 in cash and prizes up for grabs in Daytona, including a Ford Falcon, Ford stock, television sets, and two Plymouth engines. While all of the Big Three car manufacturers were realizing the potential of selling more cars

An ad for Daytona Beach shows the total purse and all of the many other awards that a racer could win.

through the promotion of drag racing, thanks to GM's ban, only two acted on it.

Ben Brown literally devoted his whole week's column of the March 7 *Drag News* issue to Arnie, as the "Flying Farmer" related his trials, tribulations, joys, and sorrows about the whole experience.

Not So Smooth Sailing
There was no such thing as

This year, it wasn't the Snow White Motel; instead, it was the Carousel. Work had already begun on the cars.

from A to B, racing, and then coming back home from B to A with Arnie. The 1964 Daytona trip was a prime example. Spencer and Gary were in the "freight train" with the Tempests, and Howard Maseles was with Arnie in the new Knafel Catalina, which was pulling the S/C Catalina.

The first dilemma occurred just east of Morrison when the hitch ball came off the truck as the car and hauler were going across the scales. A spare made for a quick fix and that long day's travels had no other issues. The first night stop was with friends in Atlanta.

The next morning, the two parties were separated in traffic while leaving Atlanta. That was no cause for concern, however, because both drivers knew where they were going. What was cause for concern was that just after crossing the Florida state line, the weld on the trailer hitch broke. The loaded trailer started dancing all over the place— held to the tow car by only the chains. As Arnie described it, the whole thing was almost up on the two left wheels, then the two right ones.

"Finally, the hooks pulled out of the crossmember on the '64," Arnie explained to Brown. "We quickly pulled off onto the shoulder, and the trailer and Catalina went right on by us! About that time, we figured we wouldn't be racing the car at Daytona that week or any other."

Oddly enough, the rig traveled down the highway for a little bit before going down into the ditch. The ground was muddy, and the trailer came to a peaceful stop with nothing damaged. Arnie was extremely thankful for Southern hospitality, as the locals helped get the rig back on the road. A welder came from a nearby town and fixed the hitch, and they were back on the road.

Arnie and Howard barely made it in time to compete the first night, but the Catalina won that night and every other night except one.

Arnie remembered that the coupe and the wagon also dominated, running in U/SA and A/SSA.

"Those Tempests also won every night except for one each because of ring and pinion troubles and some transaxle issues," Arnie said.

The Bonanza races were held on the final night, and the coupe ran like a Swiss watch and took first place. It was a huge race for Arnie not only because of the cash but also all the extra prizes.

As one would expect, Arnie was going to be protested. Since Ford was putting up a lot of the prizes

The whole crew in front of the cars are (from left to right) Gary, Spencer, Arnie, and Howard Maseles.

The whole gang unloads the cars at Daytona.

The brand-new Falcon Sprint convertible, complete with a V-8 and 4-speed manual transmission, all in resale red. Dave Jamison, a tech inspector for Bartel from Sterling, Illinois, had the pleasure of driving it home from Florida.

and, seemingly every Thunderbolt built was there, being protested was as sure as the sun coming up the next day.

Carl Brandt was a tech inspector for Bartel at Cordova, and he was there in Florida in that capacity that year. He recently recalled the event.

"When Arnie won night after night, the Ford people got mad as hell," he said. "They were sure he was cheating and went to extra lengths to prove their point."

Try as they might, the Swiss Cheese Cat was 100-percent legal, and on top of the money and other prizes, Arnie won the Falcon.

Head West, Young Man

The next big stops for Arnie were his first West Coast swing in mid-March after a match race gone awry in Houston. In California, he registered in the 1964 Smokers event in Bakersfield. There was money to be won at this show, so he pre-entered.

Arnie was actually the first name on the list shown in *Drag News*. Both of Arnie's cars continually won, and in the finals, they had to race each other. Rick Lynch, a fellow Pontiac owner, drove the wagon, reporting a win.

The Swiss cheese Catalina is at Houston in what is believed to be right after the Florida races. Arnie remembers that he was supposed to race Frank Sanders in his Z11 Chevy, but Frank was a no-show. Since there are no pictures of the car in California, an educated guess is that Spencer Knox, Gary Wagner, and Howard Maseles took the Catalina back home afterward, while Arnie continued westward.

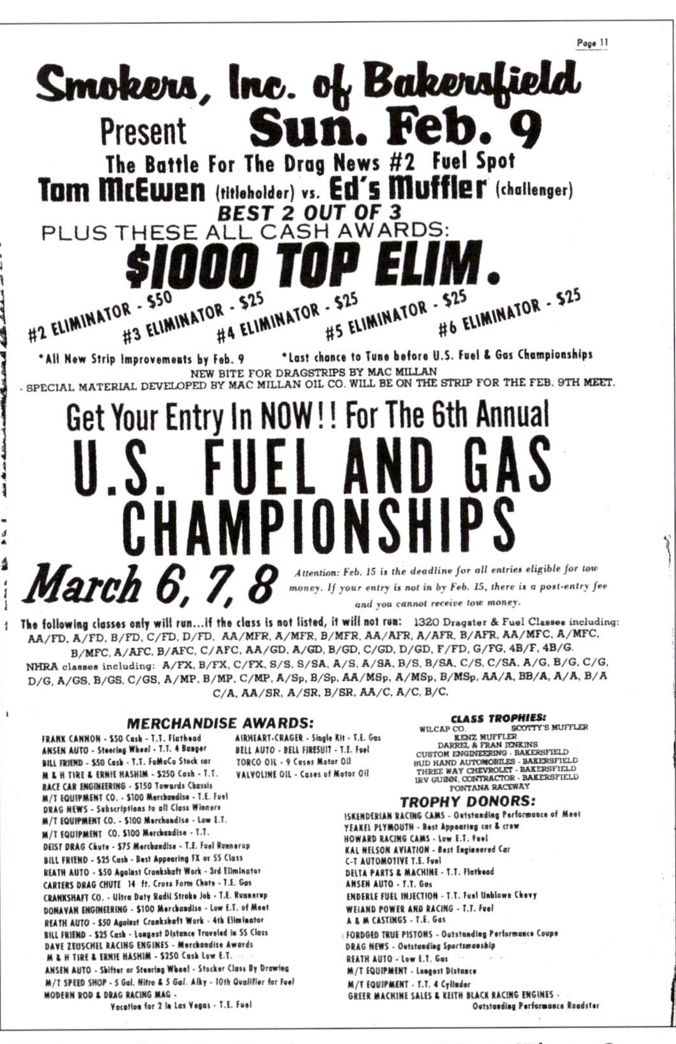

This is an ad for the Smokers race out West. (Photo Courtesy Beswick Archive)

A LeMans coupe versus the Tempest wagon is pictured. One might wonder which car Arnie drove; the answer is not the winning car but the coupe. Arnie almost always drove the LeMans instead of the others. There are stories about Gary Wagner starting out in third gear in the Catalina and still winning. The Tempests with their unique transmissions never had that problem.

Out in California, the "freight train" poses for pictures.

A close-up of the coupe on the trailer with the lettering is shown as it appeared out West.

Arnie headed south to Long Beach, California, where he downed the supercharged *Dodge Chargers* car of Jimmy Nix. Next, it was up to Northern California in Fremont, where it was a repeat of Bakersfield; however, this time Arnie in the coupe crossed the 1320 line first. As the West Coast tour ended, Arnie left an indelible impression on their drag racing fan base. The Farmer came to win!

Back to the Midwest

Illinois was the next destination, but again, this was not an "A to B then back to A" trip. It was also not without incident—again involving the car on the trailer. This time, Arnie was not as lucky as he was while heading to Daytona.

Terry Kuchel (pronounced Q-kel), a longtime friend of Arnie's, was in the US Army and was stationed in California at the time. Terry took military leave to help Arnie drive back home to Morrison. Arnie's brother, Jim, was living in Denver at the time, so they took the northern route through the mountains, rather than going through Arizona, New Mexico, and Texas. As often happens in the winter, a storm developed as they were traveling.

Not So Smooth Sailing Round 2

"We came out of Los Angeles with the truck," Terry remembered. "The wagon was on the truck and the coupe was on the trailer behind. We were up in the mountains and it had started to snow. Back then, we didn't have the interstates like we have today, and I could tell that the roads were getting pretty slick. I was about to tell Arnie that we were maybe going a little too fast when all of a sudden, he started losing control of the truck and trailer and it started to jackknife.

"I looked out the mirror and could see the whole side of the coupe swinging right around, coming right toward the truck. Pretty soon the trailer broke loose from the truck and started doing circles in the road. It all happened so fast, but from what I remember, the car broke loose from the trailer, crashed into the guardrail, and went up and over it."

The bad news was that after going over the guardrail, a tree stopped its descent. Yet, the good news was that after going over the guardrail, a tree stopped its descent. Looking at the glass half empty, the coupe now had body damage that went all the way up to the rear window. If the glass is half full, the tree had stopped the LeMans from going down a cliff that was at least a 500-foot drop. That tumble would have definitely made the rare car irreparable.

Although the damage was rather quickly fixed, for a time, only the new GTO (still normally aspirated) and the wagon were able to race, as the Catalina had been sold right around this same time.

Supercharged

Arnie had a problem, and he needed a permanent solution. The problem was that the new cars coming out of the factory were faster than the previous year's models. Whether or not it was Ben Brown's

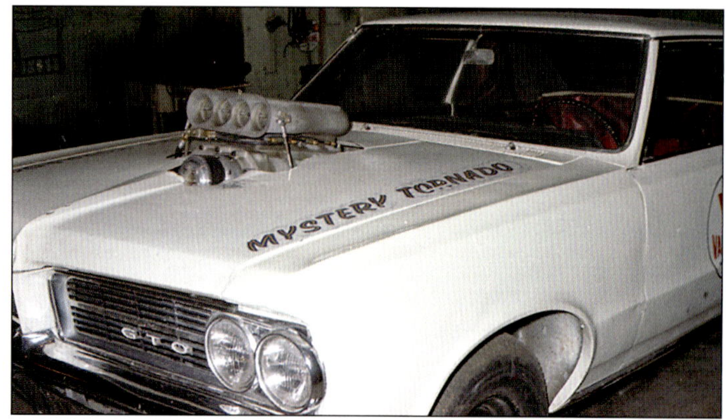

This photo was taken just after the installation of the GMC blower and Hilborn bug-catcher fuel-injection unit. The hood lettering did not last long.

Collectors of old car magazines might recognize this as the cover shot from the June 1965 *Super Stock & Drag Illustrated*. Sunny California was the location where John Raffa wrote a whole article about both the GTO and the Comet.

Shot at Cordova in mid-1964, Arnie is ultra-proud of the new race car.

Arnie was always looking for promotional pictures. He undoubtedly had that in mind while posing for this shot and was undoubtedly disappointed when the lighting wasn't better.

advice to put a supercharger on his GTO, that's what Arnie elected to do. Ben made the suggestion in the first part of 1964 when he wrote about how GMC made the blowers [superchargers] for GMC trucks, and since GMC trucks used Pontiac engines, the fit was made in heaven. The only difference was that Ben foretold of a supercharged Catalina.

Periodicals showed that Arnie used pistons with lower compression, but basically he used the stock Super Duty engines. He merely added the GMC 6-71 supercharger and fuel injection "bug catcher" Hilborn unit to it.

Exhibition match race wins and losses were about 50-50 as Arnie worked to develop the *Mystery Tornado* GTO. It's biggest issue was the transmission. The factory 4-speeds were not built to handle all the extra power, and he quickly and regularly destroyed them.

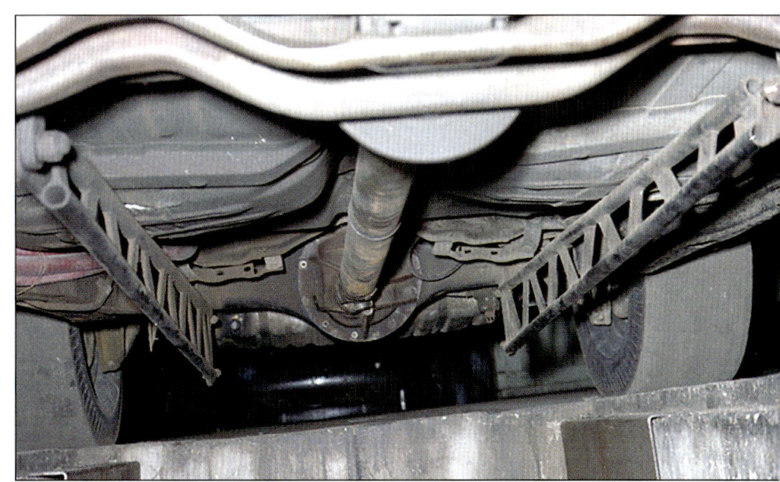

Up on the rack, this is quite a unique view of the long ladder bars used to keep the differential from wheel hopping. (Photo Courtesy Beswick Archive)

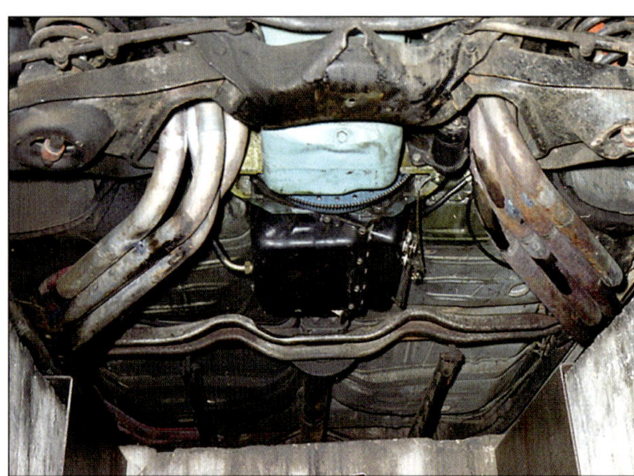

Looking up at the late Bill Wirges's work on Arnie's headers for the Mystery Tornado.

This was taken at Houston, Texas, on October 25. The caption from Drag News *tells of Arnie taking on the flying Falcon of Phil Bonner. It was supposed to be a best-of-five match race. Rain began after three with Arnie taking two and Bonner taking one. Arnie claimed the low ET of the meet with a 10.36 at 140.84 mph.*

At Rockford Dragway, Arnie faced Ed Rachanski's Marauder Comet during the autumn-held UDRA event.

Taken on the same day, this photo made the cover of Drag News *for the November 7 issue. Forrest explained that he used a 135-mm lens, close to where the spectators were behind the return road. (Photo Courtesy Forrest Bond)*

Arnie and "Ohio" George Montgomery had a match race in Houston on December 13. The Drag News *caption read that Arnie got George off the line in a big match race. Both had trouble all day with Arnie ending up winning one of the races. (Photo Colorization by Dean Fait)*

In July, Arnie switched to an automatic transmission. This came about thanks to "Ohio" George Montgomery coming to Cordova for a match race with Arnie. Even though the race was rained out, George recommended and graciously helped install the better-known automatic transmission on the market at the time: the Hydra-matic.

In mid-August, local, longtime supercharged Gas class racer Mike Marinoff helped Arnie out with the engine, which produced delightful results. All year long, thanks to help, patience, and perseverance, the car became quicker and quicker.

The competition was starting to catch up with the title-holding, naturally aspirated coupe though. Arnie raced everyone who was in the biz, including NASCAR star Fred Lorenzen, winning two straight!

Ronnie Sox and Arnie were scheduled to race, but it was canceled, much to the disgust of Bob Bartel. As the year ended, Lee Smith was in 10th place when he challenged Arnie. Oddly enough, despite the fact that they are both local to Cordova, Dallas, Georgia was the location for the challenge. Lee only won one race, and Arnie's title stayed intact.

As the 1964 calendar year ended and the development of the GTO continued, two things hadn't changed. Arnie's Catalina was still No. 1 on the East Coast *Drag News* list, and it still held the record as the fastest B/FX car in the country on the "Standard 1320" reports.

There was one thing that had really changed. For the first time in his career, Arnie and Fran Hernandez from Lincoln Mercury were talking about adding the Farmer to the team.

Upping the Ante for the Pontiacs

As 1965 began, word got out about the plan of Dodge and Plymouth to release some special cars that were going to have altered wheelbases. Six Dodge Coronets and six Plymouth Belvederes were going to be available to a dozen lucky racers, and Chrysler issued blueprints to anyone who wanted to build his or her own.

Thanks to Arnie's recommendation, Lee Smith was to get one of the Plymouths through Learners dealership of Rock Island, Illinois. The January 16 issue of *Drag News* told of how Ben Brown had talked with Lee, trying to pry information about them, but Lee was secretive about how much they planned to alter the wheelbases.

Arnie knew all, and he gave Ben all the answers he needed. Arnie knew that the rear axle was going

Houston, Texas, is the location of this shot, as Arnie defends his title on the Mr. Stock Eliminator list against the DeTar & Rupp machine. A similar shot with the cars in the other lanes was on the cover of Drag News *in the January 30 issue. (Photo Courtesy Forrest Bond)*

The coupe does its burnout at Houston. You'll notice no lettering on the door, indicating that this was before the Tempest was sent to the paint booth for that year's lettering. (Photo Courtesy Forrest Bond)

to be moved up 15 inches, the front up 10, and all the body panels were going to be acid-dipped to reduce weight. The cars would be formidable in the traction department, as roughly 56 percent of the weight was right over the rear wheels.

Defending the Title

Arnie's first event for the year was in Houston, Texas, to defend his Mr. Stock Eliminator title. The Wichita-based Ted DeTar & Dave Rupp's *Big Money* Hemi Dodge was the challenger with Dave driving. *Drag News*'s rule was the best of three, and Arnie took rounds one and three to satisfy the paper and the public.

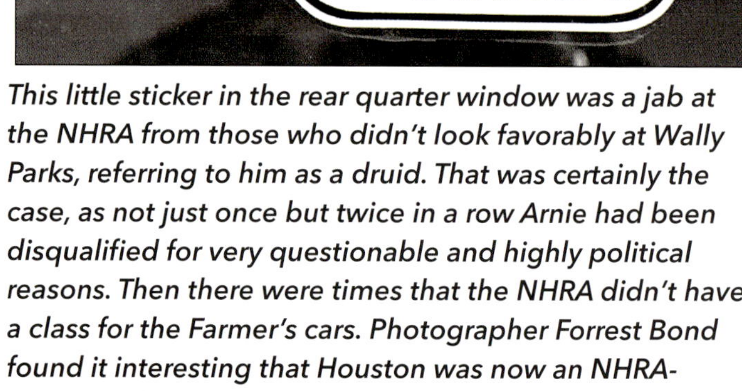

This little sticker in the rear quarter window was a jab at the NHRA from those who didn't look favorably at Wally Parks, referring to him as a druid. That was certainly the case, as not just once but twice in a row Arnie had been disqualified for very questionable and highly political reasons. Then there were times that the NHRA didn't have a class for the Farmer's cars. Photographer Forrest Bond found it interesting that Houston was now an NHRA-sanctioned track when Arnie showed up with the decal. (Photo Courtesy Forrest Bond)

It's the Mystery Tornado in front of the tower at Houston. Long gone are any mentions of Anderson or Knafel Pontiac after a major falling out.

Again, Houston, Texas, is the location where Arnie's seen pushing the GTO. Helping him out is none other than Don Gay's crew chief, James Osteen. The photographer, Forrest Bond, is rightfully proud of this shot. He explained why. "The proximity of the spectators (accentuated by the short telephoto lens), the women with head scarves so typical of the time, the impending action implicit in pushing the car forward, the blower and injection hat sticking through the hood so typical of pre–Funny Cars, and a shot that humanizes Arnie: it's all there." (Photo Courtesy Forrest Bond)

Burning in the rosin at Houston for a solo pass. (Photo Courtesy Forrest Bond)

Complete with its final lettering before the wheelbase is altered, this photo was taken at Beeline Dragway near Scottsdale, Arizona.

Another shot leaving the line, presumably at Beeline Dragway.

This is obviously Pomona during the NHRA Winternationals. Complete with his druids sticker, another change is that there are two drivers listed: Arnie and Phil Reichard. In 1964, Phil ran a new GTO called the Little Farmer. It also had Arnie's name as the tuner with Spencer's Automotive as a sponsor.

Just for insurance, they raced a fourth time, and Arnie won again. The story, written by Forrest Bond, ended with the fact that Dave felt like he got a real fair shake. He told Forrest to relay that the Farmer was one of the nicest guys going. Forrest agreed.

Arnie's next stop on the first of February was Beeline Dragway in Scottsdale, Arizona. He won there before heading to Pomona, California, for the NHRA Winternationals. He mainly went to pick up the Comet before making the mad dash across the country to Daytona.

Racing an Unexpected Friend

This was the fourth year for the Bob Bartel/Ed Otto Speedweek event. The Comet was one of the only new cars in Daytona that could be left in the Stock classes because it didn't have an altered wheelbase. Then the Mercury dropped a valve, which according to Arnie, did a lot of internal damage.

Thankfully, there was still the Unlimited class that a lot of the faster supercharged and experimental cars were in. Arnie's GTO downed the Gary Dyer–driven/Mr. Norm–owned new 1965 Dodge in the finals to take home the Unlimited Class Eliminator title and $300 in prize money.

Up to York Against Ronnie and Buddy

Another big race for the fabulous flying Farmer took place on April 18. Sox & Martin, Arnie, and Don Gay headed to the York US30 Dragway in Pennsylvania.

Joining her husband in the Daytona Beach area was Arnie's lovely wife, Evelyn. This was a car show where a lot of the other racers were showing off their tools of the trade.

An unknown author for *Drag News* wrote about how Sox's Plymouth got the jump on Don Gay, who was driving the supercharged GTO, but Don took a first-round win on the top end. Arnie decided not to let Don Gay have all the fun, and he drove for round two. The Mercury contract was forgotten temporarily.

"To the line they stormed with the usual little rosin here and a little rosin there, then to the line with RPMs high," the *Drag News* article stated. "Once again Sox shot from the line, front wheels

This oil painting replicates the events of April 18, 1965, at York US30. (Illustration by Chris Fait)

Arnie and Gary Dyer were probably the two biggest draws available at Midwest tracks. This is Rockford Dragway.

Taking on Bob Harrop's 1965 altered-wheelbase Dodge in Greensboro, North Carolina. Two separate lanes with grass in the middle made this a distinct facility. "Barefoot" Bobby Starr said it was, "Cow pasture racing at its very best."

reaching for the heavens. This time, the GTO was right beside him. At the 1/8th mile, it was anyone's race with the GTO's blower forcing moon gas into every nook and cranny of the big Pontiac mill. At the first mile-per-hour trap, it was still as close as two peas in a pod. The winner light flashed Beswick [as] the winner. The crowd roared then quickly got silent, waiting to hear the times. The announcer, so excited he could hardly talk, broke the silence with, "He did it! He did it! Arnie Beswick has broken into the 9s! Beswick is the first ever to turn in the 9s with a stock-bodied automobile."

The best ET for the meet was 9.96 at 140 mph. As the article stated, Arnie set two new strip records but couldn't finish the last three runs because he'd broken all the Gilmer (blower) belts that he had with him. It was almost a repeat on June 12, when Arnie took the first and third rounds to win versus Sox. The best ET was 9.75 at 145.98.

Next was a May 2 trip to Houston that happened between the two Sox match races. Since it was Don Gay's home track and Arnie was under contract with Mercury, Don, with the help of "quickie dust," drove the *Mystery Tornado* and defeated Butch Leal three straight with ETs in the 9s. The best run of the day was 9.70 at 143.76.

With the passage of time, it's easy to see the transformation of the GTO as Arnie tried to lighten it up. The headlight assemblies were replaced with pieces of aluminum. The inner fenders disappeared and often Arnie ran the car without its hood, even though it was aluminum.

What wasn't visible was the switch in transmissions from the clunky Hydra-matics to the new Turbo Hydra-matic 400s that General Motors released in 1964. Arnie was working with them to help develop what would later be one of the most dependable, reliable transmissions for the next 20 years at least. It wasn't without cost.

Into the 8s and the Hospital

It was August 28 when Arnie, running at Cordova, did the impossible while running against Mr. Norm's car from Grand Spaulding Dodge. Even though Gary Dyer got a hole shot on the GTO, Arnie drove around him, getting a time slip in the 8s! It read 8.92 at a tick over 162 mph.

The Norm Kraus car broke on that run, so Arnie made a solo pass, pulling out all the stops. He blasted an all-time low of 8.69. The white *Tornado* had never gone that fast. At first, the accuracy of

THE FARMER VERSUS THE KING

Our story regarding Richard Petty began in late 1964, when NASCAR banned the Hemi for 1965. Richard still needed to put food on the table. Since he had Chrysler's blessing, he decided to go drag racing in support of the boycott from the corporation of the circle tracks. History has proven that two specialty-built Barracudas were made, although there were conflicting stories about the timeline of the second car. Both had the potent Hemi engines.

Richard took a jab at Bill France's organization, and the first car to be seen had "Outlawed" on the bottom of the doors. His association with NASCAR had brought him legendary status, and it was rumored that his appearance/race money was more than what the others saw.

The first time that these two legends faced each other as opponents rather than just friends was February 28, 1965, in Dallas, Georgia.

"As I remember that ugly day, I was invited in by Southeastern International Dragway to run Richard Petty in a three-out-of-five match race," Arnie said. "While it was promoted as me using the Comet in one newspaper, the reporter got his facts wrong. It was true, I did have both the Comet and the *Mystery Tornado* GTO with me, but given the track owner's wishes, there was no way that he wanted me to use the Comet because of all the other Ford race cars back then. He wanted me to use the *Mystery Tornado,* and so did I.

"There were so few of us still in GM cars, so running the Pontiac was the obvious choice, as it was definitely the fan favorite. The reason for a lack of any GM cars goes back to the ban of early 1963. Before the ban, General Motors had nearly 57 percent of the automotive market, and there were more than just rumors that the US government was going to break up the corporation for having a monopoly on the car market. General Motors decided that it would no longer allow any of its divisions to build or endorse any kind of race-related cars, programs, or teams.

"As we know now, that had a major impact on the whole motorsports world. Yet back then, never in my wildest dreams did I ever have a clue of what would happen as the 1965 season started. It wasn't long before the tracks that I had commitments with called and told me their predicament. They were losing customers, fans who were loyal to General Motors. I didn't even need to think twice about my decision to run the Pontiac at that or almost any other race that year.

"The race was widely promoted in many of the Atlanta-area newspapers as well as the local radio station. As you might guess, there was a huge amount of traffic traveling the roads from the town of Dallas and surrounding communities to the drag strip, not to mention trying to get into the track. It was a madhouse just trying to get to the parking spots the track had reserved for Richard and me. That was a battle in itself.

"A lot of the spectator traffic had to use the same narrow track roads to get to their parking spots as the race car entries. I heard many times that day that Charles Hardy, the track operator, and other staff people never dreamt they'd have to control that many cars that contained all those spectators. They knew they'd have a large crowd, but not to that degree.

"There's no way for me to completely describe the excitement that was in the air that day either. The fans were waving their arms and throwing their hats in the air when Richard and I were trying to wiggle our way to the staging area. The spectator emotions were as high as I had ever seen at any drag race that I'd attended in anticipation of the race they were about to see between me and King Richard. Southern people are huge race fans.

"I had my share of fan following, but it wasn't anywhere close to what Richard Petty had, especially in that part of the country. That, of course, was mostly due to Richard's NASCAR track record in that time period. While there was some isolation from all the fans on the NASCAR circuits, this was a whole different arena, and he was right there amongst them all. Even back then, a lot of those fans would go to extremes beyond belief to get an autograph or a picture taken with Richard. There's simply no way to describe the amount of fan loyalty that man had and still has in the racing world.

"Once the starter got our race off and running, my GTO started pulling away from Richard's *43 Jr.* Plymouth. Luckily it did because at about 300 or 400 feet down track, Richard's car suddenly made a quick, hard left. He came over into my lane, narrowly missing my back bumper. His car kept going that direction, proceeding down through the small ditch and up the dirt bank where many spectators were sitting or standing. There were some pickups and other kinds of flatbed trucks there, along with a few small motor home–type units, and the fans were sitting and standing in them too."

"Unfortunately, some of the fans were not able to get out of the way of the *43 Jr.'s* travel path and were injured with another spectator passing away as well. A few of the fans who were close enough to witness this happening and had more than their share of alcohol thought Richard should have been able to avoid hitting people before hitting the back of a vehicle parked next to the spectator track fence. They got quite belligerent and mouthy at Richard until his crew chief, Dale Inman, stepped into the picture and quickly changed anyone's efforts of doing any shoving or swinging at Richard. Even with a lot of alcohol in their system and thoughts that they were pretty big or tough, after a few quick punches from Dale, they changed their minds and were looking for the quickest way to get out of his reach."

Petty admitted that it was his darkest hour. He was so distraught over the whole deal that he took the hulk of that first car back to his shop and buried it, never to be used again.

A month later, Arnie faced Richard again. Petty used the second car when the team of Bartel and Otto hosted an event at the Charlotte Motor Speedway in North Carolina on March 28 for the second straight year. It was a Super Stock Bonanza where Arnie, this time, raced Richard on a 1/8-mile track. Big problems unfortunately developed when Arnie gave a local sports commentator a ride. Jack Musilli wrote the article that explained how Arnie blew "the innards" on the 421 Pontiac. He told of how Arnie worked the whole weekend without sleep to race Petty on Sunday afternoon.

According to Jack, "Without the opportunity of a time run, Arnie came to the line with the blown Tempest and proceeded in wiping out Petty with an almost unbelievable run of 6.95 at 113 mph. When I mentioned earlier about Southern enthusiasm, they gave Arnie one of the biggest ovations I have ever heard, and this with beating a local favorite."

Petty won round two, but Arnie closed the deal in round three with a win that set the track record (6.89) for the lowest ET ever recorded at the facility! Arnie faced the NASCAR legend several times before Petty's retirement from drag racing and his return to the roundy-round tracks.

Arnie raced Richard Petty several times over the course of 1965. This race at Dallas, Georgia, was the last time this particular 43 Jr. car was on a racetrack.

LOCAL TESTING

As the white GTO became quicker, many test passes were needed to check changes and improvements. One of Arnie's favorite places to do that was the "Fenton blacktop," a stretch of paved road that was as flat and straight as an arrow for at least a couple of miles. John "Woody" Bramm and Andy Perry were two of the lucky ones who experienced Arnie's Fenton blacktop tests.

Andy remembered his ride like it was yesterday.

"So, we went down to Fenton Road south of Morrison," he said. "That was our test track, in those days, just before dark. There were a couple of other guys along. Arnie started the car and said he needed a volunteer to check the fuel pressure. So, I guess I was elected and wanted to ride in the car, or at least thought I did. I got in this car and got down on my knees. Mind you, there's no rear seat in this car. I'm thinking that if I fall back there, I'll be cut to ribbons. Arnie fired this thing up, and since the gauge is on the dash, I put my fingers up under it to hold on.

"Arnie hit the accelerator, and off we went. You can't imagine the ride this thing gave you. As he took off, my fingers were slipping off from under the dash and peeling the skin off because of the unfinished metal underside, the way it's made, not machined off. I had visions of me flying into the back-seat area. I thought we were about ready to be done. I think he was running mid-9s at about 160 mph.

"We were about topped out, so we had to be doing 140 to 150 mph when all of a sudden the car went sideways in the road. That was pretty much the biggest thrill of my life. I didn't know what was going to happen. Well, he straightened 'er out and, thank God, it looked like we were both going to make it home alive. He looked over at me and grinned, and I wondered if either of us was going to have to clean our underwear out that night!

"We slowed, he turned around, and he punched it again. This time, I was a little more ready for it. We got back to where the boys were standing. I was ready to get out! The crew people told us, 'Well, ya know, when you was going along, when you went sideways on the road, we could read GTO, for those who think young.'

"So how Arnie got 'er straightened out, I don't know, but here we are."

Complete with broomed-in rosin, Gary Dyer and Arnie launch into the history books at the World Series of Drag Racing in 1965. It was a better year there for Arnie than it was for Norm and the Grand Spaulding Dodge. (Photo Colorization by Dean Fait)

with Bob Sullivan's blown fuel-burning Barracuda that was, according to Arnie, merely a dragster covered with some sheet metal to make it look like a car.

During round two, while shifting into high gear, a new experimental high-stall torque converter exploded, causing an instant flash fire inside the passenger compartment. Arnie reported that the fire only lasted an instant, but then the transmission started spraying hot converter oil all over the car's interior.

"He was wearing no protective clothing of any kind," one article in *Drag News* said, "only a pair of overalls and a white shirt. Beswick stopped the car without further incident."

The *Drag News* article continued, "Beswick was rushed to the local hospital and treated for 2nd and 3rd degree burns on his face, hands, neck, and ankle. His arms were burnt up to the elbows. Beswick is reported in fair condition and is staying in room

the clocks was questioned, but they proved to be accurate.

The following day, Arnie journeyed to the US30 strip in Gary, Indiana. There, he had a match race

More than likely, this photo was taken during time trials at the 1965 World Series.

Interest ran high from coast-to-coast....all eyes were on the re-match of a featured match race between Arnie Beswick with his terrific GTO and Mr. Norm's stocker. The first match race, held 2 weeks earlier at Rockford, Ill., ended in a tie. SATURDAY NIGHT, AT THE WORLD SERIES, HELD IN CORDOVA, ILLINOIS, BESWICK MADE QUICK WORK OF SHUTTING DOWN MR. NORM'S GRAND-SPAULDING DODGE CAR IN TWO STRAIGHT!!!!! On the first run, Arnie's GTO came on like a drag-ster, turning a fantastic 8.63 E.T. at 163 mph!! This is the lowest time ever recorded by a stock-bodied car. (Not too many years ago, an Isky equipped fuel dragster was the first car to run in the 8's.)

It became common practice for the manufacturers to brag about the wins that their product helped facilitate. Such was the case from the Isky ad in Drag News following Beswick's triumph over Norm at the World Series.

It's certainly not in focus, but this is what the Mystery Tornado looked like from the stands as the torque converter exploded.

218-2 of (the hospital) in Valparaiso, Indiana. Doctors estimate that he will be there for only one week, telling him to use crutches upon his discharge."

When asked for an explanation, back then Arnie simply stated that "the safety factors of the unit [transmission] were exceeded by about three times the allowable amount." In a recent interview, Arnie said that it should be raised to about 10 times the limit.

During the hospital stay, Spencer added shields to the transmission tunnel, and Arnie soon bought a fire suit, to which a Drag News commentator added the caption, quoting Arnie. "It's sure stuffy."

Bill Wirges drove the GTO at Kahoka, Missouri, the next week because Arnie was out of commission, sprained and wrapped ankle and all.

The Youngster Joins the Ranks

Meanwhile, Don Gay built his own GTO based on Arnie's. The only difference was that Don's had the axles moved forward slightly. There were letters to Drag News from Don and Norm that challenged each other, both talked about their credentials and belittled the other in typical all-star wrestling fashion. Two match races were set for them, the first at Great Lakes Dragaway and the second at Rockford Dragway. Norm went on to be declared the winner in Union Grove, Wisconsin. Despite the fact that he crossed the centerline and even went off the track on the third and deciding race, he was given the win for the meet.

Arnie had just been released from the hospital, and he was still bandaged and ordered to walk on crutches. He was one of the loudest and most noteworthy people cheering Don on. As the match

This is Rockford Dragway and the second of two match races between Don Gay and Mr. Norm. Arnie was still recovering from his torque converter explosion. (Photo Courtesy Bob Slaymaker)

continued, Arnie heard his "buddy," special events announcer Ron Leek, telling of the many accomplishments of the *Flying Ram* Funny Car, thanks to prompts from Norm.

Ron had done this before to Arnie. Remember back to 1961? Now, the more Ron went on, in his usual fashion, telling how great the Chicago car dealer's racer was, the madder Arnie became. Jim Osteen, crew chief for Don Gay, told him to calm down. However, Leek kept pouring more gas on the fire! Finally, Arnie couldn't stand it anymore, and crutches and injuries be damned, he stormed the tower.

Leek, either out of normality or being fearful of what the deranged Arnie Beswick might do, had locked the door. Arnie hobbled up the stairs, found the door locked, and pounded on the door to let him in. Leek was having nothing to do with that and continued to bestow kudos on Norm and Gary, driving the Grand Spaulding Dodge. Arnie was furious and literally kicked the tower door. He would not be denied. Finally, he elbowed the window, breaking the glass. He quickly reached through to unlock and open the tower door, rushing Ron. He snatched the microphone away from the somewhat-startled announcer.

"NONE OF THAT'S TRUE!" Arnie screamed into the microphone. "Now you tell the truth and not the way that Norm wants you to tell it!"

Arnie ranted and raved for a while.

Oddly enough, Leek had hoped for just such an occurrence. He literally doubled over with laughter, watching and listening to Arnie and not doing a thing to stop him. It was truly just like all-star wrestling, as after Arnie finished, Ron told him that was

While there are black-and-white photos of Arnie and Don racing at Yellow River, Joel's colorized artwork brings the cars to life. (Artwork Courtesy Joel Naprstek)

one of the best experiences he'd ever had at the track!

Back at the pits, Osteen profusely thanked Arnie for his boldness and sticking up for Don.

Back to Business with a New Car

During the next few months, the *Mystery Tornado* performed pretty well, but plans were in the works for some new iron. Ben Brown had started working for *Drag World* by now, and this was his story from October 15.

"As has often been said, there are no secrets in drag racing, although the Farmer's latest project has been as closely guarded as any," the article stated. "What has been happening in western Illinois of late is the complete rebuilding of the 1963 Tempest [LeMans] coupe. [There's an] altered-wheelbase front and rear, fiberglass fenders, doors, trunk lid, Plexiglas windows, automatic transmission, straight big car rear axle assembly and etc., PLUS another 421" blown, injected engine. Why all this?"

"You might say that my GTO is a mite too heavy at 3,400 pounds to be a consistent 8-second car," Arnie was quoted as saying in the article. "On a good biting strip with the engine really sharp and 25-percent nitro, I can practically guarantee upper 8-second runs. But, those ideal conditions aren't always the case. We would alter the wheelbase on the GTO, and maybe get the car into the 3,200-pound bracket, but so what? If I'm going to have to go up against 2,500-pound cars with the ultimate engines, then I'm going to have a similar setup. 2,500 pounds and an ultimate engine, in this case my Super Duty 421 Pontiac wedge engines."

Ben muses jokingly, "So speaketh the Farmer!"

The truth of the matter was that even with the new "bird catcher" Enderle injection system and other engine improvements to help performance, the lightened car would still be 300 to 500 pounds heavier than most all the factory competition. It was becoming more and more evident that sometimes being an independent had its drawbacks.

Finishing the Year on a High Note

It was roughly two to three weeks after the explosion that Arnie was able to drive again, even if it was with some pain. With the 1965 year coming to a close on October 17, a Midwest United Drag Racers Association (UDRA) meet was to take place at Rockford Dragway. Arnie and the fast crowd were all there.

SUNDAY, OCTOBER 3rd

CORDOVA DRAGWAY GRAND FINAL

Arnie "The Farmer" Beswick
VERSUS
The Guzler Charger

ARNIE BESWICK Morrison, Illinois in his unbelievable supercharged, injected Pontiac GTO, warmed up Friday night at the World Series with 8.92 seconds at 163 miles per hour. Saturday of the Series, against Grand-Spaulding, Beswick backed it up with 8.69 seconds and 161 miles per hour.

Remember the GUZLER-CHARGER at the Series? They tried it out Saturday night and when the smoke cleared — well - it was the wildest ride you ever saw. The posi-traction on this fuel burning, blown, hemi-Chrysler powered Dodge was "goofed" up and so round and round went the entire car.

★ ★ ★ ★ ★

CORDOVA DRAG STRIP WILL NOT BE OPEN
September 24 - 25 - 26 Weekend
Support the U.D.R.A. Meet at Rockford that week end.

★ ★ ★ ★ ★

SUNDAY, OCTOBER 3rd AT CORDOVA

OPEN 9:00 A.M.   ELIMINATIONS 2:00 P.M.

Bartel plugged the upcoming race between Arnie and the Guzler Charger *almost as the season closed.*

Watching old 8-mm film of this race was unbelievable. Arnie's GTO launched so hard that it looked like he was out to the 330 mark before the Hemi Charger passed the 60-foot point.

Arnie, in the *Mystery Tornado*, took home $1,000 by taking out Mr. Norm, John Farkonas, Ron Pellegrini, the Guzler car, as well as Ed Rachanski, not to mention a few others. It was a great way to end the year on top of a few other wins down South.

A Different Aspect for 1965

We'll back up to the close of the 1964 racing season now. It was at Detroit Dragway where Beswick was approached by Fran Hernandez with the Lincoln-Mercury Division. Fran took him out to dinner to sweet-talk him into driving one of the four single overhead cam (SOHC) Comets being built for the 1965 drag racing season.

General Motors had been out of racing since its self-imposed ban of March 1963. Most of Arnie's racing peers had already switched camps in 1964 to either Ford or Mopar. Because of that, Arnie ended up with Cotton Owens's GMC car hauler.

Difficulty with the Pontiacs

In Arnie's case, the Super Duty parts and pieces for his Pontiacs were getting harder and harder to find. The ring and pinions for the 4-speed transaxle *Grocery Getter* wagon and the LeMans coupe were practically nonexistent. Even though almost everyone else who drove the year-old cars had gone to conventional rear axles, Arnie stuck with the factory drivetrain.

Development of the blown, injected *Mystery Tornado* GTO was slower than Arnie wanted. He knew something was going to have to be done to keep up with the competition. Arnie and his Pontiacs had just gone through at least three or four years of the greatest and winningest years of his racing life, but Mercury's offer began to look more attractive by the day, and he made the decision to make the switch. However, it wasn't made without a Plan B.

The Racing Industry

Up until then, the racing associations would pretty much accept anything that the factory built and they made sure there were classes for these specialty cars. The exception, however, was the NHRA at the start of 1965 with the advent of the altered-wheelbase Mopars. Most of the rest of the organizations welcomed whatever the factory put out with open arms because it drew fans in droves. Going to the track as an independent, Arnie never knew how they might classify the car or if they would even let him run.

Negotiations

Even in that first sit-down, Arnie had a couple of conditions for Mercury. First and foremost on his mind was that if parts and pieces weren't available to keep this very new and experimental SOHC engine running for every week of his racing commitments, Arnie would have the option of filling these dates with one of his Pontiac race cars.

Another condition was that he didn't want to play second fiddle to any of Mercury's other drivers. Dyno Don Nicholson had already switched over to Mercury in early 1964, and Arnie was worried that Don would get preferential treatment.

Hernandez assured Arnie that he would be treated as well as the others who were receiving these specialized cars. Additionally, Fran told Arnie that he could indeed race the Pontiac if the Comet was in the shop. He was confident, perhaps overly so, that the 427-ci SOHC Ford engine would be fine and never have issues.

Hernandez did put a condition on Arnie. If the engine had problems, Arnie was not to repair it himself. He was to get the engine to Mercury, and the company would either repair or replace it.

The New Car

Both parties were happy (although, maybe a bit leery) with the arrangement. Regardless of any apprehension by either party, on February 1, 1965, Arnie and the Lincoln-Mercury Division of Ford Motor Company signed a six-page contract. Per that agreement, it said that Arnie Beswick gave them $50

Bill Stroppe's shop was headquarters for anything race related starting in 1947 for Lincoln-Mercury. He worked on everything, including road race, off-road, Indy cars, NASCAR, and drag racing. After his death in 1995, his son took over the business in Paramount, California.

Even though this might have been its only pass all weekend, the unique new SOHC Comet received lots of attention from both still and 16-mm cameras. The NHRA cameras caught some action during their filming, and there were stills taken of both the Comet and the Mystery Tornado that appeared in the June 1965 issue of Super Stock & Drag Illustrated. (Photo Colorization by Dean Fait)

down with the final payment of $2,950 to be made in November of that year. As Arnie remembered, he only gave them $1 upon signing.

There's no doubt that this promotional shot was used during the restoration of the Comet in the mid-1980s. The black-and-white version appeared in the Super Stock & Drag Illustrated magazine.

The Snow White Motel was Arnie and company's favorite place to stay while in Florida. All three cars wait patiently to do battle. (Photo Courtesy Evelyn Beswick Archives)

After the contract was signed, the car was to be picked up at Bill Stroppe's Enterprise Shop in Southern California just before the NHRA Winternationals in Pomona. Arnie's car had been top coated, changed from the original red to white, as were the others driven by Hayden Proffitt and George DeLorean. Only Nicholson's was left the original red.

Although Arnie had hopes of going up and racing at Irwindale a week before, it was not to be, as he had to wait for them to finish the car. Finally, when Arnie picked up the potent hemi Merc, it had already been lettered and factory readied for track use.

Further disappointment happened when, upon arrival at the Pomona facility, the NHRA wasn't entirely happy with the car. There were some miniscule issues, and consequently, Arnie's first pass in the car was during eliminations.

Despite the negativity, there were many promotional pictures taken before and during the meet because the press loved the cars.

Returning to Daytona

The Comet along with the Mystery Tornado and LeMans coupe were loaded and headed straight for Arnie's favorite wintertime event: Daytona Speedweek. In 1965, it was held at the Spruce Creek Airport, 15 miles from Daytona Beach, Florida. This year's competition ended on February 13, having started seven days earlier.

Comet Drag Team, front view.

(out of consideration for competitors who will become very familiar with the rear view).

The three humans in the picture are "Farmer" Arnie Beswick, Don Nicholson and Hayden Proffitt. Maybe you've seen them wail at a strip near you.

The three beasts in the picture are 1965 Comet Cyclones, very specially equipped for drag racing. They're 427 CID SOHC-powered cars, to be more precise. And the gents mentioned above have plans for them. Their plans include track records and winners' cash at strips all around the country.

Why Comets? Because these guys like to win.

You'll be a winner too, when you see the Comets at your Mercury dealer's. There are eleven kinds of street Comets. And they all look fine— not just from the rear, but from the front and side, as well. We designed 'em that way.

Fran Hernandez was very proud of the team, and this ad appeared in numerous magazines. The question was asked if it was real champagne in the glasses. Don was adamant about never letting liquor touch his lips. Arnie went along with him, so it was only water in their glasses. Hayden didn't mind—more was left for him.

Once in Florida, after a few nights of running, Arnie started to feel more comfortable with the car. During the third night, in time runs, an intake valve decided to let go, and, as Arnie mentioned in 2000, "proceeded to change the original shape of the piston and that portion of the cylinder head."

Needless to say, that put a quick end to any racing Arnie could do with the Comet at Daytona. As it turned out, the car was out of action for that week. Luckily, and thanks to the loophole in his contract, the weeklong competition was not a total loss because Arnie had the Pontiac with him and managed to win the Unlimited Class award for the event.

Unfortunately, Ford determined that the cylinder head was not repairable and a whole new engine must be sent. FoMoCo didn't send it to Morrison though because Arnie was still down South. The new mill was flown in from Detroit and arrived on February 20.

Still Racing Down South

Bill Connell was the track owner at U.S. 19 Dragway in Albany, Georgia. He wrote a little story and told *Drag News* how he and Arnie worked all night installing the new engine at the local Lincoln-Mercury dealership. Then, in front of the next day's record crowd, Arnie took first place at the event with a 10.88 E.T. at 130 mph.

As Bill put it, "Man, it sure wasn't in vain, as Arnie only had to readjust the Hurst linkage and zip—first place."

Incidentally, Arnie's GTO took second with the Farmer driving, and it was followed by a new local Hemi Plymouth in third.

The next reported run and win was on March 14. Arnie towed the car in to Helena, Alabama (near Birmingham), to run at the track there. The *Drag News* article that headlined with "Beswick wins with 8.88 E.T. blast" warned readers not to be too shocked, as the strip was only 1,020 feet long. According to the article, Arnie took two straight with 9.01 and 8.88 elapsed times. The local fans who packed the stands that day were amazed at the factory hot rod Comet's performance, as none of them had ever seen a hemi-powered Ford product before.

David Allan was the president of the Cincinnati District Mercury Dealers. Arnie and the car stopped by for some publicity shots.

Politics of Corporate Sponsorship

As the seasons changed to spring, it was quickly learned that the Chrysler Corporation's altered-wheelbase cars had a definite advantage on the drag strips in the way of traction.

Right from the get-go, the people at Ford and Lincoln-Mercury made up their minds, and they were adamant about it. Word came down from management that no one driving one of their cars could make changes to the engine and especially alter the wheelbase of one of their cars. Further instructions made racing the Comet even harder. Orders came down from above that the Comet drivers were not to race against any of the altered-wheelbase Mopars. This further shackled Arnie's hands to the point of desperation.

Step by step, his livelihood was being taken away because the majority of his competitors drove Mopars, and as one might expect, most of them were those altered-wheelbase A990s. It's interesting to note that Ford had the big engine to do battle with anything that the Plymouth and Chrysler cars could put together, but even with all the Ford hemi's muscle, it wasn't enough to overcome the traction advantage.

The reason for the mandate of not racing against the altered-wheelbase cars was spelled out to Arnie in no uncertain terms. It was the opinion of Lincoln-Mercury and Ford that the Chrysler Corporations altered-wheelbase cars should be outlawed.

This was a way that Ford thought it could impose its will on the racing world and the sanctioning bodies.

However, track owners and race promoters couldn't get enough of these new lightweight Mopars. It was more about the brand wars of these factory cars. Consequently, as the 1965 racing season went on, track owners and promoters were calling Arnie but telling him to leave the Comet at home and just bring the GTO. Any competitive GM car in 1965 was scarce, as Arnie and only a handful of other drivers had stuck with anything from that corporation.

Arnie was under contract, and he wasn't supposed to drive the Pontiac if the Comet was working. His way around that was to show up with both cars and have Don Gay do the driving for him in the GTO. At least that's what was reported in a few articles where both cars were present. I'm sure it was true for the bigger nationally reported ones, but for the smaller events, only Arnie will ever know for sure who was actually driving.

I'm sure that Fran Hernandez might have been a little suspicious. He must have known from reports what was really going on, especially after

Arnie's Comet takes on the Dan Smoker–Dan Lewis–Merrimac Motors Big Red A990 1965 Plymouth from Newport News, Virginia. The Mopar had a big Hemi under the hood. The track is thought to be Richmond, Virginia.

Arnie and his Comet take on the 1964 Infamy *Hemi Plymouth at the Gay Drag Strip in Dickinson, Texas. The Mopar was campaigned by J. D. Feigelson out of Sutton Motor Company in Beaumont, Texas. (Photo Courtesy F.E. McKinzie)*

the story written about the April 18 happenings. York US30 track in Pennsylvania was the stage where it was reported that Arnie drove the Pontiac in the second round to put down the Sox & Martin altered-wheelbase Plymouth.

The end was near. *Drag World* broke the story first about the end of the Comet for Arnie. The headline in the May 21 edition read "Beswick-Merc split." While the story told that the Comet had been picked up from the Beswick farm on May 15, according to Arnie, no such thing happened. However, what *did* happen was just as dramatic.

While Arnie most likely received the call that they'd pick up the car, Hernandez still didn't have a replacement driver. The article said that Paul Rossi had been commissioned to go and get the car. As Arnie remembered, he brought the car to Rossi, towing it to a race at Martin, Michigan. Nobody from

Lincoln-Mercury was there in an unceremonious transfer in mid-to-late June.

Arnie expressed his deep regrets in that article, which he repeated 35 years later, about giving up the car. As he stated in that original article, "I just couldn't do the car justice while racing the GTO, and with only 50-percent effort, I would never equal Nicholson, so that was my choice."

The *Drag World* article then mentioned that there was some conjecture as to who was driving the Pontiac during the past few weeks of record-breaking performances. It went on to say, "Don Gay, Dickinson, Texas, friend of Beswick's was supposed to handle the car," but then said, "but seldom did."

The last ironic line from that article (about driving the *Mystery Tornado*) read: "'Farmer' says his appearance schedule is full through the season!"

THE REST OF THE COMET STORY

Arnie Beswick's Comet has quite the history. After it left Arnie's possession, Paul Rossi indeed took over ownership and driving duties. That only lasted the rest of that year's racing season. He renamed the car *Goldfender* for the last part of 1965 and painted it red.

From there, it went through various names, color changes, and owners. First was Dick Oldfield from Buffalo, New York. Then, the car went north into Canada to Jim Melsted. It returned and reentered the United States after that. Cary Sullivan of Hibbing, Minnesota, was the next owner. He sold it to David Kunz in 1984.

David owned it for the longest period of time. He was responsible for returning the car to its original glory and correct restoration. His attention to even the slightest detail did not go unnoticed, right down to the misspelling of "Jardine" (regarding the headers). He was the one who cut the hole in the hood and added the Hilborn fuel injection.

In 2010, David said, "It would have been the next step in the evolution of the car."

David took the car to the Mecum Auction in 2010. The gavel fell with the signs reading $315,000. The auctioneer said, "The bid goes on." The reserve hadn't been met. The car has since been sold, and, as of late 2018 (at last report), is in a museum owned by Doug Gonder in the Yukon.

The Comet was almost finished when this picture was snapped at Great Lakes Dragaway in roughly 1984 or 1985. David Kunz applied the paint himself. His addition of the Hilborn injection stacks, putting in the headlights, and a few other details were all that was left.

David Kunz and Arnie posed for this photo at the 2010 Mecum Auction. The whole weekend was buzzing with excitement about this rare car. Then to hear Arnie's regrets about turning the car over to Rossi in 1965 when Dana Mecum handed him the microphone . . . It's just like yesterday in my mind.

A look under the hood at the sterile, first-class restored engine bay, all done in-house by Dave and friends.

How many of us wouldn't jump at the chance to sit in this seat? Not many of us have. It was certainly my lucky weekend!

CHAPTER 5

RACING THE FUNNY CAR

O n New Year's Day 1966, Arnie headed out West because he'd been booked into Fontana and a few other Southern California tracks in the early months. The Pontiac dealership owned by the Gay family was sponsoring him, so he was off to Dickinson, Texas. Coincidentally, there was a match race there.

Once again, it was never just going from A to B. Arnie always preferred traveling at night. So, it was fairly late when Arnie had a flat tire on the outside, driver-side rear tire of the truck. Fortunately, he was close to a town with a small garage. Their mechanic was a young kid who fixed the tire and quickly reinstalled it on the truck.

Arnie and Clyde Wentley, his traveling companion on this trip, were well into Texas at close to 3 a.m. when all of a sudden, the same tire that was just repaired passed him on the highway. Arnie managed to safely pull over the "freight train." They found the runaway tire with hopes of putting it back on. Unfortunately, they were not able to do so because in addition to the tire being damaged, so was the wheel. All of the lug nuts were gone,

These three pictures were all taken at that same photo shoot. It was pointed out that the tiger-striped Tempest was the latest addition to Arnie Beswick's family with a wheelbase of 104 inches and blown Pontiac Power.

Both the new Tiger *car and the* Mystery Tornado *received the sponsorship lettering applied at the Gay's dealership in Dickinson, Texas.*

and at least three of the six studs were damaged from the wobbly, loose wheel. There was no way that they could travel this way and no way to fix the problem with the resources at hand.

Arnie's only hope was that a passing motorist would stop and offer assistance; they were completely stranded. There was very little traffic at that hour in the morning, and desperate for help, Arnie literally lied down on the road as if he were hurt. His only hope was that someone would stop and help. Granted, he didn't lie in the middle of the road, just in case an approaching car didn't see him. Still, Clyde was deeply concerned. He told Arnie that he would surely get hit and die.

Fortunately for Arnie, it wasn't long before approaching headlights appeared, and they were even from the right direction. Whether or not the driver saw Arnie lying on the road was unclear, but the driver stopped at the sight of the rig with the two race cars. The sedan's young driver was heading home with his wife and two sleeping kids in the back.

Fate had found the perfect Good Samaritan. He gave Arnie and the wheel a ride into his hometown.

Once there, he called his favorite shop owner very early and asked him to help. Even at 4:30 or 5 a.m., the owner came in, fixed the wheel and tire, and supplied Arnie with lug nuts. Then, the kindhearted man took Arnie back to his truck while his wife and kids were still in the car. The racing journal of the day simply reported that the delay made Arnie miss the Houston meet.

Heading West for the Second Time

After stripping off the old lettering and applying the new words to the car's doors with the Gay Pontiac name, Arnie was off to California.

His first stop was at Jess Tyree's shop for a set of headers and to fix the steering problem on the *Tiger* car. While Tyree fabricated the headers, his logo was applied to the car. Even moving the car around

A roadside stop in Arizona made for an opportunity to take a quick snapshot of the "freight train" heading to the coast.

The trip complete in California, Arnie poses like a proud father with the two cars. (Photo Courtesy reproracingposters.com)

BESWICK BREEDS A FUNNY TIGER

Arnie 'Farmer' Beswick cultivated 421 inches of Pontiac roar power that has the competition crying

from shop to trailer or vice versa had its issues. The front wheels hit the front edges of the aluminum fenders and weren't able to turn more than a couple of inches on the steering wheel. Arnie's solution was more primitive, as he found a pair of tin snips to cut away the front part of the fenders so that he could steer the car onto and off of the trailer as well as on the track.

The first meet that Arnie was scheduled for was at Lions Drag Strip in Wilmington, California, on January 22, when he'd be match racing the "Flying Dutchman" (Al Vander Woude). As was often the case, mechanical issues plagued both Al and Arnie's two cars.

Round one was between Al and the *Mystery Tornado*. According to the *Drag World* article, Al had a frequent problem of going left upon launch. He was forced to lift but was able to get back on the loud pedal after "swinging the jib sail around." Arnie's GTO had a good start but leaned out and blew an oil cap off, covering the windshield with oil and rendering Arnie blind. Seemingly guided by only a sense of smell, Arnie won the first round with a 10.42 at 129.31. The Flying Dutchman's time was 11.31 at 122.95.

As this was Arnie's first time match racing in California, he was not familiar with some of their procedures. One of which was that you were expected to know when your next round was (1 hour later). Everywhere else in the country, the officials came and got you for your next run. That was not the case at Lions, and Arnie worked on his car right through the second round with Al.

Arnie was not going to make that mistake again and made the third round with the tiger-striped LeMans.

The Tiger *burns in the rosin at Lions Drag Strip.*

The Mystery Tornado *suffers mechanical issues with a big pool of fluid under the car.*

Arnie's going through the necessary evil of maintaining transmissions. They often suffered breakage from the extreme horsepower that the engines were producing.

While the Mystery Tornado *had a class at the NHRA events (Pomona here), the LeMans did not.*

Al was on 90-percent pop, literally smoking the tires even in high gear. Arnie, in the meantime, was quickly learning that he had to really drive this wild animal. It was a real tiger for sure! Arnie's *Tiger* was darting this way and that, right on the ragged edge of a spinout. At the lights, the Flying Dutchman ran 10.80 at 129.44. Arnie was a scant foot behind, tripping the beams at a 10.99 at 144.92. Arnie pulled the chute, but it didn't blossom. On top of that, the throttle stuck wide open! Al reported that he saw Arnie plow into the sand trap, spin around at least twice, and jump over a sand dune before there was nothing but silence.

Arnie was furious! Angry because of the loss, mad because his car hadn't performed as it should, and steaming because he was in the sand! Arnie re-fired the car, and while to Al and others it might have looked like the throttle was still stuck wide open, it wasn't. It was Arnie's foot firmly planted to the floor that made the LeMans leap out of the trap with huge rooster tails of sand flying. Never mind that the car glanced off a power pole (as Arnie remembered it) before getting back on the pavement and finally shutting off.

Arnie made sure that never happened again in typical Farmer fashion. He tied an extra-heavy piece of twine to the top of the gas pedal and kept the other end close at hand so that he could pull the pedal back up if that ever happened again.

The next day, Arnie headed to Fontana for a match race with Tom McEwen's new Hemi Barracuda. Even with extra nitro and a head start, the overly heavy GTO running mid-9s was passed both times by the lightweight Plymouth. Such was the case, as the mere two-year-old *Mystery Tornado* was

Rich Sawyer told how he was supposed to take the Tiger car through tech inspection, but the car was classified with the Fuel Altereds. Arnie couldn't talk them into reconsidering and decided to just run exhibition. (Photo Courtesy Forrest Bond)

Arnie works on the untamable tiger-striped beast, although these photos are at two different West Coast tracks. Arnie's number was 729 at Irwindale.

The photo caption that inspired this painting read "Photo for framing." The caption told how Arnie would rather fight than switch from Pontiac. The original photo was shot at the AHRA Nationals in Irwindale. (Painting by Tim Frederick based on Al Yates Photo)

now an obsolete relic in this fast-paced, innovative world. Wins for the white GTO only came when the competition went red, went off the track, or had mechanical issues.

Arnie made good use of his stay in California, racing at a number of the big drag strips. While the GTO was outdated, the lighter tiger-striped LeMans took wins here and there when Arnie could keep the front wheels down to apply maximum throttle.

"WE ALL LOVE AN UNDERDOG"

Pete McCarthy is as well known in Pontiac circles as anyone, having written books that included part numbers for heads, blocks, and other engine specs. He was at Irwindale to witness the runs and meet Arnie personally. His assessment of being an independent with the tiger-striped LeMans was as accurate as can be.

"At that time, many of these so-called Funny Car drivers were getting serious contracts from the manufacturers," Pete said. "The one that I remember most vividly was Dyno Don, who was with Lincoln-Mercury. His new [and revolutionary] flip-top Comet was getting enormous publicity from everybody. Other drivers too all had factory rides. Arnie had what was considered a cobbled-up, backyard effort. While none of the other drivers would admit that they feared Arnie, they certainly didn't give him any slack. But, when he ran the numbers that he did, well, we all went berserk and so did the fans, 'cause we all love an underdog."

Back East to Florida

After his share of wins and losses, it was time for Arnie to head to the traditional Daytona meet. Once again, he was to face Gary Dyer in Norm's blown Hemi Dodge. The 1966 season didn't go as well as 1965 did for Arnie. He went red for the first round of the best-of-three match race. Dyer just flat outran him for round two.

Roughly a month later, Shug Campbell, the manager of Georgia's Yellow River Dragstrip, scheduled Arnie and Dyno Don for a match race on March 20. While full of controversy, it was one of the tiger-striped LeMans's finest hours.

The April 15 *Drag News* issue in "Dixie News" from Harold Springs reported, "Down at The River [the Yellow River Dragstrip], Nicholson and Beswick had their go today. The first run was exciting to say the least. After the rosin burning and track sweeping, the thundering fuelers came screaming off at the green with both front ends at least 5 feet in the air. Nicholson lifted first as the lightweight Comet started into the other lane and Beswick eased down and on through the lights in front. I have no idea who the winner was. If the normal rules about crossing the center line were in effect, both cars lost, as neither stayed in the lanes. The second round saw Dyno Don pull the 1965 Comet out of the pits as the front end on the new [1966] car was slightly damaged on the wild wheelie from the previous run. Beswick was the winner this time, as he made a straight pass all the way with Don getting crossed up and wisely

Arnie and the crew often stayed with Red Lawler when he raced at tracks near Atlanta, Georgia. The Mystery Tornado *and the* Tiger *cars can be seen.*

The race at Yellow River with the new Tiger *car against Dyno Don was a big feather in Arnie's hat. Here the cars are getting staged with Don in the new flip-top Comet.*

The Tiger *car working in the rosin proves that there was a lot of* hook.

shutting off. Nicholson and crew had the front end corrected by third round time, and the new car was once more brought into the fray. [It's the] same tale. Nicholson touched the center line and lifted, and Arnie sailed home the winner. Arnie's best elapsed time for the meet [was] an astounding and unbelievable 8.35!"

Mr. Springs went on to tell of the Comet's potential and mentioned that, as he saw it, Arnie had found the answers to the Tempest's problems.

The following week in the same column, Harold Springs stayed on the topic. "Let's talk about the 8.35 turned in by Beswick at Yellow River last weekend. I don't believe it. So there. As a matter of fact, I haven't talked to anyone who did, including the track owner and all the race officials. This is not to say that the clocks did not read this, as they did. I saw it myself as 8.35 seconds but somewhere down in the innards of the timing equipment, I'm convinced something went wrong. It was no doubt one of the strongest runs ever made by a stocker, but, as far as I'm concerned, it was not that quick. Of course, I've been wrong before and will be again but as I said, I don't believe it."

Bob Cruse was skeptical as well but remembered the *Mystery Tornado* running an 8.60 at the World Series against Norm. He congratulated Arnie, saying, "Let's just say it must have been one fantastic run." He went on to say that Arnie and Norm were the two biggest contributors to making Factory Experimental (F/X) exhibition as popular as it had become.

Jess Tyree took advantage of Arnie's big win to promote his company's services with this ad.

Described as a "well-rehearsed dance step," both cars leave with wheels in the air. This was one of the most-published photos from the match race between Arnie and Don at Yellow River.

The lanes have switched for the pair, with Don using the 1965 Comet. It was pressed into service, thanks to damage incurred during the new car's first round.

The Tiger car burns in rosin at Dallas, Georgia. Since there was no other car in this and another similar picture, it's unclear if Arnie was alone or not.

This close-up clearly shows where the leading edge of the aluminum fender had been cut away to make steering the car possible. (Photo Courtesy Dwight Garnhart)

This is one of the very first shots of the newly completed 1966 Star of the Circuit GTO. While the front air dam proved to be unneeded, after dealing with the wild wheelstands of the Tiger car, Arnie didn't want to take any chances. (Photo Courtesy Red Lawler)

The fact of the matter was that Arnie didn't believe it either. The run was never backed up; so, we'll never know!

Back in the Midwest

The May 6 issue of *Drag News* promoted the upcoming UDRA Nationals at Great Lakes Dragaway on Memorial Day weekend. Arnie was there among many, and "Broadway" Bob used Arnie's GTO as the poster child. *Drag News* also wrote about the April 3 win that Arnie took over the Ramchargers at Alton, Illinois. Then, coming from another meet, Arnie was too late to compete but made a great exhibition pass to the delight of the fans.

There was a match race on May 14 at Cordova against Dyno Don, who took the win as Arnie did a

The Beswick versus Mr. Norm marque was always something worth promoting in the local newspapers, as seen here in the Dixon Evening Telegraph, circa May 7, 1966.

wheelstand equal to any wheelstander. He came down and crushed the oil pan. Meanwhile, Don's prototype transmission broke (as was evident by a gaping hole in the case). Both Arnie and Don repaired their cars within two hours and were back up to the line. The heckling began between the two, driving all the fans wild.

Even during rosin burnouts, Arnie did 3-foot wheelstands. Finally, it was green and go with Arnie pulling a hole shot on Don. Arnie had a good run going when his transmission let go from second to third and Don passed him to win. There was no third round except for congrats to both racers and crews from Bob Cruse. For you statisticians, Don's best was an 8.85 at 149 mph.

This shot was taken on May 15 at Great Lakes Dragaway in Union Grove, Wisconsin. Arnie is racing against Gary Dyer in the Mr. Norm altered-wheelbase Dodge.

This is the Mystery Tornado *racing against Terry Culligan. The date is Sunday, May 22, and the location is Neita Dragway (now Cedar Falls Raceway).*

Arnie and Gary Dyer go at it again. This is obviously Rockford. (Photo Courtesy Dwight Garnhart)

Although James Ibusuki was unable to find documented proof of this exact pair racing at US30 in Gary, Indiana, he wanted the bright tiger-striped car doing battle with the Grand Spaulding car in his painting titled The Sunday Funnies. *James felt that the US30 strip was more iconic than Rockford, where a race between the two had just taken place. (Illustration by James Ibusuki)*

Snapped on Friday, June 24, at Great Lakes Dragaway, it is plain to see that there was always a crowd around Arnie's cars. Rich Sawyer mentioned that often there would be five people around Arnie's cars to every one or two around his competition.

Taken a short time later, Arnie and Don line up here at Thompson. (Photo Courtesy Robert Goldstein)

Accomplished during the summer, this painting illustrates the difference between the original aluminum front end and the longer fiberglass version. While it helped, the front end still wouldn't stay down. (Illustration by Joel Naprstek)

Still in primer after the longer front end was added, the stress on the subframe is evident here. This shot is at Great Lakes Dragaway in Union Grove, Wisconsin, during a match race with Dyno Don. (Photo Courtesy Robert Goldstein)

Heating up in Summer

As the weeks went by, reports came in that Arnie was match racing many of the nation's top names. There was a tie with Norm's car at Rockford Dragway on May 8. The following weekend, May 14, Arnie was at Cordova Dragway again facing Dyno Don and losing two out of three in the match race and attributing the losses to handling/mechanical problems.

The GTO was mentioned as taking two out of three at Neita (now Cedar Falls) on May 22. It was early June when Arnie lost two straight to Eddie Schartman at Cordova thanks to a huge bumper-dragging wheelstand. When he came down, he broke a front spring shackle. Arnie was still the crowd favorite, however. The next day, still at Cordova, the Flying Farmer took John Farkonas's blown Plymouth, *Ply Mouth Galore,* two straight. The Tempest was broken, so the GTO was used for round two.

On June 25 (still at Cordova), Arnie downed the Darrell Droke Mustang in two straight out of three. On July 23, Arnie downed the new Farkonas/Minick

Funny Car, believed to be the *Chi-Town Hustler*, taking the first and third rounds. In that same issue of *Drag News*, there was a report that the Ramchargers downed Arnie on July 24 at Great Lakes Dragaway. It was the best of five. The article mentioned that if Arnie could keep the front wheels down, he'd do well. This was even after Arnie extended the front end.

This was just a small snapshot of recorded events with many more filling in the dates between. The luxury of being Arnie Beswick was that many of the biggest stars were now coming to his area of the country for match races.

Heading East

As the summer continued, there were ads in *Drag News* promoting the big upcoming events out East. They listed Arnie as attending the *Drag News* S/S Invitational Championships in Atco, New Jersey, and the King of Kings event at Capitol Raceway on August 13.

There was also an ad for the upcoming Super Stock Nationals in Long Island, New York, on August 5, 6, and 7. To everyone's surprise, Arnie showed up unannounced to race.

The late John "Woody" Bramm went with the Farmer and talked about this event. Woody put it this way:

"The second Super Stock Nationals might have been the weekend that made Arnie Beswick," he said. "I remember reading an article where it said there were 39,000 people at that race. One particular race against Dick Landy, probably 1,000 feet of the quarter, Arnie was on the back bumper, all over the track, sideways, every which way. When that race was over, that crowd was Arnie's! They fell in love with him right there.

"On Sunday against Bill Shirey, they called him the Professor, Arnie had to spot him a half second light. Probably at about half track, Arnie went completely off the track. We were following him down in the tow car, probably about an eighth-mile behind. All we saw was Pontiac Tempest . . .

The paint job complete minus lettering that would later be added. This photo was taken at the Super Stock Nationals in Long Island, New York. (Photo Courtesy Harry Pinkard)

Arnie's Tiger *car is here against "Dandy" Dick Landy at the second-annual Super Stock Nationals. (Photo Courtesy Harry Pinkard)*

The Tiger *car is pictured here on a solo pass in Long Island's Super Stock Nationals.*

Taken the following weekend after the S/S Nationals at Capitol Raceway in Crofton, Maryland, the spectators went wild over the wheelstands that the Tiger car always seemed to do.

As the date on the edge of this photo confirms, this is one of the first known pictures of the '66 at a race-track. This shot is likely again at Cordova, as Bob Bartel's station wagon is in the background.

Go west, young man! The "freight train" is loaded, and the cars are lettered with the new sponsorship for the upcoming California races. (Photo Courtesy George Houraney)

Fiberglass Ltd. was so proud of Arnie's new car that it used the car in an ad for Drag News.

Notice that the injection unit does not stick out of the hood or the base of the windshield. Arnie wanted the car to be as stock appearing as possible. Bill Wirges came up with the idea of using a self-priming system (similar to an airplane) so that the hood wouldn't have to be opened every time.

This Jules Meyers Pontiac advertisement was on the back page of Drag News.

The Tiger *waits to pounce at Bakersfield.*

Warming it up at Bakersfield.

Dust flying everywhere, we heard him hit the throttle again. He'd come back on the track. When all the dust cleared away, the crowd went absolutely nuts as it looked like Arnie had won the race. That whole weekend was absolutely wild! Even though Arnie did not win on Friday night, Saturday night, or Sunday, including the Super Eliminator race held that day, Arnie was probably the most popular car there."

It was little wonder that after events like this, Arnie made it all the way to number 1 on *Drag Racing* magazine's National Drag Racing Poll under the "Exhibition Stockers – Blown" category.

As the year closed out, Arnie was back in California, this time thanks to help from Jules Meyers Pontiac racing. He not only brought the tiger-striped Tempest but also the new *Star of the Circuit* 1966 GTO as well.

1967 Begins the Same Way

The year began as it had for the past two racing seasons with Arnie and a couple of cars in Califor-

nia. There was not only a change in the cars but also the sponsorship. Jules Meyers out of Los Angeles had helped Arnie out this year, and the dealership's name was on both cars.

The *Tiger* car, now proudly named the *Tameless Tiger* by suggestion from a GM executive, had the Jules Meyers logo on the doors. The new 1966 *Star of the Circuit* had it on the big air dam in the front of the car.

The first big event was the AHRA Nationals at Beeline Dragway in Scottsdale, Arizona. Plagued with either engine or driveline problems, Arnie lost with both cars. Schartman took out the *Tameless Tiger*, and Nicholson downed the 1966 *Star*.

There were events where Arnie raced every single weekend through the month of February. While his speeds and ETs rivaled those of his opponents, it seemed that mechanical issues plagued the Pontiacs. Don Nicholson, Larry Reyes, "Jungle" Jim Liberman, and Doug Cook in the Stone, Woods, & Cook Mustang all can say that they beat Arnie while he was out West.

The Tiger *is shown here taking on the* Chevy II Heavy Nova *at Bakersfield. The little Chevy II had just been recently purchased by Ed Carter and Bob Little. This photo was used by the Charlie Hunter Quartet on their "Ready . . . Set . . . Shango!" album cover. (Photo Courtesy Jere Aldadeff)*

Taken during time trials at Lions in 1966 from way down track, the Tameless Tiger *car is burning in rosin.*

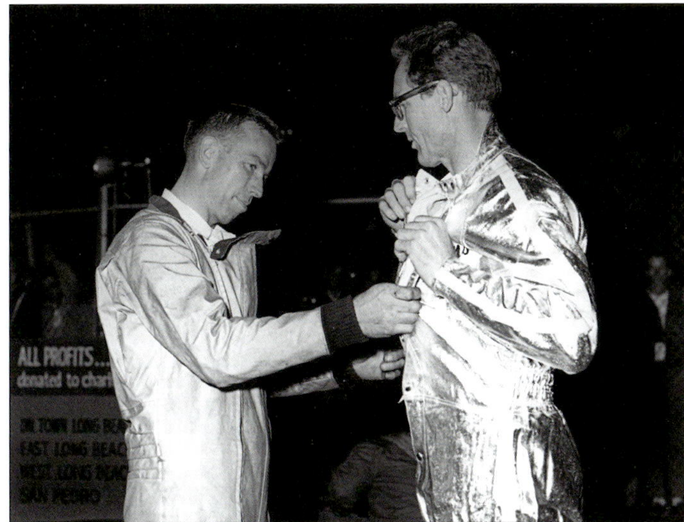

This is not the only photo of Arnie and Don helping each other with their fire suits. This one was taken at Lions. (Photo Courtesy Jere Aldadeff)

In another shot from Lions, this time we see that Arnie is running against the Brutus Funny Car, *driven by "Jungle" Jim Liberman. (Photo Courtesy Joe Kerr)*

The new Star of the Circuit *gets its turn at the track in Lions. There was only one place to put the sponsorship logo for Jules Meyers Pontiac: on the spoiler.*

It wasn't until he was at Irwindale on March 5 that Arnie won with both cars. That's not to say that the fans didn't enjoy the showmanship put on by the Farmer and the other drivers. While the runs themselves only lasted between 8 to 10 seconds, it was all the preparation of the day that was part of it.

Using rosin (or *gold dust*, as it was commonly called) was the norm in those days. Each driver had his own canister of it and "shook out" two strips of the powder onto the track surface. Then, using a push broom, it was carefully evened out. Once that was done, the car was fired, and they did burnouts until they felt that their slicks had enough bite to launch properly in front of their opponent. As much as Arnie dominated the competition in 1963, 1964, and 1965, match racing was where the money was, and the more of a showman you were, the more promoters craved your car at their tracks.

Arnie is racing Gary Dyer and his new G-S 1966 Charger at Fontana. According to the February 1967 issue of Super Stock & Drag Illustrated, *Arnie took the first round with a 9.37 ET at 155 mph thanks to a blown transmission in Norm's machine. Rounds two and three went to Norm.*

Arnie and Al Vander Woude have just pulled onto the track at Lions Drag Strip.

There's always someone who wants to take your picture, and Arnie was always kind enough to oblige. This was snapped in California.

Another angle of the Star of the Circuit *preparing to take on the* Flying Dutchman *during the rosin procedure. Notice the broom out front, most likely for burning in rosin. (Photo Courtesy Jim Demmitt Jr.)*

"Jungle" Jim

Bill Stoermer has been an Arnie Beswick fan and a drag racing fan all his life. Growing up in Morrison, he went to races and helped the Farmer out as a teenager. Here is his take on the subject, especially concerning Liberman.

"Jungle Jim idolized Arnie in those days. Jungle was a real showman. He could have easily been considered the John Force during that time, so he drew a lot of attention. But Arnie was Jim's hero, and he loved to race against him.

"There was one particular race in Detroit where the Farmer was out quite a ways in front of Jungle when all of a sudden, Arnie got sideways, first one way then the other. Jungle went off the track to get around him, blowing dirt all over the place. Of course, the crowd went crazy 'cause they just loved it. Finally, Arnie got it straightened out and went on down [to the finish line]. He lost the race of course, but it was all so exciting.

"Later on, Jungle Jim was doing fire burnouts too. They'd pour gas down, throw a match, and then he'd drive through it, so the showmanship of that time was always unbelievable."

Yet another view of the start of the race between Arnie and Al. The GTO lifts the wheels, ever so slightly. (Photo Courtesy Jim Orloff)

This is another still photo at Bakersfield. The car is so colorful that it's easy to see why everyone wanted pictures of it.

It's a good launch at Bakersfield. An almost identical photo made the centerfold of Super Stock & Drag Illustrated in June 1967. It's interesting that even before he left California, the big front spoiler was gone.

The notes that went along with this photo shoot mention the Winternationals.

An example of this happened on April 15 at Capitol Raceway in Towson, Maryland. Arnie's '66 won round one as the Stone, Woods, & Cook Mustang broke. Don Gay was on hand, mentioned as an announcer at this particular event. Jungle Jim in the *Brutus* GTO Funny Car filled in and ran Arnie's *Tameless Tiger.* Liberman was quicker to the finish line due to a hundred-yard wheelie.

The author for *Drag News* put it this way:

"The wheelie that Arnie pulled is one of the longest I have seen at Capitol in a match race and still continue in a straight hard run." Jim ran a 9.05 at a tick over 159. The Farmer was right behind, stopping the clock at 9.21 at 135.33.

Back in the Midwest, Arnie poses again for this night-time shot.

The Tameless Tiger *sits on the trailer getting ready to be unloaded at Cordova.*

Since it's still smoking, I'm guessing this was the first in the series of pictures showing the wrecked Tiger *car. (Photo Courtesy Skip Norman of Gold Dust Classics)*

Untamed Tiger

As the year went by, Arnie campaigned all over the United States, whether it was the Midwest, the South, out East, or all the way out West. He delighted not just Pontiac fans but drag racing fans everywhere. Then, Arnie made the headline of the May 19 issue of *Drag World* with, "Dyno, Arnie Crash at Cecil."

Bruce Young was credited with the photos from that event, so we'll assume that he wrote the article that told the story of what happened while Arnie was racing the Ramchargers. It reads, "Stay Loose! The next two were the Ramchargers with Mick Buckle driving and Arnie 'the Farmer' Beswick in his tiger-striped 1963 Tempest.

"On the green it was like this: the 'Chargers had no power and left last; Arnie lifted the wheels as usual and went to the middle of the track with wheels still up in the air. Then, he got sideways, and the accelerator stuck to the floor. This, plus the low-pressure tires, caused the car to run off the track sliding sideways, flipping over and rolling through the guardrail, landing on its side in the pit return road."

While the Ramchargers passed Arnie and crossed the finish line safely, the *Tameless Tiger* was badly hurt.

The columnist continued:

"Arnie scrambled out, grabbed a fire extinguisher, and put out a small fire around the injectors. The complete front end was wiped out and all the fiberglass was ripped away. The Farmer said that his door hit the guardrail, came off and hurt his side and hip, but other than that, he was okay."

The writer also mentioned that because Beswick wiped out the timing wires, they had to run the rest of the meet with ET clocks only.

In regard to the headline, while running separately, Dyno Don's car lifted the wheels a lot higher than normal. He came up so high that the body ripped off the chassis, sending sparks flying. The commentator said it was like the body disintegrated. Don crossed the finish line in just the tube frame chassis, eventually flipped end over end once or twice, and landed right-side up in 4 feet of mud. While he was being pulled out of the car, Don's true colors showed, and he asked what his ET was, just like Arnie would have done. When he was told an 8.04, he said, "Well, that's low ET of the meet!"

Both the operable *Star of the Circuit* and the wrecked *Tameless Tiger* were loaded up and headed for Canada. The '66 made its own headlines, com-

The damaged Tempest is shown from a variety of angles at Cecil County. (Photos Courtesy Fred Welch)

Loaded on the trailer to tow it back to the farm, the damage doesn't look quite as severe here. (Photo Courtesy William Zinkhan)

This was taken out East at the Super Stock Nationals in 1967. There was a reason the LeMans had its picture in the 1967 program with wheelstands like this. (Photo Courtesy Skip Norman of Gold Dust Classics)

ing out on top of the field of four cars and setting low ET of the meet with an 8.63 at 164 mph.

The next day, Arnie was back in the States, racing at Thompson, Ohio, on May 22, getting beat by Don Nicholson's Comet.

Arnie Behling

It was midsummer when the *Tameless Tiger* was repaired, and in the following weeks, Arnie Beswick was approached repeatedly by Arnie Behling. He wanted to drive for the Farmer. He wanted it so

Arnie Behling stops for a picture with the Tameless Tiger. *Arnie Beswick's pickup is behind him.*

Most likely, this is Behling driving the Tiger *car in this sequence from Oswego, racing the Chapman Camaro.*

bad that, according to Beswick, he just gave in and decided to let him give it a try.

Even though Behling, or "Little Arnie" as he was called, didn't know much about the mechanics of keeping a nitro-burning Funny Car running, he was fearless behind the wheel. As Beswick remembered, it was to the point of being reckless.

The first mention was an instance where Fred Coopman, who had been with Beswick on again and off again since 1958, and Little Arnie were at Cordova. Arnie Beswick was with the '66 somewhere else because the team could then make bookings at two separate tracks. At least two different people filmed the incident as Little Arnie did a huge wheel-stand. Being new in the car, Little Arnie wasn't ready for what the *Tiger* always did.

When Little Arnie got out of the throttle, the car, of course, came down hard and did a lot of damage to the fiberglass front end. Since the way to get paid was to complete the runs, he ran without the front end.

This is the last version of the Tameless Tiger *with the tiger's head on the door before it met its demise.*

Arnie heats the hides while racing Dyno with the '66 at Yellow River.

When Arnie heard about what Little Arnie did, he was livid because the car's appearance was almost as important as the completion of a run to him.

The Tameless Tiger Is Tamed

Little Arnie was responsible for the death of the *Tameless Tiger*. News of the new 1968 car being built, the *Star of the Circuit II,* had just been released, even though *Drag News* incorrectly reported that Arnie was switching to Chevrolet power. Arnie was convinced that it was just Little Arnie overdriving the car in typical fashion, but three eyewitnesses remember it differently.

Bob Lendman, nicknamed "Super Duty" because

This is what was brought back to the farm after the big wreck.

of his ability to stay awake while driving long distances, and Little Arnie towed the *Tameless Tiger* down South. Their destination was Sportsman Park in Farmington, North Carolina, for a match race with Roger Gustin. Roger was driving the Gustin Brothers' injected flip-top Cyclone.

Lendman remembered it this way:

"Arnie Behling was running in the right-hand lane. I was following in a pickup truck that we were using for a tow vehicle. There were fire extinguishers under my feet. [He paused.] Something broke, and he made a hard right just before he got to the lights [finish line]. The car went off the track and, *mmm*, hit something on the edge of the track, went airborne, and went backward through, *uh*, between two trees.

"It was high enough up in the trees that the car cleared, going through them, but when we towed the car back out to load it, we had to go around them because the rig wouldn't fit between them on the ground," Lendman said. "The battery ended up being imbedded some 20 feet up in one of the trees. When it stopped, the car was turned around, facing the track at such an angle that I couldn't see him. I ran through a patch of blackberry bushes with a fire extinguisher in each hand, both my arms getting ripped up with blood running down them. I hit one of the trees with one of the fire extinguishers, and it

bounced off and came back around to smack me in the jaw and broke a tooth.

"By the time I got to the car, I couldn't see him. I was afraid he had fallen on his fire mask against the steering wheel. Actually, that car still had doors and he had fallen out the driver-side door. I got him set up next to the car. I didn't know if the blood was his or mine. It turned out I got hurt worse than he did.

"All of the locals then descended upon the car, which at that point, still had things burning on the front end. The fuel tank had been split. They started pulling parts off the car for souvenirs. One guy picked up a hot piece of metal. I saw him pick it up then drop it. It was just kind of amazing to me that that kind of thing would happen."

Laverne Zachary told a similar story. At the time, he was one of the locals. While he didn't descend like a vulture to get souvenirs, he still has a few pieces of that original *Tiger* car to this day.

Another eyewitness recently surfaced, thanks to social media. I was privileged to talk with the track owner's son, "Little Jim" Renegar. As was often the case, he worked for his father in just about every capacity at Sportsman Park. He took 8-mm footage of the episode and watched it repeatedly. While he told me that this footage is now gone, scooped up by the new track owners in 1969 or TV or production people some years ago, he remembered the

One of the souvenirs from that fateful day is owned by Laverne Zachary. The Farmington, North Carolina, track was close to home for him. (Photo Courtesy Laverne Zachary)

As the 1967 season was coming to a close, Arnie traveled up into Canada to Grand Bend for a match race against Dyno Don Nicholson. The score ended up 2-1 in favor of Don. Arnie won the first round on a redlight start by Don, then lost the last two. (Photo Illustration by Dean Fait)

event like it was yesterday.

"It was the most spectacular thing we ever saw," Little Jim recalled. "The right wheel came off the car. That made it go that way with the left one still driving. The 'Goat' grew wings, as the whole car got airborne, getting as high up as the telephone poles! When it came down, because it had recently rained and the ground was soft, it only rolled once or twice. If the ground had been hard, there's no doubt that it would have rolled maybe as many as five or six times."

Laverne Zachary sent me the clipping about the accident from the local paper. The facts were wrong, as the reporter thought Beswick was driving the car.

"Beswick Escapes Spectacular Crash," the headline read. "FARMINGTON – Arnie Beswick, a nationally known drag racing personality, had a close brush with disaster yesterday at Sportsman Park, but he came out of it with little more than a couple of bruised ears.

"Beswick's supercharged fuel-injected 1963 Tempest rolled through the clocking devices at 155.17 mph, hit an embankment across the track, and sailed an estimated 1,000 feet in the air before striking a tree 30 feet from the ground."

The article reported that the driver was taken to Davie County Hospital and continued with an interview.

"You couldn't tell it had ever been a car," said Track Manager James Renegar. "The only things left were the roll cage and the seat."

Renegar informed the paper, "He [Behling] defeated Roger Gustin in the first run in the match race and the accident occurred on the second run."

The Farmer, now down to one car for the first time in four years, crisscrossed the country with just the '66. He would not have Behling drive for him again, convinced that the wrecked hulk was Little Arnie's fault. Behling's name surfaced in subsequent years driving other people's cars. Another racer who knew him added that he was never with one owner for very long. He was hard on equipment, to say the least.

It was an unfortunate tragedy that Arnie Behling and Arnie Beswick's 1964 *Mystery Tornado* aluminum front end both met their demise in a similar fashion after Beswick had given him this unique piece. Additionally, and most likely needless to say, work on the '68 was prioritized and moved to the front burner.

1968 and the *Star of the Circuit II*

The *Star of the Circuit II* was completed in the first part of 1968. The paint and bodywork were similar to the '66, and the car was absolutely stunning. It was the chassis that made it completely unique. Arnie had been talking with Don Schumacher on occasion. Due to the fact that he'd ordered a new *Stardust* Barracuda Funny Car, it was Don's idea to use the Chicago-based shop of Romeo Palamides for his build.

When Arnie visited Don's shop, he was envious of all the Hemi engines that were scattered about that Don considered junk. Some of them had maybe only one cylinder gone. The handwriting was already on the wall, as the Pontiac engines that Arnie was using were becoming increasingly rare, not to mention, obsolete. The Pontiac blocks didn't respond well to the increase in blower pressures and the nitromethane fuel like the Chrysler-based engines.

The most extreme example was when Arnie was out East with the *Tameless Tiger*. After one particular run, the engine was leaking every fluid that it had. When Arnie took the blower and intake off, the

Arnie and the crew: Fred Coopman and Joe Palsgrove.

engine literally fell in half, leaving two 4-cylinder pieces. Arnie was now dealing with heads and valves that were failing on a regular basis. The Pontiac heads with their restrictive ports simply could not flow enough to keep them cool. New round-port heads were released in 1968 that were an improvement over the old S/D 980 heads, but it was still almost too little, too late.

Thanks to the promise of a quick turnaround time and less of a bill, Arnie bought in to Don's suggestion and went with longtime Chicago-based racer turned chassis builder Romeo Palamides. It was this shop that built what Don considered a "cutting-edge" car.

Not So Cutting Edge

History showed that this was not the case, however, as less than a handful of front-hinged cars were ever built. After Don Schumacher's car was finished, Arnie's was the only other one built to have the engine in front of the driver's seat. Another unique aspect about the car was that the rear axle was welded directly to the frame.

As Arnie remembered, after having his

This is one of the earliest pictures of the 1968 Star of the Circuit II *GTO fresh out of Romeo's shop. This is a publicity photo.*

Another early shot shows the front-hinged body.

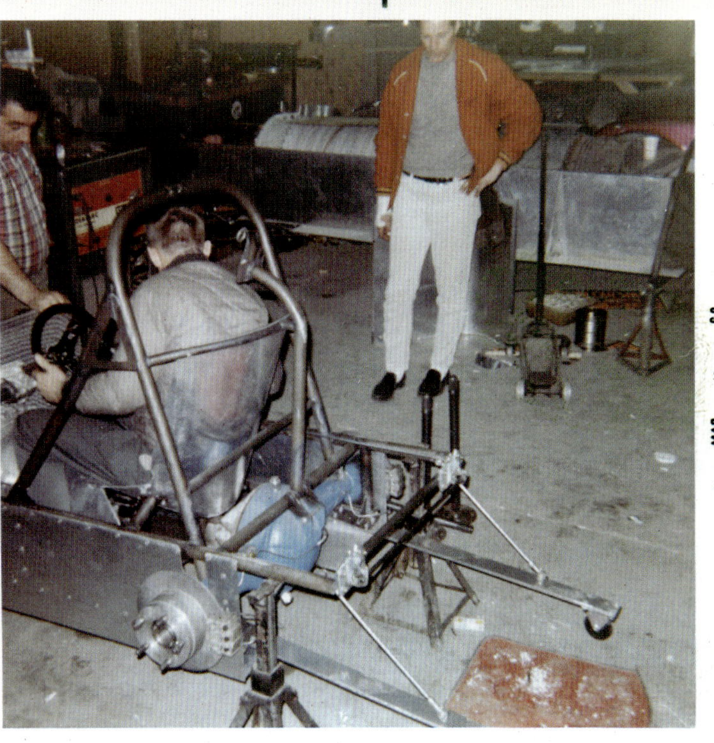

Working on the problems of suspension, Arnie moved out of Spencer Knox's shop into his own, which was a 1/2 mile or so west in Morrison. The solid-mounted rear axle is clearly evident.

Barracuda built, Schumacher found out that the cars were doomed from the start. Don sold his very shortly after, buying an already built car with a traditional design out of California.

Along with Joe Palsgrove, Fred Coopman was helping Arnie out in these years. Fred told of some of the problems.

"The car may have been way ahead of its time in certain aspects, but it didn't have any rear suspension at all," he said. "It was solid mount. If it would have had a clutch system like they have today [1996], it would have run. We'd have been in the 6s while everybody else was still in the 7s. The car was foul handling right from the start. The first time we took it out to test it at Cordova, it came up three times and went immediately to the left. After the third time, Romeo came over to me and asked, 'What are we gonna do with this car?'

"After I gave him a smart-ass response, saying, 'What do you mean *we?*' I told him what I thought needed to be done. It was my opinion that we needed some way to load the chassis and that a rear suspension should be added. As it was, the only thing that helped out was with tire pressure. If the car went one certain direction, we took air out of that slick. Sometimes it got so bad that we were almost running flat tires, which didn't help performance any."

While Fred remembered it that way in his interview in 1996, he also mentioned that Palamides took it back and added coilover shocks to the rear. Richard Durlack reported in *American Rodding* that

Arnie is shown here racing at Beeline Dragway in Arizona in early 1968. (Photo Courtesy Laverne Zachary)

what actually happened was that Arnie proceeded to chop off the front of the frame, replacing the front suspension with coilover shocks. Arnie was quoted as saying, "The original front end was as grim as the rear, so we completely rebuilt it."

The article said that the handling didn't improve much even after the change in front suspension. Arnie remembered it differently in that it all depended on how well the track was prepared. The more slippery the track surface was, the better the chance would be that the car would go straight.

AHRA Nationals

The first outing that Arnie attended was the January running of the AHRA Nationals in Arizona. While Richard Durlack reported that the car didn't do too badly and initially the announcer reported that Arnie had qualified fast enough to make the field, it turned out to be a mistake. Durlack wrote that it wasn't a surprise since it was only January and the oats that farmers sowed weren't harvested 'til June.

Things went a lot better in the spring on Arnie's home track of Cordova, according to *Drag News*. The issues had, for the most part, been sorted out when he was racing against Mr. Norm, as an article from April 14 read:

Arnie presents Mr. Norm with his new car. Bob Atherton would later be the mayor of Morrison, and he lettered both the car and the "honey wagon" up. He wasn't really a sign painter, but he was good enough for this.

"Easter Sunday will be remembered by many people for many reasons at Cordova Dragstrip. Arnie Beswick, [from] Morrison, will remember it because of the new record he set for the 1,000- foot drags. The first real "power all the way" run on Arnie's new supercharged nitro-fuel injected 1968 Pontiac GTO resulted in 161.58 mph in 6.601 seconds."

There's a lot more to the story about hyping the match, Bill Stoermer said.

"That day, Arnie was going to race against Mr. Norm," he said. "He'd always had kind of a rivalry with Norm, actually any of the Chicago cars, whether it was *Mr. Norm* or the *Chi-Town Hustler*.

"Arnie found this old junk Dodge that was all rusted and beat up. He literally put it on a manure spreader. They took it to Cordova, and they made it a big deal about Arnie presenting Norm with a new race car. It was all just part of the showmanship.

Stoermer continued, "I remember another time when he gave Pat Minick, the driver of the *Chi-Town Hustler*, a roll of toilet paper and said that he'd better take that with him, as he'd need it when Arnie blew past him."

That same *Drag News* article about the Easter Sunday race continued:

"Jim Riggio, driving the Mr. Norm's Grand Spaulding Dodge Charger, will have vivid memories of his spectacular crash and the resulting broken leg."

The writer explained that after the run of 7.04, Riggio lost control. The car careened off the left side of the track first, then cut over to the right side, sliding sideways for approximately 1,000 feet and completely destroying the car.

It's Easter Sunday with Arnie lining up against the new car of Mr. Norm.

It was not a good day for the Grand Spaulding Dodge Charger with the driver breaking his leg and totaling out the new car. Such was the cost at times of doing business on a racetrack.

Losses outnumbered the wins for the next few months, thanks mostly to the handling issues. There were also engine problems or an occasional redlight start. Some of the handling issues had apparently been worked out by mid-May, although it sometimes meant frying the Turbo 400 transmission. The Farmer was at Cecil County's Funny Car shoot-out on May 18. Arnie took round one over a *sleepy* Malcolm Durham. While Jungle Jim beat Arnie in round two, the reporter told how the GTO ran "arrow straight" all night.

Win, lose, or draw, Arnie was always all about the show and was never about letting the fans down. After all, he knew they'd paid good money to see a show with him and the others running. A great example of this happened at US30 in Gary, Indiana, on August 11. The GTO was not firing on all cylinders, and Arnie could have easily let Mr. Norm's car make a solo pass. Even though he had to shut it down half-track, he still gave it his best.

Spring Cleanup

The next report showed Arnie with a win at Motor City Dragway on March 31. The headline was "Farmer downs S-W-C." The story told how Arnie took rounds one and three. The first round was Arnie with 8.83 at 161 to Stone, Woods, & Cook's 9.02 at 151.86. Ron O'Donnell in the Mustang took round two with an ET of 8.86 at 163 to Arnie's 8.99 at 158. Arnie turned on the win light then with an 8.57 at a whopping 171 mph to the Ford's 9.01 at 162.

While Arnie denied this, Bruce Larson gave another example of this when Arnie was racing his 1966 *Star of the Circuit* against him in the *USA-1* car at the Pennsylvania-based York US30 track.

"I'd finished my burnout and Arnie did his," Bruce said. "As he came to a stop, he must have accidently hit the parachute lever, and it popped out and fell out onto the track behind his car. His crew guy acted quickly, gathered it up, brought it around the side of the car, and showed it to Arnie. Now most of us wouldn't have run, but Arnie motioned

Burning in rosin at Oswego against the Chapman Camaro.

for him to give it to him. The crewman stuffed it inside the car and Beswick lined up. The light turned green and we both went, after which he literally threw the chute out the window, it caught, blossomed, and Arnie stopped just fine."

Bill Stoermer told a "behind the scenes" story from the 1968 World Series, an event that was always held in late August.

"On Thursday before that year's race, Arnie wanted to make a test pass in the car," Bill said. "The seat had been sent out earlier to an upholstery shop and was not going to be ready until Friday. Fred Coopman made a seat out of cardboard that would allow Arnie to be in the car and not sitting directly on the frame rails of that Romeo Palamides chassis. They made the run and the car blew a head gasket going through the lights. The engine was rebuilt overnight, the new seat installed, and they raced Friday night at the Series."

While Bill mentioned the car blowing a head gasket, he didn't mention that there was also a fire in the car. This was the second time that Arnie suffered burns.

Jim Flynn was the assistant sports editor for the *Moline Dispatch*. In the Friday, August 23, paper, he told it this way:

Bruce Larson's USA-1 *Camaro and Arnie's GTO do burnouts at the Super Stock Nationals. (Photo Courtesy Ted Pappacena)*

This view is from before the light turned green from the other side of the track at the Super Stock Nationals.

Arnie poses in front of the unique Pontiac at the Super Stock Nationals in New York. (Photo Courtesy Ted Pappacena)

"Morrison's Arnie Beswick incurred first- and second-degree burns about the eyes and hands yesterday when his 1968 Pontiac GTO Funny Car caught fire at the end of a practice run during the opening day activity at the 15th-annual World Series of Drag Racing at Cordova Dragway.

"Beswick had just passed through the timing lights at the end of the course and recorded the fastest elapsed time and top speed of opening day time trials when a piston broke, rupturing the head gasket and thus allowing the oil from the oil pan to ignite," the *Moline Dispatch* story continued. "The resulting fire engulfed the machine in flames for a few seconds. But the fire went out as quickly as it started, and the veteran driver was able to bring the car to a halt at the end of the strip. He was taken to a Morrison doctor and treated for second-degree burns about the eyes and first- and second-degree burns about the

This photo from the Super Stock Nationals at New York National Speedway shows the body open. (Photo Courtesy Jim Caputo)

Here's a close-up of the Pontiac mill at the Super Stock Nationals. (Photo Courtesy Jim Caputo)

A close-up of the driver's cage is pictured here, still at the Super Stock Nationals. (Photo Courtesy Jim Caputo)

Taken at his little shop on Route 30 in Morrison, Arnie sits in the driver's seat of the '68. (Photo Courtesy Brian Harmon)

Mike Rutherford helped out Arnie, and the Farmer helped him get a very special 1968 GTO. Here's the Funny Car, complete with the saying on the side in Mike's driveway. (Photo Courtesy Mike Rutherford)

Back in the Midwest, Arnie was sick of the handling problems and decided to have some fun with it. He lettered the side of the car, as seen here, with "Chassis by Mickey Mouse."

It was unbelievable that Arnie's Star of the Circuit II was able to go this fast.

hands. The car body was scorched, and the inside of the machine was damaged. Crewmen spent most of [Thursday] night working on the car, and a Beswick aide said the Flying Farmer would race in [Friday night's] supercharged Funny Car eliminations unless it was utterly impossible."

When the 1969 model year arrived, Arnie started on a new Funny Car that would absolutely not be built by the Mickey Mouse company of Palamides. He took delivery of a rare factory lightweight GTO. Pontiac marketing pushed for a new version of the GTO that was being released called *The Judge*. Arnie immediately placed an order.

The year ended on a high note, as the *Star of the Circuit II* had its best 15 seconds (or should we say, 8.12) of fame in Orlando, Florida. Arnie's car made the front page and the headline of the December 27 issue of *Drag World*.

Recently, Arnie was asked why the car did so well. Had he done anything to the engine or transmission? The short answer was, "No."

"Every now and then there was a track that was

just right," Arnie said. "It was slippery enough that the car didn't go to the left or right and yet all the rest had trouble hooking up because they were used to better tracks that hooked."

The article went on to say that Arnie had flat outrun the finest field of S/FX stockers ever assembled with a run topping out at 194.36 mph. The Farmer also set the low ET for the meet.

As the year closed out, there was also the promise of new and much better engine parts coming out of the Pontiac skunkworks that shed a ray of hope in the performance realm for the future.

A New and Better Outlook for 1969

Thanks to John DeLorean's vision, Pontiac came up with a fun version of the GTO, named "The Judge." While it had been told that the car's name was based on the widely popular television program of the day *Laugh In*, there was more to it than that.

As the late Paul Zazarine stated in an article from *Pontiac Enthusiast* magazine in the January/February 2002 issue, "The Judge also came with the brawn to back up its curious appearance. The standard Ram Air III was rated at 366 hp, and the optional, virtually hand-built Ram Air IV was whimsically rated to 370 unruly horses."

Don Keefe, an author with many years of experience and the current editor of *Poncho Perfection*, explained the Ram Air engines this way:

"It boils down to performance versus drivability," he said. "The Ram Air III (1969–1970) engine has the most torque. It's the best all-around street performance engine and would beat the other two, stoplight to stoplight. The Ram Air IV (1969–1970) was less streetable but better at the strip. It had no low-end torque and couldn't be ordered with less than a 3.90 gear. Prepped, and let's say with 4.10s or a 4.56 ratio, it could run high 12s. The Ram Air V (1969) was a race engine and was barely able to be put out on the street at all. They were dreadful engines at a stoplight but on the strip could rip a low 12 or even a high-11-second ET, if you really let them rev."

Paul Zazarine went on to say that some of the limited few who had access to the Pontiac engineering department's dyno area actually observed pulls in excess of 400 hp.

Part of Pontiac's strategy came with instructions to make these Ram Air IV cars available to the active and serious Stock class drag racers. Paul, in his article explained, and I loosely quote content from several paragraphs here:

"For the lucky few drivers who received these very special vehicles and campaigned them, Pontiac implemented a policy of replacing parts, should any piece in the engine or drivetrain fail."

As Arnie had done with most all of his other new Pontiac race cars, almost every option was purposely left off. There was no radio or power steering, not even power brakes, as the drum brakes were lighter and reportedly had less drag. Remember the saying, "Brakes don't make a car go any faster." Arnie knew how to order his Carousel Red Judge and went one step further, making his car one of even fewer—a factory lightweight. There was no seam sealer (dum-dum, as it was called).

The only option that Arnie wanted was hideaway headlights. Despite a little increase in weight, they gave a cleaner look to the car. By now you know of the appearance aspects of any car that Arnie was going to bring to the track. They all needed to look as good as they performed.

Initially, as the people at Pontiac Motor Division were very proud of the pop art graphics and

This is an early photo of the D/Stock Judge. Bill Stoermer talks of his dad picking up the car just after Arnie got it. He would bring it into Morrison and use it to promote sales of the 1/25-scale models of the car. (Photo Courtesy Steve Reyes)

emblems, they really didn't want Arnie to change much. Arnie knew the cars needed to make clear statements, and initially the *Super Judge* had scallops painted down the middle.

As the year went on, a third car was added to the stable: a Funny Car. The lineup ran like this: a street version (D/Stock class car), the (Pro Stock) *Righteous Judge,* and the new Funny Car that was dubbed the *Super Judge.* The Funny Car was sent to Dick Scully for a face-lift (as were the others). The Farmer told Dick to be flamboyant and create something that nobody would mistake for anything but a Beswick racing machine. Scully did not disappoint.

Articles published back in the day already told how Arnie learned his lesson with Funny Car chassis and had gone the more traditional way. He'd gotten in line and waited for one built by the Logghe brothers. The Logghe shop was the one that built Dyno Don's first flip-top Comet back in 1966, and business snowballed for the company when its cars really worked and went straight. According to Arnie, saying that the difference between Palamides and Logghe was like night and day is probably the understatement of the century.

The Traditional Daytona Beach

The first race for 1969 that was talked about was the February 21–22 running at Daytona Beach, Florida. Down from lasting a whole week, this two-day-only event had lost its importance in the world of drag racing. It received no press or promotion whatsoever in the local paper.

One of the reasons for that was because the month before some 198 racers had gained illegal access to the Spruce Creek abandoned airstrip and were arrested for wildcat drag racing. It was Georgians Charles Hardy, Marvin Jones, and Buster Couch who got together to put drag racing back on the good side of the law. Arnie was still driving the '68 and had the upper hand both times on Friday night over Bobby Wood's Camaro only to have the tables turned on him on Saturday night.

Tough Sledding in the Midwest

As the weather warmed up and racing in the Midwest resumed, it was reported that Arnie, still waiting for the *Super Judge,* was at US30 in Gary, Indiana, to go at it with Mr. Norm's car. There were no results printed, but handling problems were responsible for the April 13 losses to Fast Eddie Schartman's Cougar. Arnie lost three straight while the Mercury set a new low ET for the track at 189 mph.

The '68 has lost a lot of its shine shown here down in Florida.

Manufacturers' Funny Car Championship

The first reports of the *Super Judge* finally showing up occurred at the third running of the Manufacturers' Funny Car Championship race during the early summer months of the year. Rockford Dragway was the location where roughly 10 teams competed with no less than a dozen Funny Cars to put on a show for 9,000 eager fans, despite the 100-degree heat.

Jon Asher was preaching to the choir when he penned that while Arnie's 1968 GTO was a very colorful car, it wasn't the best of performers. It didn't help when for round one he was paired up against the eventual winner: the Candies & Hughes Barracuda. Asher reported that Arnie's car didn't do too badly that day, running a 7.92, but Leonard Hughes annihilated the track record on that run, turning a fantastic 7.37 at 205 mph.

Winners faced winners and losers faced each other at the meet. Arnie won a round, destroying the engine at only 900 feet, turning an 11.61 ET. It was 200 feet farther than Don Schumacher's *Stardust* Barracuda made it when he broke his second transmission of the day.

Arnie has never been one to test 'n' tune in front of a large crowd, but he made an exception here. He unloaded the *Super Judge* and began preparing for a

These photos were taken at the manufacturers' race at Rockford. Arnie's brand-new Super Judge *can be seen in both photos. This was the practice for all the feature cars to be put on display at the track prior to competition.*

This made such a great photo from that first Rockford event that Arnie used it as his promotional photo to send to the tracks for his upcoming events. (Photo Courtesy Jon Asher)

Here is another photo from Rockford where the rear opening 1968 Star of the Circuit II GTO is quickly spotted down toward the other end. (Photo Courtesy Jon Asher)

The whole crew of the **Super Judge** *from left to right: Mike Farrell, Arnold W. Beswick, Maurice "Maurie" Mauer, and Charlie Carter.*

This was the way the **Super Judge** *first looked with the lace down the center. When the other two Judges, or at least the D/Stock version, were at the same track, Arnie wanted them all to look the same and had them all painted to match. This is believed by some to be Dallas, Georgia, taking on Charlie Allen's 'Cuda.*

run. That was after Asher told of the death for the day of the Farmer's '68, having a rod hanging out of the block. Arnie and Don weren't the only ones to have breakage, as carnage reigned supreme over almost all the teams there. Most of the others were implementing their backup cars.

As the meet went on, Dean Lapool in Larry Christopherson's wildly painted Chevy II was ordered to the line to race against the Ford Torino of Larry Coleman with Sidney Foster behind the wheel. Lapool made one burnout and the car refused to go into reverse. He shut the car off and was pushed off the track. Foster could have singled and taken an

easy win, but Sidney was a racer above all else and he, like Arnie, wanted the fans to see a good show.

Christopherson's replacement was none other than Arnie. According to the article, the *Super Judge* was brand new, maybe never having run before. Arnie made two short burnouts, and the Pontiac seemed to hook. Foster made one long one. Jon wrote that when the light turned green, Foster blasted for the big end while Arnie blasted into the sky with a 6-foot wheelstand. Arnie wasn't quite prepared for that, let off, and came down hard. Foster turned a 7.85 to Arnie's 9.46.

The *Righteous Judge* Plus One

In mid-1969, Arnie found two new GTOs. The first was a flood victim from New Orleans. The second was one that had some front-end damage from a Pontiac engineer's mishap on the GM Proving Grounds. The second one was driven by Arnie late in the year but was used by Father Leake for his youth ministry program. The flood victim went on to become the *Righteous Judge*.

Even though the interior was ruined from the water damage, Arnie didn't care. The body was straight and good and something he could use to start entering the new Pro Stock class that the AHRA started that year. The NHRA added it in 1970.

Pro Stock gained popularity quickly, as it was still heads-up racing but at a fraction of the cost and danger of what running a fuel Funny Car was. In an interview conducted years later, Dyno Don stated that was the reason he switched and got out of the Funny Car ranks.

Maurice "Maurie" Mauer talked about the car in the mid-1990s.

"So then Arnie decided we outta get in the Pro Stock business along with the Funny Car," Maurice said. "[This GTO] had been a strip-out job. So, he bought a fiberglass front end for it. He put a 428 into it originally with Ram Air V heads, switching to a 455 when they were released in 1970. He had the car sent to Scully, who painted it the "Judge" orange, adding the stripes like the others. It ran two 4-barrel carburetors on it with two different intakes, one for an eighth-mile track and one for a quarter-mile track.

"So, we played with that for quite some time, and I started doing the driving on it," Maurice said. "We campaigned that little car pretty hard. It wasn't all that competitive with the Chevrolets and the Hemis in those early Pro Stock days, but, being a

Taken during the 100th anniversary Whiteside County parade in Morrison, Illinois, Darrell "Growler" Okken is sitting on the step with an Arnie T-shirt. Since it's a red machine, there's not much doubt that it was the Beswick family combine pulling the Righteous Judge. *The reference to "Big Daddy" is interesting.*

This is an early picture of the Righteous Judge *at Rockford.*

Morrison, and they had to turn right around, heading to the first event. Rich noticed that the 6-cylinder-powered GMC seemed to be making a lot more noise. They'd no sooner left the first track, losing the engine in the race car when the engine blew in the truck.

"So here we are, a blown-up truck and a blown-up race car, trying to get to the next date," Rich said.

They did manage to get the car back together for US30, as *Drag News* reported that Arnie lost round one against the C-K-C Camaro out of San Antonio, Texas. Arnie managed an 8.52 at 178 to their 8.11 at 198. Such was sometimes the case with the adversity that came due to Arnie's hectic schedule.

Super Stock Nationals

The fifth-annual Super Stock Nationals, now held at York US30, was from August 8 to 10. Tom Stephens made the short trip to be there to see Arnie run. Tom was a fan of Pontiacs, as his family drove them, and he first met Arnie in 1966.

"Everybody was there—Don Schumacher, Jungle Jim, Gene Snow, everybody," Tom said. "Arnie was there with both cars, the '68 which looked terrible by then. The beautiful cobwebbed paint job by Dave Puhl had faded so badly. The *Super Judge* was brand new, and boy, was it ever beautiful. He had the new Judge on the back of the truck, and the *Star II* was on a trailer if I remember right.

"He did real well. He went three rounds, running like a 7.89, which was fast for a Pontiac-powered Funny Car. I think 7.50 was low ET for the meet. That would have been set by Larson, Schumacher, or Jungle. They were the quickest cars there. But Arnie won his first two rounds, first over Al Graeber in the *Tickle Me Pink* Charger and then Hayden Proffitt in the *Grant Rebel* SST machine. I seem to remember that in round three, Bruce Larson took

Beswick car, it certainly got its share of attention and would draw a crowd."

Eight Days a Week

Once again, Arnie's cars could be at more than one track as the season continued with an unbelievable schedule of anywhere from 75 to 100 events a year. It wasn't uncommon to have three or four dates in a row.

Rich Sawyer told of a weekend in mid-May that began with Arnie scheduled in Milan, Michigan, on Friday. He was booked into Detroit Dragway on Saturday, then US30 in Gary, Indiana, on Sunday. The Farmer and crew had just returned home to

Taken at Great Lakes Dragaway in September of the year, this has long been one of Arnie's favorite photos of the Super Judge.

The Super Stock Nationals is the location for this picture showing both the '68 and '69.

him out and then went on to win the whole event."

That was indeed the case, and every manufacturer that had parts on Larson's *USA1* Camaro bragged about the win in the August 16 issue of *Drag News*.

The Coca-Cola Cavalcade of Stars had already been formed by this year, and just like the UDRA, Arnie was often booked into events with a lot of other cars and drivers. The September 6 issue of *Drag News* talked about an August 20 event at US30 in

This slide is dated October 12, 1969, from Oswego. John "Woody" Bramm is in the driver's seat, warming up the car. (Photo Courtesy Mark Van Osdol)

The truck with the Super Judge loaded sits in front of Arnie's shop on Highway 30 in downtown Morrison. (Photo Courtesy Mark Van Osdol)

Arnie looks on while Don Smith's mechanic (sunglasses) and more than likely Mike Farrell finish some adjustments on the Pro Stock Judge in Florida. (Photo Courtesy Marty Johnson)

The original caption read, "Arnie 'the Farmer' Beswick and Don Smith had a good run going for the 'Mr. Pontiac' title until Smith's gold-leaf Firebird lost a rear end at Thunderbolt Raceway. Beswick took the match three straight at 11.95, 11.78, and 11.70 after Smith warmed up with a 10.98." (Photo Courtesy Marty Johnson)

A number of companies used Arnie to endorse their products. This ASL advertisement is one of my favorites from the era.

Gary, Indiana, where Gary Dyer won the championship, downing Arnie with a 7.32 ET at 204 mph to Arnie's 8.07 at 180.

The last known event for 1969 happened on December 21 and appeared in the January 1970 issue of *Drag Times*. Marty Johnson supplied the photos and story titled "Arnie Beswick Wins Florida 'Poncho' Match." The story was about Arnie coming down to Jacksonville's Thunderbolt Raceway without the *Super Judge* Funny Car. Instead, the Farmer brought what Johnson called a 1970 Judge. It was in reality the 1969 *Righteous Judge*. He was correct when he reported the displacement as 400 ci.

Arnie was there to race Don Smith, who was driving a 1969 Firebird called *Canadian*, as it had power from a 427 Chevy. Don was quick, and on his warm-up lap turned a 10.98. Arnie's warm-up lap was not without incident, as the car had no front brakes and he went long to "mire up safely in the mud and weeds." His warm-up ET was exactly 2 seconds slower than Smith's.

Marty's *Drag Times* story read, "After a quick shakedown on Beswick's car, the match racers pulled to the chute. Beswick's car sounded sharp and rapped quick as did Smith's. Beswick was out of the gate first with a lead over Smith. Beswick's Judge breezed through for the win at 11.95 with the Firebird coasting off the track. The rear end was lunched on the 'Bird. Arnie was on the line in the agreed 30 minutes in between runs and made a bye at 11.78 for round two."

Don found another car, a J/PSA classed Firebird, for round three. Even given an almost 4-second handicap head start, the Farmer took the stripe at 11.70 to Smith's 16 flat. It was a nice Christmas present for the Farmer team and a great way to end the year.

"The Wheels Are Always Turning"

Our story continued for 1970 with a start in late 1969 and a slight change in geography. We move to just over 100 miles east of Morrison to Algonquin, Illinois, where, Dave Boncosky, a young 20-something-year-old decided that he wanted to keep racing as a car owner. Dave had gotten his start in the business as a driver in the Richter/Bolger Camaro Funny Car. He saw an ad in the trades and drove down South to plunk down $5,000 and buy the "never before ran" Ford Torino Funny Car of Phil Bonner. Dave had barely brought the car home when he bumped into our hero, Arnie Beswick.

While Dave didn't remember specifics, he did recall that a deal between him and Arnie was all worked out within half an hour. Arnie would supply the body if Dave would change the car over from

A proud Dave Boncosky poses for a promotional picture next to his brand-new Hemi-powered Boss Bird. *(Photo Courtesy Ray-mar, Mark and Laura Brudelre Collection)*

The setting for these photos with the brand-new Super Judge *is an indoor car show in Sterling, Illinois.*

a Ford with an SOHC engine to a Chrysler-based Hemi-powered Firebird. Both parties walked away with smiles, and shortly thereafter, work began at Fiberglass Ltd. on the new body, another of which Arnie would also soon use.

Business as Usual

Meanwhile, Arnie began the year 1970 right away on January 2, 3, and 4 at the *Drag News* Championship races at Central Florida Dragway in Orlando, Florida. Rain interfered with the event on Friday and Saturday, making it a one-day event on Sunday.

All the biggies were there, according to the report, including Don Garlits, Chris Karamesines, Connie Kalitta, Steve Carbone, Ray Marsh, Arnie, Roger Lindamood, Shirl Greer, Sox & Martin, Bobby Wood, and many more. Sunday's races began when the rain finally quit as the racers rolled into the facility at 8 a.m. Since the rain had cleaned the track surface, it was mentioned that quite a few engines and other parts were lost. The traction must have been unbelievable!

A clean surface was key here, and while sometimes in the future Arnie preferred a more slippery surface, the *Super Judge* was running well enough to qualify. Shirl Greer was the number-1 qualifier, making the distance in just 8.23 seconds.

Arnie was the last to run in round one against Tom Smith's *Super Camaro* with Huston Platt driving. It was a competition single, as the Chevy broke on the line. Arnie's solo pass was a lot better than his qualifying run, as he crossed the stripe with an 8.49 at almost 176 mph.

Fate smiled on Arnie again for round two, as the "Custom Body Enterprises" Castronovo Dodge mini-Charger blew up halfway down. It was an easy pass for the *Super Judge* at only 11.02.

Only three cars remained for the semifinal round, and more than likely because he was number-1 qualifier, Greer received the bye. It was Arnie Beswick against Larry Arnold in the *Super Cuda*. Arnie got a little anxious and went red, missing out on the chance for the $1,500 first-place money.

Just in case you're wondering how the race ended, Larry Arnold lost control and had to shut off as Shirl Greer got a well-deserved win, setting low ET and top speed for the event at 8.11 and 198.48. The caption on the unusable photo taken by Gene Blythe of the *Super Judge* mentioned that Arnie's best was a very respectable 8.34 at 176.5 mph.

Shot at Great Lakes Dragaway, this was Arnie's hero card for the first half of 1970, showing the Boncosky Boss Bird and the Super Judge. (Photos Courtesy Ray-Mar, Mark and Laura Bruderle Collection)

the venue ever had, as 7,800 people were counted at race time with more pouring in. Arnie was one of eight cars there, most of which are all UDRA fuel-injected, blown Funny Cars.

Arnie's first race was against the Nova of Bobby Wood. The Chevy had a hole shot on Arnie with a good lead when Wood's engine let go. Arnie ran the 1,000 feet in 6.45 seconds with Wood coasting through with a 7.01. Shirl Greer, in his Dodge, was among the eight and took an easy competition bye run over when Malcolm Durham's Corvair broke on the line. However, thanks to an unusual breakage rule, Durham was back to race Arnie in the finals, as Greer's Charger was ailing and unable to make the call. Malcolm was determined to win, literally smoking the tires the whole way down the track. His pass was good enough to tie the strip record with low ET of the meet at 5.97.

There were still no reports of the *Boss Bird* as the August 8 issue of *Drag News* was released. It had Arnie and 15 other Funny Cars back at Dallas, Georgia, on July 26. Things didn't go so well for the Farmer as in round one; he lost to Charlie Allen's Dodge. The

Back in Dallas . . . Georgia

The next big race was in Dallas, Georgia, at the Southeastern International Dragway for its season opener on March 1. It had the largest crowd that

All of these photos were shot at the AHRA Springnationals at New York National Speedway. That event took place on the weekend of May 24. Charlie Carter is seen backing Arnie up. (Photos Courtesy Ted Pappacena)

reporter listed the cause as "ill handling." In March, the distance was said to have been 1,000 feet for the Funnies and Fuelers; 900 feet was reported here.

Remembering how popular his match race with Malcolm was back in March, he challenged the Corvair driver to a grudge match. The article said, "The two most frequent contenders at Dallas, Arnie 'the Farmer' Beswick and Malcolm Durham, had at it in a special grudge match. Durham's fans went wild as the announcers Jim Mosteller and Doug Hicks said, 'Malcolm, the man, done put some of that black power and soul explosion on the ole Farm Boy.'"

These are the times for you scorekeepers: Durham a 6.72 to Beswick's 6.87.

The last report of the *Super Judge* was from August 5 in Memphis, Tennessee, where Arnie lost two straight: first to the Flying Dutchman and then to the *Warlord* Funny Car driven by Tony Wahley.

The Ups and Downs of Racing a Pontiac

While the Hemi-based engines were the absolute norm by now, Arnie learned to adapt and work with what he had. While Maurie made dates with the *Righteous Judge*, Arnie kept busy with the *Super Judge* and continued on with the chassis when the car was rebodied as the Firebird.

There was one advantage to the Pontiacs: low-end torque. Consequently, Arnie preferred eighth-mile tracks where the GM product could get a jump on the Hemi-powered machines that caught and passed him at quarter-mile facilities. There were also unique and sometimes unusual opportunities presented to the Farmer.

Larry Quinn, a longtime Pontiac racer, remembered one such incident.

"I remember Arnie Beswick coming to the Illinois State Fairgrounds [in Springfield] with his 1969 GTO nitro car to run a quarter horse, of all things," he said. "I remember vividly that Arnie had a set of snow tires on the back, as it was a dirt track. When Arnie fired that Funny Car up, that horse almost jumped out of the state of Illinois! They stood around for a little bit, trying to figure out how to make this work.

"They finally took Arnie and put him on the back straightaway and put the horse on the front stretch," Larry said. "And they ran. It was about half track before Arnie caught up and passed the horse, but I don't think that horse was ever the same after that!"

Finally, the New Body

In very late 1970, the heavy *Super Judge* body was replaced with a lighter Firebird/Trans Am body. Some of the extra weight of the GTO was due to all the extra paint that made the car so pretty, not to mention patchwork from mishaps. Add to that the fact that car bodies in 1970 were thinner and weighed less.

The car first appeared in early fall at Great Lakes Dragaway with a paint job that would quickly be changed to almost match Dave Boncosky's version. As the year ended, the partnership that Dave and Arnie had wasn't discussed, even though Dave continued to race his Firebird for another couple of years.

Again, Great Lakes Dragaway is the scene for these photos of a wrecked Super Judge. *Amazingly enough, it didn't keep Arnie from racing for very long, as there were always shops around eager to help put it back together again.*

This is the very first paint scheme on Arnie's Boss Bird Funny Car, taken here on the return road at Great Lakes Dragaway.

Pontiac Parts in 1971

It has been stated numerous times that as the 1960s came and went, not only Super Duty pieces but anything high performance from Pontiac became extremely scarce and cost prohibitive. Ram Air IV and V equivalents to the S/D parts of the early 1960s were also quickly becoming extinct. While Hemi and Chevy parts were a dime a dozen, a lot of parts for a Pontiac needed to be hand-built or were one-off, including magnetos, blower manifolds, and cams.

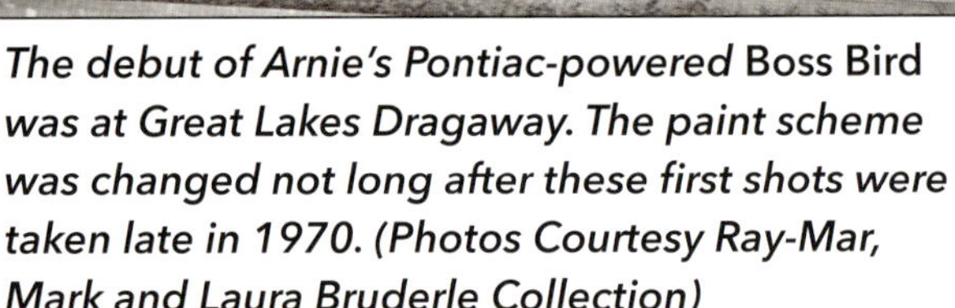

The debut of Arnie's Pontiac-powered Boss Bird was at Great Lakes Dragaway. The paint scheme was changed not long after these first shots were taken late in 1970. (Photos Courtesy Ray-Mar, Mark and Laura Bruderle Collection)

Dave Boncosky does a nice smoky burnout at Great Lakes Dragaway, more than likely in early 1971. (Photo Courtesy Ray-Mar, Mark and Laura Bruderle Collection)

More than likely shot the same day as he debuted his new Firebird, Arnie helps line up Boncosky. Again, Great Lakes Dragaway is the track. (Photo Courtesy Ray-Mar, Mark and Laura Bruderle Collection)

Racing in Florida early in 1971, Charlie Carter looks over the Boss Bird, *being towed by a Mustang of all things.*

Another shot from sunny Florida.

The lack of new and improved transmissions was also a factor. Crower-glides had recently come out, which allowed enough slippage to not go up in smoke, yet they automatically reacted fast enough to make for very quick runs. The Pontiac had no such technology with it.

Armed with the best that Pontiac engineering and his shop could assemble, Arnie and crewmember Charlie Carter loaded the *Boss Bird* on the truck and headed for the warmer February climate of Florida. This time, they were headed to Orlando and the fourth-annual Central Florida Winter Championships on February 13.

A Newcomer with a New Car

While Arnie's race in Florida was against "Big Mike" Burkhart, among the other competitors was Vic Ferris. Vic's new and small team pitted next to Arnie and belonged to Charles Revson, of Revlon Cosmetics fame. Vic had persuaded Revson to buy the year-old Woody Gilmour *Ramchargers* Challenger Funny Car and go drag racing. It had been a backup car and didn't have any runs on it, as Arnie's crew people remembered. It was most likely a publicity stunt for the company that would turn into advertising.

Arnie knew that they were newcomers to the business. He recognized immediately that they ended up with a Challenger that was in sad shape. That fact combined with the lack of experience made it hard for the Revson team to even get the car down the track at any speed.

"The car was so weak, I don't even think it could do a burnout," Charles recalled.

Arnie had always been a helper, and the Challenger team members were more than eager students. Someone from their camp was constantly asking for help or advice about something. The Farmer helped them locate a new fuel pump and magneto to give the Hemi at least some power. Arnie was even asked if he would drive the car, as the rookie driver was apparently a bundle of nerves and was more than likely afraid of the car.

Arnie declined. The engine constantly smoked, as he put it, "like a freight train." While at first glance, there didn't appear to be any major internal problems, Arnie didn't want the responsibility of complicating matters further. He put it best, "They spent a lot of time pulling on my ear, realizing that they were out of their league."

By the meet's end, they decided to let the racer race and turned the car over to Arnie. If anyone could make it race-ready, it was him. Arrangements were made to deliver the car to Arnie's shop in Morrison. At this point in time, he was only to make the car ready for track use.

A week or so later, the car arrived in the Beswick Enterprises shop. Charlie was slower in arriving home, and when he got there, he found the whole engine and car scattered all over the shop, completely disassembled. Arnie was happy that he'd decided not to drive the car in Florida. He had been incorrect in the assumption that nothing much was internally wrong with the engine.

The block was cracked up the number-2 and number-4 main webbings all the way to the cam journals. To make matters worse, the Hemi's crankshaft was cracked. More negotiations were needed with Revson through Ferris, the spokesman for the company and car.

Dallas, Georgia, is the scene here with the Boss Bird *about to leave against Bobby Wood's Super Camaro.*

What looked like a good way for Revlon to advertise was turning out to be a bigger money pit than anyone could have imagined. As Arnie explained the cost of everything, Vic decided that the first loss was their cheapest, and he pulled the plug on the project. A company rep picked up the junk engine, and he did try to get new parts from the Ramchargers, but like any used car, the Funny Car had been sold "as is."

The Challenger's chassis and body was left sitting in Arnie's shop, collecting dust for the time being.

More than likely having left the *Boss Bird* at Red Lawler's shop in Atlanta, Arnie returned on February 28 for a 10-car shootout at the 1,000-foot strip at Dallas, Georgia. The other cars were the top runners in the country. Marty Johnson's article listed the *Blue Max* and the *Chi-Town Hustler*, strangely enough driven by Jungle Jim, while Arnie Behling drove Liberman's Nova. Jake Johnson drove Gene Snow's Challenger. Bobby Wood was there along with Tommy Grove, Frank Oglesby, Malcolm Durham, and Mike Burkhart.

In round one, Arnie downed Oglesby's Mach 1 at 7.19 and took out Malcolm in round two but lost to Burkhart in the semifinals.

Upon returning home, Arnie found that Revson and company were pretty easygoing, and a deal was struck. They decided to let Arnie use the car in a partnership fashion. Arnie would supply the engine, but since there was no additional funding, no company logos were to be used.

The Difference Is Night and Day

Arnie was in a whole new world for the first time in many years. Now, instead of scrounging for or nursing the rare Pontiac parts, a couple of phone

calls was all it took to find Hemi parts. The whole Funny Car world was using them! A new block, rods, crank, and pistons came shortly, but initially many parts came from friend and fellow drag racer Don Schumacher. As Arnie remembered it, he was advised to go with Ed Pink rather than Keith Black regarding the speed parts, and he never regretted that decision.

The 426 Hemi was so different from the Pontiac in the way it responded. The best example was in the timing. The Hemi loved lots of advance in the distributor as opposed to the Pontiac wedge, and after doubling the initial numbers of timing degree, the Hemi really came to life and started to cackle.

While he'd been around the various Funny Cars since 1966, the young Tom Stephens joined Arnie's crew during the summer of 1971 after school was released. He had been in contact with Arnie for some time now, and as Tom put it, "Arnold said that if I wanted to come out and work for free, yeah, we'll take the help. Well, I couldn't wait!"

Tom went on to say, "He'd had the car [Challenger] since March, as I remember. It was right after Memorial Day weekend when I got out there to Morrison. We took it to US30 [Gary, Indiana] for one of those Wednesday-night deals. There'd be like 10 cars there. It'd be Gary Dyer with Mr. Norm, [Tom] Hoover, maybe Claire Sanders, [Roger] Lindamood, [Les] Richter, and [Chuck] Folger, all the locals. Dickie Harrell and others would be there too. They'd schedule 15 cars, of which 10 to 12 would show up. Arnold and Charles [Carter] had the car set up by then, and he ended up winning the whole thing that first night I was there."

Tom Stephens remembered: "Arnie found a painter in Rockford or somewhere up there that painted the car for free. It wasn't nearly as breathtaking as his previous cars, but it looked good, especially at night."

Back on Top in a Mopar

While Arnie ran the Challenger, the *Boss Bird* wasn't going to just sit around and collect dust. Like he'd done for years, if there was money to be made by having the two cars at two different events, they made that happen. While Arnie was running the Challenger, Maurice "Maurie" Maurer ran the Pontiac-powered *Boss Bird*. He made his license passes on April 11.

Tom Stephens explained that Maurie stuck close to home, as the Pontiac wasn't as fast as the Hemi cars. Together, they were able to cover many of the appearance requests that were constantly coming in. Again, the team was making anywhere from 75 to 100 dates a year.

Tom listed them off.

"There were the normal Wednesday, Saturday, Sunday dates every week," he said. "Throw in some Tuesday night races at Alton, Illinois, and then Thompson, Ohio, on some Thursdays. On top of that there the specific dates at Martin, Rockford, Cordova, or what have you.

While everyone associated this picture with Arnie, it's really the Boncosky car going long at Oswego. That facility had such a short shutdown area that it was impossible to get stopped on pavement, even with the parachute. The original caption talked about the Farmer combining drag strip performance with his agricultural background. (Photo Credits to Dennis Scott)

Everyone associated with Arnie was at Rockford on April 11. Maurie was there making the required passes in the Pontiac to get his competition license. Dave Boncosky was there with his car, so Dave and Arnie stopped to do at least half a dozen promotional shots. Arnie was running the Challenger and ended up setting a new track record that day in the Dodge. Ironically, the Drag News article said that all the fans are there to see the Chi-Town Hustler run.

Maurie Mauer proudly poses next to his ride for the first part of 1971. He made his license passes in April at Rockford and was excited to drive a faster car than just the Pro Stock Righteous Judge *and later the* Boss Bird Jr.

This is a pair of Challengers at Great Lakes Dragaway as Arnie leaves on Mr. Norm's car.

We ran a massive amount of dates that year in 1971—massive."

Charlie Carter especially loved the speed of the car and said this about the Challenger:

"Unlike most Funny Cars and Arnie's earlier ones, the Challenger was not a flashy car. It wasn't just plain, it was just plain fast. It was the kind of car that never attracted much attention when we first pulled into the pits at the tracks. When Arnie made his first burnout and then the following quarter-mile pass, he had more than his share of onlookers and curiosity seekers. If the car didn't set low ET and/or top MPH, it certainly knocked on those doors wherever it went."

Tom remembered Arnie taking the car out East.

"He took the car to York, and he only got one run in before it broke the rear end," Tom said. "But the next week in New York, it hauled ass, running like 6.8 or 6.9 at like 219 or 220."

Arnie racked up several wins and set no less than eight track records along the way. He was definitely in hog heaven with the Dodge.

Thanks to the continued lack of any sponsorship, Arnie was continually on a shoestring budget. That led to some interesting problems that required innovative and often unorthodox solutions. Charlie recalled one particular event where a rare puncture somehow happened in the sidewall of the rear slick. Believe it or not, duct tape was called into service. The tire was filled with air and the tape was used as a patch. That along with the centrifugal force from the high-speed run of the car kept it usable for that day's runs. Although it was completely flat when Arnie came to a stop at the end of the track, the car made its normal quick passes, and no one went home disappointed.

As Tom Stephens remembered, the Challenger came to an untimely end exactly halfway through the year on the big Fourth of July race at Union Grove's Great Lakes Dragaway. Earlier on that fateful day, Arnie had set the low ET and top speed records for the event. It was the final

Rockford is the location where this great smoky burnout happened.

Getting the Challenger ready to run. It's a fact that all of Arnie's Pontiacs were named but the Challenger was not.

Arnie had boldly flaunted the fact that he wasn't in a Pontiac as he'd lettered the front spoiler, "Would YOU Believe." He joked many years later that maybe his association with another brand of car was not properly ordained. Were the Pontiac Gods upset and put a hex on him for driving a different brand of machine? There were certainly Pontiac fans who thought that back in the day.

round of a 16-car shoot-out of Funnies. Arnie was paired up with Gene Snow to decide the winner and runner-up honors.

It had been a long day already with this final run happening at about 1:30 or 2 a.m. Beswick did his burnout and backed up only to find that Snow hadn't even fired his car. It was a long wait before Gene's crew finally managed to get his car fired, and he made his burnout.

Thanks to the late hour, the engine heat didn't mix well with the cold night air and started producing a terrific amount of fog on Arnie's windshield. Rich Sawyer remembered that they would usually put a thin film of Dawn dish soap on the windshield to keep it from fogging up, but they'd forgotten it that fateful night.

Arnie could not get the starter's attention, as the official just stood there with an outstretched hand over Arnie's front end. His eyes were on Snow's progress. Instead of not running, Arnie waited, but by this time, Arnie's engine wasn't the only thing that was hot, as his temper boiled. Still, the show must go on.

The lights flashed green, and the Farmer jumped out to a car-length lead. Not being able to see out the windshield, Arnie was driving blindly, trying to

This is the scene of the wrecked car. Then, it was hauled away by the track truck.

judge where he was through the side windows. At two-thirds track, he could see Snow's front end right near where his rear quarter panel window would be. He started using Snow's Funny as a gauge. Gene's car was close, too close.

Arnie compensated and steered to the left a bit, figuring that he must have been close to the centerline. What actually happened was that Arnie was very close to the center of his lane. He was where he should have been, but Snow wasn't. Gene was too far over to the left.

It wasn't long before the Challenger got out of the groove and into the marbles. Then, the worst thing happened: the left wheels touched grass. With the right tire still grabbing, the car made a hard left into the guardrail. Several tumbles later, the Challenger came to rest on its wheels; the body having gone skyward. Thanks to the safety equipment, Arnie wasn't hurt, but the same couldn't be said for the Mopar. The accident destroyed the car's body and bent up the chassis.

Oddly enough, while there was an article about the event in *Drag News*, it only mentioned that Arnie had indeed set the top speed record for the meet and that Gene Snow had indeed won the event.

The Hemi was still good and was quickly removed. Already the *Boss Bird*'s brackets, mounts, and other differences were being changed to accommodate the Hemi mill. Gone were the troubles and tribulations of finding those needle-in-a-haystack Pontiac parts—the *Boss Bird* benefitted from the destroyed Dodge.

Since the body and chassis weren't Arnie's, there were still consequences to be dealt with. That required Arnie to fix the chassis and replace the body before Revson's people came and picked it up. The Revson crew loaded the repaired Dodge onto a truck, where it disappeared into obscurity, never to be seen again, ending the Chrysler chapter of Arnie's life.

Pontiac Body Under Hemi Power

The *Boss Bird*, now Hemi powered, would have to finish the racing year, and it did that with pride. Tom Stephens remembered one of the more unusual races for the car.

"We'd come off of a three-day run that included Alton on Tuesday and US30 on Wednesday," he said. "Arnold

had double booked, as he sometimes did back then. It was either the state fair in Davenport or Thompson, Ohio. He actually asked Charles and me where we wanted to go. Well, we obviously picked the closer race."

After that, it was back to the normal racing. There was a July 11 date in Saint Paul, Minnesota, against Bill Schifsky's Pinto. While Arnie lost the first round, in round two the little Ford had problems and Beswick made a solo pass with a 7.37 elapsed time at just under 200.

One of the more unusual races that Arnie was involved in was at the fairgrounds in Davenport, Iowa. Interestingly enough, it was two bosses: Arnie's Boss Bird *against the* Boss Hoss. *It was quite the trick to get traction on that dirt, but he ended up passing the tractor. Of course, then he had to stop the car. Arnold did that by spinning out, and just like everywhere he went, the crowd went absolutely wild.*

The date was July 25, 1971. Rockford was the location. Arnie raced Tom McEwen, and Arnie crossed the finish line first.

Summertime 1971

On July 25 at Rockford, Arnie beat Tom McEwen in round one then redlighted against Gary Dyer in round two. On August 15, he was back up to the Twin Cities, where he ended up winning the whole four-car shoot-out among Dunn & Reath's 'Cuda, Mike Burkhart's Camaro, and the *Gold Digger* Mustang.

Arnie closed out the 1971 year back at Cordova for the 18th-annual World Series of Drag Racing. The Farmer didn't have the best of luck there. During time trials, he went long "into the corn."

Rich Sawyer explained that you never wanted to drag the parachute out past the shutdown area at Cordova because you'd be pulling cockleburs out of the material for hours.

The event then ended for the Hemi-powered *Boss Bird* during eliminations, as the car had severe engine problems; it literally blew up. It was vividly described as, "There was the big boom, the flame, the oil bath, and the lights got it."

Thanks to the Hemi, Arnie was now among the fast cars. Things were looking up for 1972.

1972 Begins as a Year of Promise

Although it was 1971 when Arnie began building a new shop on his own property, it wasn't until springtime of 1972 when it was finished. He'd outgrown the little building in town and the new first-class building would house not only all of the race cars and equipment on the north side but a lot of the farm equipment on the south side. It was roughly a 60x150-foot structure that had an upstairs loft with apartments for the crew. It also cut out the need to travel into town to work on the cars.

The construction kept Arnie close to home during the early months of 1972. While there was an occasional indoor car show, the racing season hadn't started yet and the NASCAR drag races in Florida in February were a mere memory.

There were plans to again have a second car. Arnie felt bad when Maurie was left without a ride after the Challenger wreck. There was also the fact

These photos show the World Series of Drag Racing at Arnie's home track of Cordova.

Indoor car shows had become routine beginning in 1969. Here's the Boss Bird in its last configuration with the Firebird logo in between the words "Boss" and "Bird."

This photo was taken during an early outing for the Farmer and the Hemi-powered Boss Bird.

that a lot of the fans loved seeing the Farmer or his cars with Pontiac power. He had planned on building another Funny Car that would be powered with traditional Pontiac power.

Fire!

It was at about 2:30 or 3 p.m. on April 5 when Arnie burst into the house telling Evelyn to quickly call the fire department because the new shop was on fire. In a 2011 interview, she said, "I remember picking up the phone only to find that the line was dead."

Evelyn drove to the neighbors to call the fire department, leaving a barely 1-year-old daughter, Michele, at a neighbor's house as well.

"It seemed like it took forever for them to get here!" she continued. After a slight pause, she went on, "I stayed in the house, unable to watch it all go up in flames."

Earlier that morning and into the early afternoon, Arnie was hauling silage toward the silos. It was just after lunchtime that he entered the driveway and went past the new, almost-finished building that was located just west of the house. He happened to glance over and see smoke issuing from the open overhead doors on the south side.

"That was the farm-machinery side," Arnie explained, "and the combine had a problem and smoked more than it should. Since it was still under warranty, I assumed that someone from the dealership had come out and started to work on fixing the problem. When I realized that it was indeed the new shop on fire, I ran to the house, telling Evelyn

to call the fire department and then started working myself, trying to put the fire out.

"The first thing I did was to find the fire extinguisher that was in the old blue GMC truck that we used to haul the race cars around. It was parked on the machinery side of the building. I also found another in the finished race shop side and slid the door open between the two parts to make my way over to the electrical junction box. I could easily tell where the biggest portion of the fire seemed to be coming from. It was the electrical box that was about in the middle of the building, on the east wall of the machinery side.

"There was a chisel plow sitting close to the area, and in my hurry to get close to the crackling noise that was issuing from the fire, I slipped and fell, hurting my leg some. I never did accomplish what I set out to do, as the billowing smoke became too intense by then. My chances of saving the building were decreasing by the second, and even the items I could save were getting smaller. There just wasn't much I could do. Yet, as I remember, it was more than the first fire truck did. I next ran to the spigot and hooked a garden hose up. When I lifted the lever, I was horrified to find that there was no water. We later learned was that the fire had started right where the electrical and phone service were brought in. So that's why there was no phone or power for the pumps.

"At that point in time, the only thing I could do was try to rescue anything out of the building that I could. It wasn't much. Pretty much the only car I got out was my daily driver and the car the daughters learned to drive in: my three-year-old 1969 Grand Prix. There was even a customer's car that had the heads off. We didn't even have time to push it out, and it was destroyed in the blaze.

"When the first fire truck arrived, it merely parked on the road, which was a long way from where the fire was. I don't know if the driver was afraid to get too close to the heat, smoke, and fire or what, but when they unrolled the hose, it was barely close enough to the north end. While the fire was more in the middle, actually closer to the south side.

"Then to top it off, they started to pour water onto the metal roof, which as you might guess, was worthless. "Despite my protests and frustration, they didn't bother to remedy their position or attack on the fire at all. By the time the second fire truck arrived, the roof had already caved in and all hope was lost."

Here is the earliest shot of the damage while the fire department and other people were still at the scene.

This was what was left of the Logghe Funny Car chassis.

These four pictures show the horrific damage done in the aftermath.

A ruined tractor sits in the midst of the debris.

quarter of a million dollars. Of course, adjusters don't want to hear about a barrel of nitro-methane kept in the structure. The misconception about nitro exploding while not under pressure might have kept the firemen at bay. We'll never know.

Hope

While the Morrison community helped Evelyn and the family, Bob Bartel wanted to help Arnie. He advertised a benefit race that he hoped

Evelyn told more of that fateful day, "Later that day, I remember dressing Arnie's wounds on the back of his head and shoulders. Burning insulation had fallen on him as he tried to rescue things from the building."

Both Arnie and Evelyn were so traumatized by the fire that they found it impossible to sleep upstairs in their bedroom for almost a week, sleeping instead on the living room floor.

"I was, and am, so grateful to all the people who helped us out during this time," Evelyn said.

The next 14 years of their life were tough. It was a difficult time in the American farm and banking industry, and Arnie was basically starting from scratch. He chose to rebuild the farm operation first, and much of the machinery was gone. Everything from the race side of the building was totally lost and destroyed.

To add insult to injury, there was barely enough from the insurance company to cover the building itself, let alone any of its contents that were estimated at almost a

This was the ad for the benefit that was posted out at Cordova Dragstrip. Dale Wiersema, Arnie's son-in-law, kept this in his possession all these years.

would raise plenty of money to get Arnie back into a race car. Unfortunately, as I've learned from working at drag strips in this century, a lot of the money that racers earn gets put into their own cars. The event didn't have the success that Bartel had planned.

There was, however, a bright candle burning that came out of the benefit. It was that Fiberglass Ltd. gave Arnie a new fiberglass Firebird body. It retailed for right around $750. While it took more than 25 years, that body was important in the future.

Other than an occasional guest appearance at a car show or as a color commentator at the 1985 World Series, Arnie's racing career had hit a stone wall that seemed impenetrable at the time. It was an extremely dark time for the family, but Arnie's drive and determination kept him chipping away at that wall until finally . . .

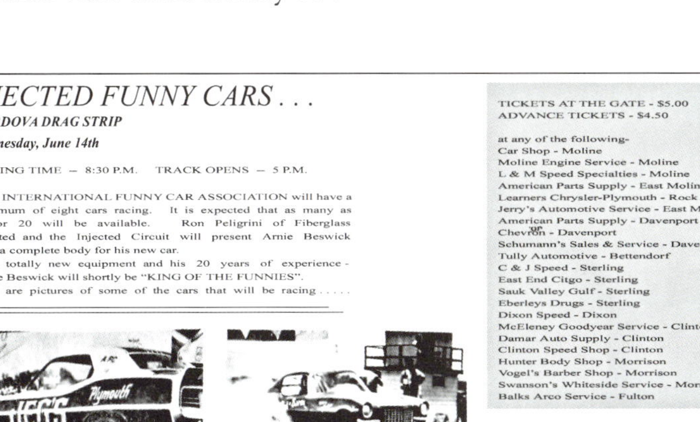

INJECTED FUNNY CARS . . .

CORDOVA DRAG STRIP
Wednesday, June 14th

RACING TIME — 8:30 P.M.   TRACK OPENS — 5 P.M.

THE INTERNATIONAL FUNNY CAR ASSOCIATION will have a minimum of eight cars racing. It is expected that as many as 15 or 20 will be available. Ron Peligrini of Fiberglass Limited and the Injected Circuit will present Arnie Beswick with a complete body for his new car.

With totally new equipment and his 20 years of experience - Arnie Beswick will shortly be "KING OF THE FUNNIES".

Here are pictures of some of the cars that will be racing . . . . .

TICKETS AT THE GATE - $5.00
ADVANCE TICKETS - $4.50

at any of the following-
Car Shop - Moline
Moline Engine Service - Moline
L & M Speed Specialties - Moline
American Parts Supply - East Moline
Learners Chrysler-Plymouth - Rock Island
Jerry's Automotive Service - East Moline
American Parts Supply - Davenport
Chevron - Davenport
Schumann's Sales & Service - Davenport
Tully Automotive - Bettendorf
C & J Speed - Sterling
East End Citgo - Sterling
Sauk Valley Gulf - Sterling
Eberleys Drugs - Sterling
Dixon Speed - Dixon
Damar Auto Supply - Clinton
McEleney Goodyear Service - Clinton
Clinton Speed Shop - Clinton
Hunter Body Shop - Morrison
Vogel's Barber Shop - Morrison
Swanson's Whiteside Service - Morrison
Balks Arco Service - Fulton

Jeg's 1970 Barracuda — Tom Kenny's Chevy Camaro — Ditmars and Moller's Buick Opel

Larry Swiatek's Pontiac Firebird — Art Cambridge's Buick Opel — Gaglione & Paulo's Chevy Vega

Performance Systems' Pontiac — Duane Muelling's Pontiac Firebird — Jim Farnsworth's Pontiac Firebird

Burton & Guthrie's Ford Mustang — Kelly & Pokrzyka's Chevy Vega

Hankinson's Dodge Charger — Arrigo's Chevy Camaro — Joe Amato's Chevy Vega

Cordova Drag Strip
BOB BARTEL
1128 - 33rd Street Court
MOLINE, ILLINOIS 61265

Wednesday, June 14th
8:30 P. M.
RAIN DATE - THURSDAY, JUNE 15th

CORDOVA DRAG STRIP
— presents —
ARNIE BESWICK BENEFIT
(PROCEEDS TO PUT ARNIE BACK INTO RACING)

ARNIE BESWICK AND THE DESTROYED "BOSS"

...s show the total de-
...on of over 20 years
...ng. Two funny cars,
...ransport trucks, an
...nearly 15 engines,
...rs, tools, 4 speeds,
...rans, injectors, su-
...rgers, 100 cases of
...vo farm tractors, a
...0.00 self-propelled
...e and picker, discs,
...- everything that was
...new 60 x 128 foot
...that burned down
...th. Loss is estimated at $220,000.00 with very little covered by insurance.

Here are some of the SUPERCHARGED NITRO FUEL FUNNY CARS that will be racing. REMEMBER -- THESE GENTLEMEN WILL BE FIGHTING IT OUT FOR A CHAMPION-SHIP -- SO THE RACING WILL BE FURIOUS.......

...NORM'S CHALLENGER — DON SCHUMACHER'S STARDUST

...RICHTER'S GOLD DIGGER — FRANK OGLESBY'S QUARTERHORSE

...Y HEDRICK'S SUPER SHAKER — MR. NORM'S CHARGER

...STIC FANTASTIC — CURT WASSON'S SUPERSTITIONS

...AZAR'S FUNNY GREMLIN — PAULA MURPHY - MISS STP

SUPER CHARGED FUNNY CARS | June 14th | CORDOVA DRAG STRIP

CHAPTER 6

THE FINAL YEARS

Our story fast-forwards 14 years and 4 months to July 1986.

A new chapter of the Pontiac Oakland Club International (POCI) formed in 1985 and had been given its charter: the Quad City–based Blackhawk Chapter. Thanks to founders Bob and Delores Hammond, Rockin' Rob and Dani Lindholme, and Gene Scheer, Arnie was one of the original signers of that petition.

The Pontiac enthusiasts traveled down to Greensboro, North Carolina, to attend the convention there and met another enthusiast, Bill Blair. The club members and Bill hit it off. It was mentioned to Bill that the club had a drag day at Cordova coming up. That conversation planted a seed in Bill's mind, and he decided to bring his Super Duty Tempest up to the Blackhawk Chapter's drag day at Cordova and let Arnie have some fun with one of Bill's cars.

Arnie was indeed in hog heaven, extremely happy to be back driving a race car, even if it wasn't a 6-second ride. Bill and Sheila Blair recounted it was Arnie's coming out of the doldrums of a disheartened past and waking up to a new future. After that first experience with Arnie's excitement, Bill brought the car back up to Cordova for the 1986 World Series of Drag Racing.

Arnie was hooked, and he wanted to indulge in the popularity of a nostalgia group. In November, he traveled down to West Palm Beach's Moroso Motorsports Park with some of the other legends of the sport. The event was immensely popular with the fans.

July 20 was when these pictures were taken with Bill Blair and Arnie in front of his little Tempest and Arnie buckling in. (Photo Courtesy Bill Blair)

BLAST FROM THE PAST

Saturday Nite and Sunday

November 22 and 23

ADMISSION $10/DAY

Gates Open 11:00 a.m. On Saturday
Elimination Starts at 4:30 P.M.
Gates Open 10:00 a.m. On Sunday
Elimination Starts at 2:30 P.M.

1960's Heads-Up Match Racing!
Meet the Stars and See the Cars!

STARS
Arnie "The Farmer" Beswick
Gas Rhonda
Phil Bonner
"Dyno" Don Nicholson
Dick Brannon
Malcolm Durham
and Others

CARS
1963 Series #1 Tempest A/FX
1963 Dodge Ramcharger
1964 "Daddy Warbucks" Mustang
1964 Mercury Comet A/FX
1963 Lightweight Ford Galaxy
1963 Z-11 A/FX Chevrolet
1962 Pontiac Super Duty
1963 Fastback Lightweight Ford

Coors $100,000
5-DAY BRACKET CHAMPIONSHIPS
NOVEMBER 21-25, 1986

MOROSO MOTORSPORTS PARK
BEELINE HIGHWAY, WEST PALM BEACH
(305) 622-1400

This was the flyer for the "Blast from the Past" reunion. (Photo Courtesy Bill Blair)

You might notice that Bill changed the lettering on the Tempest when he returned for the 1986 World Series of Drag Racing. (Photo Courtesy Beswick Archive; thanks to Gary Beard)

Back in the Saddle

Was it fate that made fellow drag racer and friend Jake Howard call? Jake was talking to Arnie about buying a little 1963 LeMans that was up in Minnesota. Jake's plan was not for him to use the car, but for Arnie to use it.

Jake and Arnie's relationship went back to the mid-1960s. Arnie first sold his *Grocery Getter* Tempest wagon to the duo of Ron Sanders and Dave Parry, and Jake bought it from them. Now, in the late 1980s, Arnie took possession of the recently purchased LeMans coupe without an engine, scraping up enough pieces to get one together.

Arnie left Jake's paint scheme alone for most of 1987 until Dave Peters in the Quad Cities offered to paint it for Arnie. The *Tameless Tiger* had returned!

The little Tempest in action in Florida takes on Phil Bonner's Daddy Warbucks Ford. (Photo Courtesy Bill Blair)

True legends, each one. From left to right, they are Arnie, Phil Bonner, Gas Ronda, and Dyno Don Nicholson (being interviewed on the line).

Just after Arnie took possession, the Jake Howard car is pictured here at the 1988 World Series. The solo pass would was taken on Friday night, and the run with the pre-historic Rat Chevrolet was on Saturday. (Photo Courtesy Gary Beard)

Shown here at the World Series in 1989, the Tameless Tiger was definitely back. (Photo Courtesy Gary Beard)

Arnie is pictured here at one of the first induction ceremonies in Virginia in 1989. Frank Spittle gave all the inductees blue polos that had their names embroidered.

There were the usual dates based around Cordova and Union Grove, Wisconsin, with one special weekend in early July 1989. "Broadway" Bob Metzler, owner and founder of Great Lakes Dragaway, booked Arnie and Ronnie Sox for match races. He also hired ESPN's Bret Kepner to announce the event. It was there that Bret and Arnie met for the first time.

"It was just two old drag racers having the time of their lives," Bret explained.

Wanting to go faster, it wasn't long after this that Arnie began building a Pro Mod version of the *Tameless Tiger*. The car would have enough power, thanks to nitrous-oxide assistance, to do half-track burnouts like the Farmer had done with the Funny Cars. Thanks to the manually shifted Lenco 4-speed transmissions, Arnie also delighted fans with backups performed at amazing speeds. He almost always went faster in reverse than the competition in the other lane did going forward on the burnout!

Bret Kepner lists this event at Union Grove as one of his top-five favorite shows. He related some 20 years ago how it was more than just a normal weekend for both Arnie and Ronnie. They ran each other no less than nine times over the course of the event.

A Protégé

During the early 1990s, Arnie began having his automatic transmission work done through the Master Transmission Specialists shop located in the Chicago metro area. The shop was run by two brothers, one of which raced. One of them was father to Sheila Cerami, a very pretty girl who had aspirations of driving a race car and was in the March 1990 edition of *Playboy* magazine. It was a good fit, as Sheila started driving the Jake Howard car while Arnie drove the Pro Mod LeMans. In 1992, *Playboy* released a special issue titled, "Career Girls." Lo and behold, there was Sheila in a photo shoot around and on top of the *Tameless Tiger*.

Sheila was looking for a more permanent driving job in a faster car, but their partnership became tougher when she moved to Las Vegas. Geography played a big

Just after the completion of the Pro Mod LeMans in 1992, Arnie brought both cars to his neighbor and friend's property for this promotional photo.

This particular shot of Sheila was taken at Gateway near St. Louis.

While this photo never made the magazine, I'm pretty sure it was shot at the same time next door to the transmission shop.

This is a promotional picture taken at Union Grove, Wisconsin. Doesn't Sheila look intent on the Christmas tree? There's footage of her racing Al DeSalvo's 1964 Dodge Polara, where she wins merely by cutting a better light than the Mopar.

This photo was taken in Arnie's driveway for his Christmas card most likely in 1992.

The Rockingham induction ceremony included some prestigious racers. Included in the list (starting with those kneeling from left to right) are: Hubert Platt, Bill Shrewsberry, Jake King, Ronnie Sox, Arnie, and Jess Tyree. Standing (from left to right) are: Billy West, Don Nicholson, Hank Thomas, Jack Bayer, Malcolm Durham, Phil Bonner, Bill Golden, and Gary Horton.

part of the problem, and she became frustrated with Arnie when he couldn't put her in touch with car owners looking for a lady driver. There was also the fact that back then, it was even tougher for women to break into the sport, especially as a driver.

Recognition Starts

The year 1988 was the beginning of many Hall of Fame inductions. Frank Spittle was responsible for many of the very first ones when he started honoring the pioneers at Charlotte Motor Speedway. Then came Rockingham in 1989. A biggie for Arnie and the rest happened in 1995 with the Super Stock, AF/X, Funny Car Hall of Fame in Virginia.

During the early to mid-1990s, the Legends of Drag Racing was formed with as many as six or seven different drivers making appearances. This evolved into Super Chevy Shows, where promoter Roger Gustin often hired Arnie and Dyno Don to match race.

Occasionally, if the show was out East, Dick "Dickie" Estevez ran too. Dickie had been involved in drag racing for many years, having crewed for Phil Bonner and Don Nicholson. In the early 1990s, he bought the car and the rights to the *Daddy Warbucks* machine from Phil Bonner.

Arnie gained a lot of satisfaction from those races. The little LeMans was quicker than either Don or Dickie's cars. Dickie was running in the high 7s, and Don was running mid-7s. Arnie's ETs were down in the 7.0 to 7.30s, and consequently, he often crossed the finish line first.

Dick Estevez spoke of Arnie's competitive nature at a "Fun Ford" weekend at Cordova Dragway Park

in the late 1990s. Keep in mind that the appearance money was the same for both Arnie and Don at this time.

"Arnie is so competitive, that for him, the finish line wasn't the end of the race," Dick said. "As long as he passed you before you turned off the track, he'd won."

Arnie stands front and center right next to the historic York US30 sign. Inductees included Dick Brannan, Roger Lindamood, Bill Shrewsberry, Malcolm Durham, Ronnie Sox & Buddy Martin, Jake King, Bill Golden, Phil Bonner, Hubert Platt, Bruce Larson, Bill Lawton, Dave Strickler, and Don Nicholson.

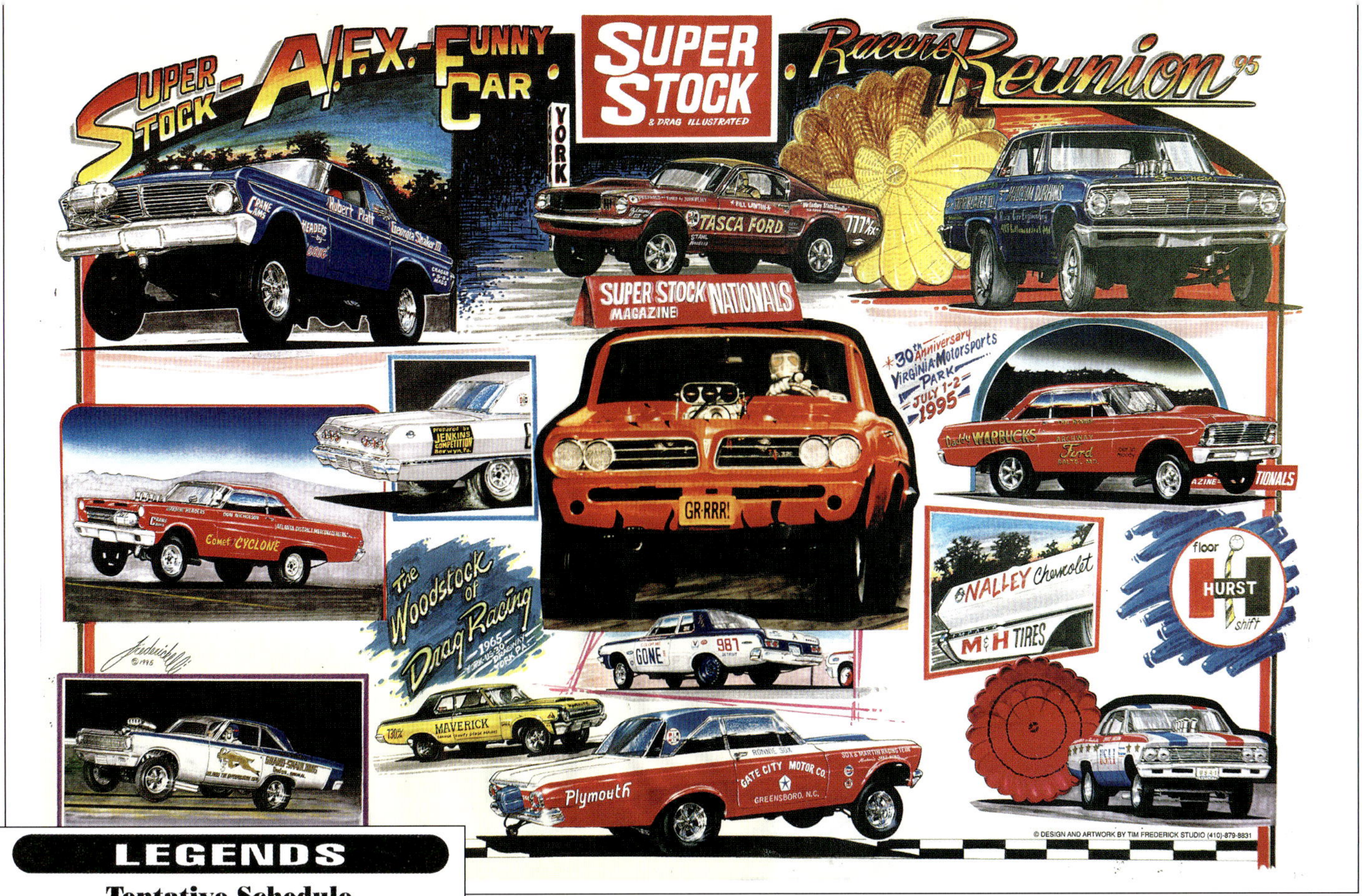

Tim Frederick created this fabulous poster for the 1995 reunion. After the ceremony, fans could have the racers sign the print.

The Legends of Drag Racing had a pretty full schedule in 1994.

LEGENDS

Tentative Schedule

April 17	Morocco, Indiana "Match Race Madness" at U.S. 41 International Dragway
April 23, 24	Ennis, Texas Super Chevy Event
May 14, 15	Kaukauna, Wisconsin at Wisconsin International Raceway
May 21	Jackson, South Carolina at Carolina Dragway Beswick vs. Bonner
June 4, 5	Martin, Michigan Super Chevy Event
June 10, 11, 12	Morocco, Indiana "Forever Blue Legends Musclecar Review"
June 18	Cordova, Illinois UDRA Summer Nationals at Cordova Dragway
June 22, 24	St. Louis, Missouri GTO AA Nationals at Gateway International
July 8, 9	Bristol, Tennessee Super Chevy Event
July 16, 17	Indianapolis, Indiana Super Chevy Event
July 23, 24	Souix Falls, South Dakota "Arnie Toftland & Earl Britt Benefit Race: at Thunder Valley Dragway
July 29, 30	Norwalk, Ohio Super Chevy Event at Norwalk Dragway
Aug. 4, 5	Holyoke, Massachusetts Yankee Chapter P.O.C.I.
Aug. 14	Englishtown, New Jersey at Old Bridge Township Raceway Park
Aug. 20, 21	Not yet confirmed.
Aug. 26, 27, 28	Cordova, Illinois World Series at Cordova Dragway
Sept. 2, 3	Indianapolis, Indiana NHRA U.S. Nationals
Sept. 4, 5	Union Grove, Wisconsin at Great Lakes Dragaway
Sept. 10, 11	Englishtown, New Jersey Super Chevy Event at Old Bridge Township Raceway Park
Sept. 24, 25	Rockingham, North Carolina Super Chevy Event
Sept. 30	Norwalk, Ohio Tri Power Sunday Event
Oct. 22, 23	Piedmont, North Carolina Legends Super Stock, A/FX Legends Reunion at Piedmont Dragway

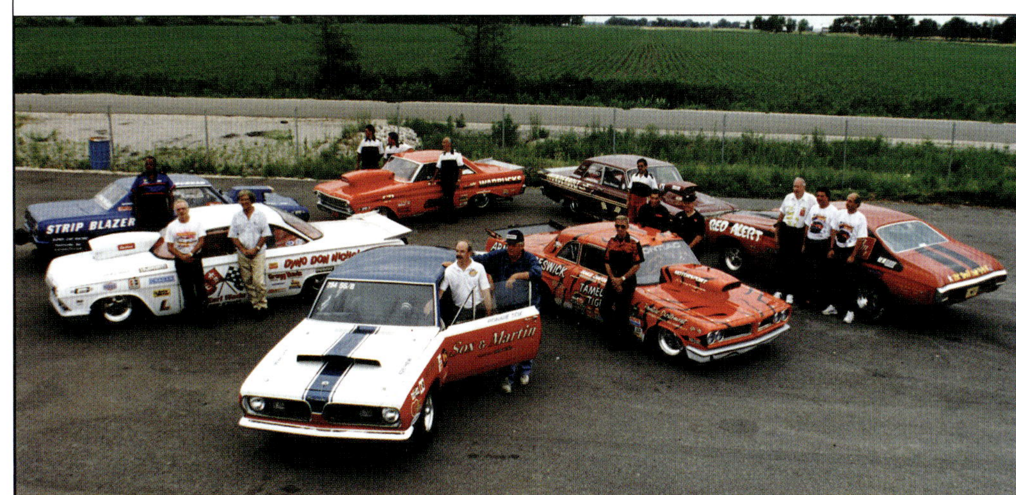

The Legends got together on June 10, 1994, at US 41 International Dragway in Morocco, Indiana. The company of CarWick & Bentley shot video of the full day's event. It aired on the Exciting World of Speed and Beauty. You can still watch this on Amazon Prime. Starting in the back (at about 1 o'clock) with Dick Brannan's Ford T-bolt is Marco DeCesaris. The Red Alert Chevelle was owned and driven by Bob Hamilton. Then, Arnie is next to his LeMans. Ronnie Sox was there with this particular Barracuda driven by Ernie Chapman. Next, of course, is Dyno Don himself with Earl Wade helping out. Malcolm Durham is next to his Chevelle. Bringing it back full circle is Dick Estevez, the new owner of Phil Bonner's Ford. Roger Lindamood was there but didn't make this picture. (Photo Courtesy Mike Caretto)

This is a great shot of Arnie and Don launching at the Milan Nostalgia Nationals in or around 1993.

Taken at Byron Dragway, Arnie and Don trade jabs on the starting line for the crowd's benefit in the mid 1990s.

This is what happens when your crew people forget the wheelie bars. Joe Palsgrove was the guilty party in this instance at a Super Chevy event in Norwalk, Ohio. Arnie said it felt like the whole car was going over backward. Needless to say, Don won that round.

This photo was taken at Indy during the US Nationals in 1994. Arnie loves this picture, not so much because Wally Parks suddenly become Arnie's best friend but because of the look on Don's face. Afterward, Don called Arnie a "kiss-ass!"

Countless kids have had their picture taken while sitting in this seat. Most of them aren't tall enough to see out the windshield, though.

During the late 1990s, Arnie learned that I had some ability in the art department and showed me a picture that someone had done of him plowing under the competition. The tractor was orange, small, and looked pretty beat up. Then the cars were none that anyone would recognize. Arnie asked if I could work something up. I knew what cars to put in the drawing and the right color for the tractor. I'll never forget the look on his face when the Farmer saw this. He left my shop grinning from ear to ear. Arnie used it for several years on the back of his kids' shirts. Even Dick Estevez got a chuckle out of it, and I think for a while he wondered if I could do something like this for him.

Back to GTO

It was because of the fans that Arnie started work on a new car in the mid-1990s. This time, it was an all fiberglass–bodied 1964 GTO. A one-man shop out of Tennessee was used to start the build. When the owner's world was turned upside down, Arnie picked up the car and brought it to Diamond Collision, which was owned and operated by Rick and Rob Bruce in the Detroit area. They finished the car, and their names along with Luke Petit appeared on the new car.

Two Memorable but Opposite Races

Two races stand out in my mind from the late 1990s. By this time, I started attending races where Arnie was running just to videotape his passes. The first one occurred at Byron Dragway in 1997.

Arnie was running against the *Bad Judgment* Hemi-powered 1963 Dodge Polara owned by Kilpat-

Arnie had just picked up the new GTO from Diamond Collision and took it to the Performance Racing Industry (PRI) show in Cincinnati in 1996. Brian Ashley's name is on the pillar. He was obviously proud of the work he'd done on this special "canvas."

rick and Stegall. Arnie crossed the finish line first with a 7.16 on the first pass and a 7.08 on the second. Just in case you're wondering about the top speed, it was 192.51 on the second pass. While I don't have any photos from that day, there's a video by Beswick1fan on YouTube if you care to watch.

The same day at the track another brand-new car was there, a bright red 1966 GTO owned by Lynwood Wood. He and the Adler brothers, Randy and Rob, had just gotten the car out of the body shop, and they were making their first test-and-tune hits. The Adlers also had their fourth-gen Firebird, and they were tuning the GTO.

All day long, there had been all kinds of banter back and forth between Lynwood and Arnie. Even

The Tameless Tiger *is just starting out on a wicked eighth-mile burnout at Byron. That's Arnie's nephew, Jimmy Beswick, looking on. Jimmy was crew chief for quite a few years in the late 1990s into this century. (Photo Courtesy Beswick Archive)*

"Broadway" Bob Metzler pulled out all the stops to promote Arnie's celebration of 50 years of racing by bringing in not only Arnie but Pontiac ad man Jim Wangers and Hurst spokesperson Linda Vaughn. (Photo Courtesy Roger and Judy Mac Zura)

Two different views show all of Arnie's cars parked on the track. A staff member told me later that doing this had really hurt some of the track prep. Nobody involved with Arnie cared. It was his day!

though big money was discussed, they decided on a one-time grudge match to see who had the faster GTO. When it came time for the grudge match, Randy was asked to drive. Randy told me that because Lynwood was such a big guy, they had to put pillows and padding to make it possible for him to reach the steering wheel and pedals. Lynwood was not going to lose to Arnie and had Rob lean out the fuel in the car to go faster.

The GTO hadn't gone any faster than the mid-7s that day, but they really wanted the bragging rights of beating a legend. Sure enough, even though Arnie redlit, Randy made a run of 6.83 at 204.29. They leaned it out too much though, and in the process, they burnt three pistons.

Longtime racer Erik Carlson was there that day. "Randy had just started doing the driving for Lynwood, and they were there making some test hits," Erik said. "When the grudge match was announced, I knew Adler had every intention of putting the Farmer on the trailer. I wondered if they turned up the blower speed and didn't get the air/

Since there are billboards next to the other side of the track, seven photos were stitched together for this historic shot. The cars from left to right were owned at the time by Mike Guarise, John and Janette Holmes, Mark Keykendall, Jeff Sams, Eric Larson and Mike Garblik, Mike Guarise, and, of course, Arnie.

Definitely the highlight for me at the 50 Years of Arnie at Great Lakes Dragaway event was going down the track in his original altered-wheelbase Tiger car. The tach was not really there; it was at zero, and what has been taken out through Photoshop is the pickup truck that's pulling me down the track. The tach was also moved up to make it look like you or I am driving the car down the track.

Arnie spared no expense using up some rubber on the tires doing his burnouts at this gala affair. He's out there way past the eighth-mile mark. (Photo Courtesy Roger and Judy Mac Zura)

fuel mixture right to make it go lean."

The next big race where something different happened was roughly a year later when Arnie was out West. One of the final stops of this 1998 tour was in Phoenix for a big event that featured a Pro Mod race. Arnie was booked for exhibition runs, but when he unloaded, he was asked if he was going to actually compete with no guaranteed prize money. He was informed that if he wanted to compete, he would need mufflers on the car. Arnie decided that rather than just running exhibition passes, he'd enter the competition. He bit the bullet and spent close to $300 on a set of mufflers. He couldn't have been happier when he then went on to win the whole event.

The Best and the Worst

Fast-forward to 2003. Arnie had a high point that year in June when he celebrated 50 years of drag racing at Great Lakes Dragaway in Union Grove, Wisconsin. The icing on the cake was that no fewer than eight of Arnie's cars were there, whether originals or duplicates. The biggest surprise was seeing the original *Tameless Tiger* there, which was completely restored by Donnie Reeves.

Legendary bluegrass musician Mark Keykendall (pronounced Kirk-en-dall), the owner of the car at that time, came up to me and said, "Hey, can you do me a favor? We're going to pull the cars up on the track. We'll have a truck to pull you, but I need somebody to steer the car.

"I'm so big that if a fire started in the back of the car and it took two weeks to get to the front, I'd still die!" Mark continued.

I didn't have to be asked twice about sitting behind the wheel and steering this piece of history down the track while Arnie told the fans about each car as we went down the quarter mile.

Tameless Tiger II

While there was a pass in a re-created Tempest wagon at Norwalk in 2005, it was three years to the

While Arnie healed, work began on the Tameless Tiger II. *A whole new fiberglass body, minus the rear decklid and spoiler, was fabricated by VFN. The Best of Show shop did the paint and bodywork. (Photo Courtesy Beswick Archive)*

ANOTHER FIRE

The absolute low point for Arnie's racing career, not only of 2003 but maybe of his entire life, happened on August 3, 2003, in Wentzville, Missouri. Arnie was brought into the Mid America Raceway there for exhibition runs. On Saturday and the first run on Sunday, the car wasn't running as quickly as normal, due to problems with the nitrous oxide system. The problem was thought to be fixed as the final run of the day got under way.

Upon reaching the finish line, Arnie pulled the chute and lifted off the gas, and the car backfired. At almost the same instant, an explosion with a huge fireball erupted under the hood. Flames engulfed the car so completely that Arnie's opponent thought the whole car was on fire. The fire then subsided to the point where Arnie thought it was out.

The car continued to slow, but within a second or so, Arnie heard a roar like a jet plane. Suddenly, fire and intense heat were coming through the engine-compartment firewall, melting and burning the dash, windshield, doors, and much of the floorboards. The fire was so intense that it started to burn through Arnie's shoes, gloves, and even portions of his fire suit.

Arnie underestimated what was happening. Still keeping his wits about him, and being conscientious, the Farmer did not want to stop the car on the track to incur the wrath of a cleanup crew. Consequently, he stayed in the car and made the left-hand turn onto the return road. That was because he did not yet know the severity of the fire. He reasoned that the fire *had* to die soon because there would be no fuel for it. What he didn't know was that what most likely happened was that the nitrous micro switch wires were melted and probably fused together along with the fuel switch wires. This kept supplying both nitrous oxide and the methanol fuel to the fire, theoretically until the tanks were emptied.

Upon making the turn, covering his mouth and nose as best he could, Arnie struggled with the seat belts as the car slowed. He couldn't unlatch them because his hands were already too badly burnt. Perhaps the fire had partially burnt through the belts or he had managed to unfasten them because as the car came to a stop, a track official approached and opened the door, and Arnie, having been throwing his entire body weight against the door, literally fell out of the car.

As more people approached, Arnie immediately asked for cold water to be poured on his hands and feet. The track people saw the severity and called

This photo was taken shortly after Arnie was pulled out of his coma, still in the burn unit in St. Louis.

The cockpit area shows extensive damage.

It's hard to believe that such a tiny relay could do this much da (Photo Courtesy Janette Holmes)

911 for airlift services. Within five or ten minutes, the helicopter arrived. Arnie was immediately given something for the pain, and he remembered the take off, but he was quickly out.

The doctors were not optimistic about him even living through the first night. Having experienced fires before, Arnie knew to hold his breath, and that, along with the grace of God, kept him alive. After being kept comatose for roughly six weeks, it was his sheer determination that helped him heal.

Most people know what transpired over the next few months, as updates on his website kept his fans informed. Thankfully, with the help of some skilled doctors, the healing continued. His celebrity status did not go unnoticed by the hospital staff, as Arnie received literally hundreds of cards, letters, and e-mails. Evelyn told me that even though Arnie was in a coma, she read every single one to him.

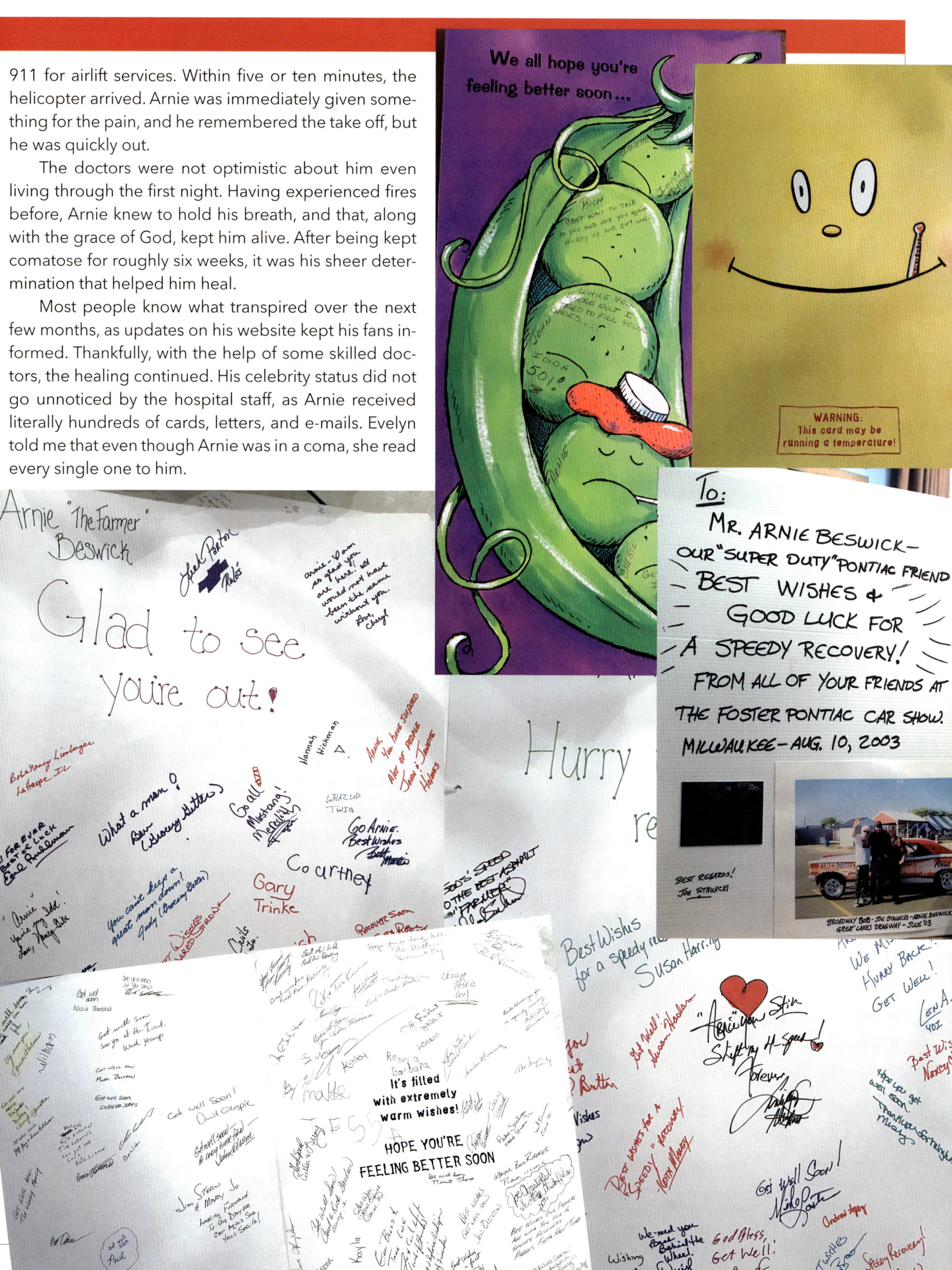

month before Arnie once again sat behind wheel of his own *Tameless Tiger*. The car had been completely rebodied and now carried the *II* after the name. It has gone on to delight race fans across the nation ever since, making its quickest pass ever at the World Series in 2012. Arnie broke the 200-mph barrier by two hundredths of a second at an astonishing speed of 7.05.

Recognition and Accolades

In the last 20-plus years, Arnie has received plenty of recognition for his achievements. In 1995, Frank Spittle held some of the first hall-of-fame inductions for drag racers. They also consisted of drag racing for those still with cars. Arnie was inducted into all of them.

Arnie was also recognized for his racing accomplishments when he was presented with the coveted award of "American Auto Racing's Best" at the National Driving Recognition Dinner in Chicago. On January 28, 2006, he received the Lifetime Achievement Award presented by the Legends of Motorsports Guild in Chicago. Then in mid-March, a huge entourage of friends, family, and crew traveled to Florida to be part of the ceremonies as he was inducted into the International Drag Racing Hall of Fame. Never has anyone had such a large group of fans present to show their support.

In early August, Arnie rounded out the year by receiving yet another award for his contributions from Super Duty Promotions at the Pontiac Nationals in Norwalk, Ohio.

In late summer of 2007, Great Lakes Dragaway also inducted Arnie into its hall of fame.

Arnie received several more awards and inductions in 2008. The first was in mid-June at the NHRA Hot Rod Reunion, which was sponsored by Holley. It was at Beach Bend Raceway Park in Bowling Green,

The driver and owner of the Royal car in the near lane is 'Nae Russo. He was the lucky person who got to run against Arnie driving this little Tempest wagon at the Ames Tri-Power Pontiac Nationals. Wally Abela painstakingly restored this car and lettered it like Arnie's original wagon. He handed Arnie the keys in 2005 for a trip down the quarter mile. Bill Bater Jr. was announcing from the line while Arnie fastened the belts and put on his helmet. His comment was, "Arnie's plenty excited!"

While all the ladies sported bracelets and tiger pins, all the men and boys wore tiger-striped ties. Even Bob Frey, the emcee for the night, couldn't help but notice. It came from a conversation between Evelyn, Chad Starbuck, and me while coming back home from the Legends of Motorsports Guild trip. I suggested that it might be cool if we would all wear tiger-striped suits or even vests. All three of us simultaneously thought, "ties." Chad found two companies, and Evelyn picked her favorite.

Arnie tells Dave McClelland about loving that ride in his Tameless Tiger Pontiacs down the quarter mile. (Photo Courtesy Fred Simmons)

The Beswick table is shown after Arnie was awarded his very special "Wally." Clockwise behind Arnie is me, Chad Starbuck, Janette Holmes, John Holmes, and Mike Ehrhart. (Photo Courtesy Fred Simmons)

The cover of the program for the 2008 East Coast Drag Times Hall of Fame ceremony lists all the recipients. (Illustration by Joel Naprstek)

Kentucky. Arnie was awarded a very special "Wally" for his lifetime of achievements. Dave McClelland was host of this prestigious event.

The Ramchargers also had been given a similar award, and the late Jim Thornton was their spokesperson. He spoke first, going on and on about how they'd never been beaten, how they were always the first car in the 10s, the 9s, the 8s and so on. Every statement was followed by a hushed, "BS" from the "Strange Engineering" table behind and to the right of us.

Next was Arnie's turn on the podium. The famous NHRA announcer asked him a number of questions about still driving and carrying the Pontiac banner among other things.

Dave finally summed it up with, "You've raced and beaten almost every other racer out there at one time in your life."

Arnie brought the house down as the whole place erupted with a huge laugh when he said, "Even the Ramchargers!"

Arnie joined a very prestigious group of people for the first-year ceremony of the Pontiac Preservation Association (PPA), which was held in conjunction with the GTOAA convention in Hatfield, Pennsylvania. (Photo Courtesy Bill Vantuono)

All four daughters made it to Greensboro for Arnie's induction ceremony into the North Carolina Drag Racing Hall of Fame. From left to right: Rhonda Mitchell, Michele Beswick, Arnie, Arnette Stralow, and Paula Wiersema.

The next induction was in York, Pennsylvania, for the seventh-annual York US30 drag race reunion where Arnie was inducted into its Legion of Honor.

The last event for 2008 was another big one, as Arnie was inducted into the East Coast Drag Times Hall of Fame and presented with the Distinguished Achievement Award. That meant a trip to Henderson, North Carolina, on the weekend of October 17. The master of ceremonies was none other than ESPN's Bret Kepner.

Two more organizations recognized Arnie's achievements in 2018. The first was in July when the Pontiac Preservation Association (PPA) had its first Pontiac Hall of Fame ceremony. Arnie was one of the very prestigious inductees along with John DeLorean, Bunkie Knudsen, and seven others. In August, at the World Series of Drag Racing, Cordova International Raceway also started its Hall of Fame. Arnie was naturally a first-year inductee.

The last induction to date was into the North Carolina Drag Racing Hall of Fame in February 2020. It was a 13½-hour drive for Arnie, the crew, two of his daughters, and me. Yet it was worth every minute to see him and his four daughters reunited and together again.

Adoration through Restoration or Duplication

Within the last 30 years or so, several of Arnie's past race cars have been restored or duplicated.

1966 Star of the Circuit

The first one was Arnie's original 1966 *Star of the Circuit* Funny Car. Russ Ottens, a longtime friend and neighboring farmer, restored the appearance of the car back to its original livery in the mid-1990s.

Having no idea about the magnitude of the popularity of nostalgia drag cars, the framework, roll cage, and drivetrain were left as original.

In early 2002, Russ sold the car to John and Janette Holmes. John was Arnie's crew chief in those years. When John wasn't working to help keep the *Tameless Tiger* on the track, he started updating the '66 for track action. In early May, after dotting all the *I*s and crossing the *T*s in the safety department, the car returned to the concrete and asphalt that it had not seen in over 40 years with burnouts just like the Farmer did in this special car.

This is one of the best shots of a wheelstand ever taken while John and Janette have had the car. This was taken at Great Lakes Dragaway in 2011 with John driving the car. (Photo Courtesy Janette Holmes)

1961 Pontiac Ventura

Next was Arnie's original 1961 Ventura. Alan Ranz of Polo, Illinois, brought out the freshly restored beauty at the POCI convention in Moline,

This is how the Star of the Circuit looked when Russ Ottens towed the car home. Arnie actually towed the car for Russ, as he didn't have a trailer. (Photo Courtesy Mike Caretto)

Alan Ranz brought out the newly restored 1961 Ventura to the 1996 POCI national convention in Moline, Illinois.

Illinois, in 1996. The car was then sold to Mike Guarise of Barrington Hills, Illinois. He auctioned it off along with three other cars, and it went out West to Lincoln, Nebraska, into the Gary Kuck collection.

Mrs. B's Grocery Getter

Mrs. B's Grocery Getter was the next of Arnie's famous cars to hit the tracks again. This updated duplicated version started in 1994, making its first passes in 1996. Mike Garblik, Eric Larson, and the late Wayne Martin teamed up to re-create and campaign this piece of history, complete with traditional Pontiac power, this time in Pro Mod form.

Eric Larson, Mike Garblik, and Wayne Martin traveled to the convention to show off their work on the Grocery Getter wagon. They took it to Cordova as a static display on Sunday while the Pontiac people raced. It was on the track shortly after.

This is an early shot in 1996 of Mrs. B's Famous Grocery Getter in action at Indy.

Little B's Runabout

Jeff Sams of Phoenix, Arizona, teamed up with Arnie to duplicate the *Little B's Runabout* coupe in Pro Mod form. It's complete with traditional Pontiac power and is often spotted in the Midwest. The car has changed hands and is still in Arnie's possession.

Arnie and Jeff Sams out of Phoenix, Arizona, got together to build this Pro Mod version of Arnie's original LeMans coupe. When the car was being built, Arnie called, asking if there was a better name than Little B's Runabout. *The car was originally named that as a tribute to the daughters. Since they were grown, I suggested crossing* Little *out and replacing it with the word* Big. *Arnie called Jeff, and that's the way it was lettered. After it went to the Holmes shop, they changed it back to the way it was originally.*

This car is often called "the Farmer Coupe." It is shown here doing a huge burnout at Cordova Dragway Park. (Photo Courtesy Mike Garland)

Tameless Tiger

The most unbelievable restoration to date has to be Arnie's original *Tameless Tiger*. Donnie Reeves purchased the wrecked hulk, and in late 1997, the *Tiger* was on the loose on the drag strip once again. The car was owned by Mark Keykendall for a while. Then, it was sold to Don Snyder Sr. and now resides in Ohio.

The Tameless Tiger *was posed on Donnie Reeves's driveway right after the restoration was finished. Donnie is a race car enthusiast and has redone other famous drag cars.*

D/Stock GTO Judge

After the D/Stock GTO Judge was restored, the car went through several owners, including Dominic Blasco, Mike Guarise, and Todd Werner. Todd recently sold the car through Mecum's Harrisburg, Pennsylvania, auction at the end of July/August 1, where it hammered for $137,500.

Righteous Judge

In 2007, for the first time since the early 1970s, people were able to see a newly finished re-created version of the 1969 *Righteous Judge*. It ran as good as it looked. It also changed hands a few times, and I believe it is now in Texas.

The Ames Tri-Power Pontiac Nationals in Norwalk, Ohio, is often the place to catch the best and rarest Pontiacs on the planet. Seeing the newly finished Pro Mod version of the Righteous Judge *was a surprise to many. It was great to see it out on the track as it was originally intended. Arnie put a huge hole shot on the driver and never looked back for the win here. (Photo Courtesy Don Keefe)*

Arnie's original D/Stock Judge posed for this photo shortly after the restoration by the late Terry Carney and family. It was unveiled on a snowy night early in 2001 at a big party that included the band Shadows of the Night.

There were a few years in the late 2000s where Arnie got a nitrous pop when he was leaving the starting line. This was by far the worst one that Arnie experienced, literally launching the hood scoop about 15 feet in the air. It happened at Norwalk in 2008. Arnie never got excited about the whole thing and just said that the Tiger was acting rudely. (Photo Courtesy Don Keefe)

Mystery Tornado Tribute

The next Arnie Beswick car that surfaced was in 2007 at the Pontiac Nationals in Norwalk, Ohio. Benny Bax and his sons did an absolutely superb job of duplicating the *Mystery Tornado*. While the original car underwent changes between 1964 and 1966, Benny chose to do the GTO as it originally appeared. Its maiden voyage was in July 2009. It was at Cordova's "Nostalgiafest" in 2010. For the first time ever, the *Mystery Tornado* and the '66 were paired up for a good old-fashioned match race that kept the capacity crowd on its feet until they crossed the finish line.

Beswick-Built Tunes

Also making its debut in 2008 was the 1968 *BossMan* GTO. Back in the day, Mike Rutherford from the Muscatine, Iowa, area hung around Arnie's shop, helping with Arnie's 1968 Funny Car. After witnessing the pull that Arnie had with Pontiac, Mike wanted something special and out of the ordinary. Mike and Arnie came up with the idea of a special 428-equipped GTO straight from the legendary Royal Pontiac. Ensuring that both street and strip were dominated, Arnie added a special set of prototype RA II heads that Pontiac was testing.

The car was painstakingly restored to perfection by Bob Adams of Joliet for Mike Guarise, who was also from the Chicago metro area. Mike sold the car in 2015, and at last report, it was in Texas.

Rick Holladay had been drag racing for some time, and even though he lived in Norfolk, Virginia, he heard of Arnie's accomplishments in drag racing with his Pontiacs. He talked with Arnie in 1965 and ordered a specially painted GTO that was named the *Jolly Green Giant*. He had it shipped directly to Arnie for him to work his magic.

After making a few passes at Cordova, Arnie delivered the car to Rick. It went on to accomplish great things at almost every drag strip at which it ran. This car, like the others, went through a few owners and was auctioned through Dana Mecum's company the following year. It now resides in Lincoln, Nebraska, owned by Gary Kuck, in the same museum as Arnie's '61.

The last car that was spotted at Norwalk in 2008 was the *TT III*. Dominic Blasco, a longtime fan of Arnie's, built this little Tempest

There are two places to regularly find Arnie's past and present race cars: Norwalk, Ohio, and Cordova International Raceway. Benny Bax and his family towed the Mystery Tornado tribute up from Mary's Hope, Missouri, to take on John Holmes in the Star of the Circuit Pontiac in 2010. (Photo Courtesy Mike Garland)

This very special one-off 1968 GTO was originally ordered for Mike Rutherford. Bob Adams restored this beauty for Mike Guarise, complete with its Royal Pontiac–installed 428. The magazines in 1968 showed Milt Schornack with Royal Pontiac installing the new engine. Bob and Mike duplicated the shot for the presentation after the restoration. Mike Rutherford had Arnie order the car for him because of Arnie's contacts with Pontiac. It was almost the same deal with the Jolly Green Giant.

Just after completion, Richard Ellis brought the Jolly Green Giant to the BOP Nationals at Cordova. (Photo Courtesy Chad Starbuck)

coupe as a tribute. Dominic owned Arnie's original D-stock *Judge* for a while. This blue accented black car is a gorgeous piece of engineering and at last report was owned by Gregory Sy of Ohio.

Tameless Tiger III Tribute

Enoch Matson, from New London, Missouri, has been a fan of Arnie's since he was a kid. In 2009, he

The Tin Tiger has a 421-ci engine with a G-force clutchless 5-speed transmission. VFN helped with the fiberglass body parts. Enoch and his father, Larry, hand built the tube chassis. The car uses a 9-inch Ford rear end with a 5.43:1 gear ratio. Enoch is part of the Ozark Mountain Super Shifter group of stick-shift racers that has a full schedule every year. The car's best time is a 5.46 at 124 mph in the eighth mile. (Photo Courtesy Beswick Archive; Thanks to Enoch)

The Tameless Tiger III tribute Tempest was first spotted at Norwalk. The flat-black paint with all the bright blue trim and accents is very unique.

At Central Illinois Dragstrip in Havana, Illinois, there was a good hard launch from the Tin Tiger of Enoch Matson. Mike Kelm captured this wheels-up shot.

loved the 1970–1972 Trans Am bodystyle.

It wouldn't matter if they built a new car or updated the *Grocery Getter* wagon, a whole lot of money was needed to go to the next level of performance. Their friendship with Rick and Rob Bruce of Diamond Collision in Flint, Michigan, also influenced their decision.

The complete story began back in June 1972, when Fiberglass Ltd. gave Arnie that Firebird body at his benefit after the fire. Due to other rebuilding priorities and directions in Arnie's life, that body stayed in a shed on the farm until the late 1990s.

After finishing a videotape session in 1997, Arnie, Gene Scheer, and I disturbed the dust and cobwebs as we moved that fiberglass piece of history into Arnie's trailer so that he could deliver it to Bruce's shop. While visions of a new *Boss Bird* undoubtedly danced in Arnie's head, I'm sure he was extremely

bought a 1963 LeMans and together with his father, Larry, built the car. Enoch talked with Arnie, asking if it would be alright to tiger-stripe it, and the Farmer gave it his blessing.

Other Tributes

Since then, three more of Arnie's cars have surfaced. The first one was the *Boss Bird* Funny Car. Eric Larson and Mike Garblik, the men who built the *Grocery Getter*, decided to build the ultimate and quickest of all the Beswick machines. The fastest Pontiac that Arnie had was obviously his 1970½ *Boss Bird* Firebird. It was an easy decision for them to build a duplicate, as they both

First spotted at the POCI convention in 2010 at Charleston, West Virginia, the Boss Bird Funny Car looked spectacular. The back wing was a debated subject between Arnie and Eric. Eric and Mike were listening to Rick and Rob Bruce in regard to downforce.

This was the original body that Arnie received in the benefit in 1972. (Photo Courtesy Ted Pappacena)

disappointed when the car emerged, painted in red and labeled *Zombie* on the quarter panel.

The *Zombie* Funny Car made various appearances for a few years until there was a blower explosion and fire that burnt the car's cowl area. Rick and Rob were forced to park it temporarily. Eric and Mike liked the body and decided to duplicate the car. They bit the bullet, fixed the original body, and then had VFN make two copies, one for themselves and another for the Bruce family as payment.

While the bodywork was taking place, Mike and Eric began working on a special Ram Air V motor for the beastly machine. Using the great airflow design that Pontiac had created back in the late 60s and thanks to the modern technology of computer numerical control (CNC), they fabricated their own heads from aluminum blocks. Their handmade heads were put on top of an *Indian Adventures II* block.

Once assembled, the roughly 480-ci mill was one of the only non-Hemi engines to power a nitro-breathing Funny Car down the quarter mile. In 2019, Mike and Eric had a monumental year, as the car broke the speed record for a traditional Pontiac-powered car in Norwalk, Ohio.

Boss Bird Jr.

The next race car that surfaced was a duplicate to Arnie's *Boss Bird Jr.* Firebird. The original car was meant to do battle in the Pro Stock arena. When the class was first intro-

duced in the late 1960s, Arnie used a GTO labeled as the *Righteous Judge*. Later, he got ahold of a lighter Firebird and began work on that. The Funny Cars and cash shortages kept the Farmer busy, and development was slow on the *Boss Bird Jr.* Even before the fire, the car was sold.

Based on one old photograph that was given to Arnie, Chris Shenuk took a Firebird and duplicated the original car—right down to the Ram Air V engine. It is often spotted at Norwalk's Ames Tri-Power Pontiac Nationals in early August and at Cordova's BOP Nationals later in the fall.

The Boss Bird does a burnout at Norwalk, Ohio, on its way to breaking the top speed record for the world's fastest Pontiac. That weekend, on roughly 90-percent nitro, the car went 5.87 at a tick over 250 mph. (Photo Courtesy Dave Bonaskiewich)

Eric and Mike's Boss Bird *Funny Car, along with Chris Shenuk's* Boss Bird Jr. *and the* Boss Bird Mini *were all present and accounted for in Norwalk in 2014. Arnie loved the pictures so much that he used one of them for his Christmas card that year.*

Le Mans Coupe

The last clone was a LeMans coupe put together by Benny Bax and family. They were the same people who built the *Mystery Tornado* tribute. This '63 was painted just like Arnie's original coupe after it had been lettered. As I understand it, Kaleb Bax drives the car in nostalgia classes, touring with Dennis Mothershed's Victory Performance–sponsored Nostalgia Super Stocks.

The second tribute car built by the Bax family is a tribute to Arnie's original 1963 LeMans. The car looks great going down the track. (Photo Courtesy Dennis Mothershed)

1960 Pontiac Ventura

While mystery still shrouds the locations of some of Arnie's cars, one of his original cars finally surfaced in 2019. It was his original 1960 Ventura. Arnie had heard from people now and again who said they'd found the old Ventura. Since Arnie possessed the original dealer invoice, he knew the VIN. Late in 2019, Arnie was again contacted about his Ventura. Finally, after comparing the original invoice and the car's VIN, Arnie's old 1960 Ventura had been located!

Sometime in the not-too-distant future, we'll hopefully see Arnie's original 1962 Super Duty Catalina. The car has been a project of his for a good 10 years or so. He recently sold the car and all the accumulated parts to a very big collector named Mike Kaufman.

Things Still to Come

As he was closing in on 90 years old, Arnie came to terms with a few physical limitations. He passed the driving torch to Anthony Layne in 2018. This move ensured that the next generation of race fans will enjoy the huge smoky burnouts, the quick backups, and the lightning-fast passes down racetracks for years to come. Both Arnie and Anthony are tickled about the arrangement, and in early

2020, Arnie had the car's paint freshened up and new graphics applied to reflect the new crew chief's business on the fenders.

As we entered this new decade, Arnie turned 90, and I can't help but again mention my admiration of all the amazing things that he accomplished. His life certainly had its share of lows from adversity, but there have been so many highs that I'm sure even he'd tell you that his life has been blessed and that it's been a pretty good ride. Over the past 30 years, I've come to feel like he and the rest of the Beswick clan are family. So, in closing I have to say, "Arnie, I love you, Dad!"

Both Anthony Layne, the new driver of the Tameless Tiger II *(pictured here with his wife, Deb), and Arnie are delighted with their new arrangement. Anthony loves driving the* Tameless Tiger, *and Arnie can talk with the fans without worrying about having to make the call to the lanes.*

This was taken in 2005, just after Wally Abela finished his version of the wagon. It was parked by the Beswick pits, and Evelyn came up with this idea for a classic shot.

In 2012, Arnie and the crew traveled to the York US30 Reunion in York, Pennsylvania. While there, Arnie's daughter Michele (middle) joined them. While looking through Arnie's picture book, she noticed and made mention that Arnette (right) and Paula (left) had the LeMans coupe named for them while growing up, while she was not mentioned. This special shirt was custom made just for her as a practical joke.

In July 2013, Michele Beswick retired from the US Air Force and threw a big extended weekend's worth of activities to celebrate. Arnie asked my wife and I if we'd like to be there. Included in the schedule was a guided trip of all the monuments in the city. This is the whole extended Beswick family in front of the Vietnam Memorial.

Arnie thinks of his own history as he stands next to the Korean War Memorial.

Arnie shows his sense of humor posing for this shot by sitting in Franklin Delano Roosevelt's lap.

In 2017, two distinct machines made it to Cordova for the BOP Nationals. One was Arnie's original IH Farmall 400 tractor that would go across the auction block later that year. The second was the Boss Bird Funny Car. David Peterson of Walcott, Iowa, restored Arnie's original tractor and brought it out for fun. Again, the fun-loving Arnie came up with the idea of a match race between the two. The author created all the smoke artificially. (Photo Courtesy Mike Garland)

Additional books that may interest you...

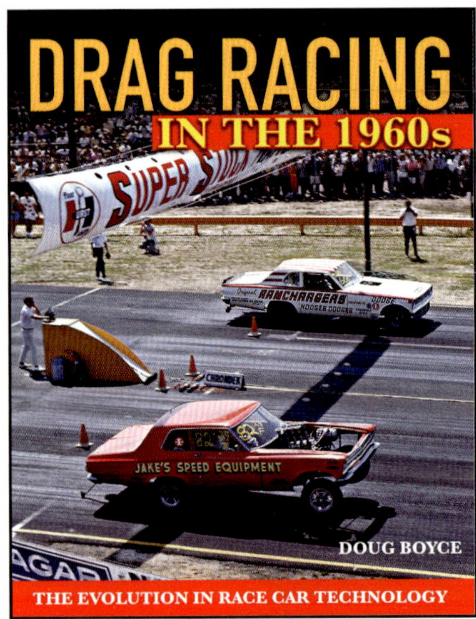

DRAG RACING IN THE 1960s: Evolution in Race Car Technology *by Doug Boyce* In *Drag Racing in the 1960s: The Evolution in Race Car Technology*, veteran author Doug Boyce takes you on a ride through the entire decade from a technological point of view rather than a results-based one. 8.5 x 11", 176 pgs, 350 photos, Sftbd. ISBN 9781613255827 **Part # CT674**

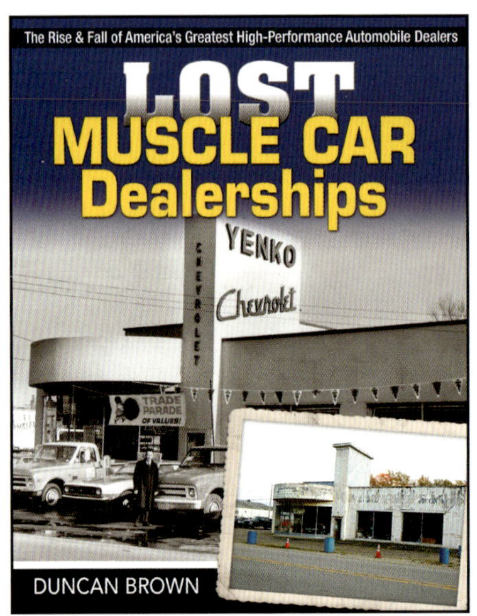

LOST MUSCLE CAR DEALERSHIPS *by Duncan Brown* Revisit the glorious 1960s and early 1970s, when cars from Reynolds Buick, Yeakel Chrysler-Plymouth, Mel Burns Ford, and others created the lasting muscle car legacy through innovative advertising and over-the-top performance. Detailed text and more than 250 historic photos and illustrations provide the history of those dealerships. 8.5 x 11", 192 pgs, 360 photos, Sftbd. ISBN 9781613254516 **Part # CT644**

MATCH RACE MAYHEM: Drag Racing's Grudges, Rivalries and Big-Money Showdowns *by Doug Boyce* Veteran drag race author Doug Boyce tells the tale of the history of match racing through the cars, the drivers, the events, the classes, the rivalries, and everything else that was fun about match racing during the golden era. It's all here, complemented by wonderful vintage photography provided by fans and professionals in attendance. 8.5 x 11", 176 pgs, 297 photos, Sftbd. ISBN 9781613253052 **Part # CT582**

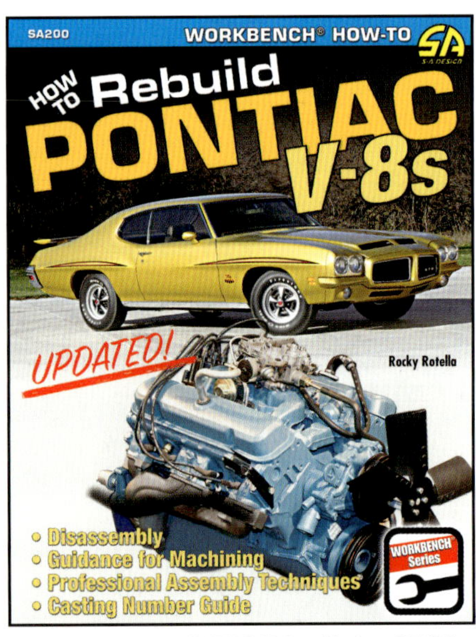

HOW TO REBUILD PONTIAC V-8s - Updated Edition *by Rocky Rotella* Drawing on his vast experience, Pontiac expert Rotella uses detailed captions and photos to show each crucial step of the disassembly, inspection, machine work, parts selection, assembly, and break-in process of a complete engine rebuild. 8.5 x 11", 152 pgs, 395 photos, Sftbd. ISBN 9781613255636 **Part # SA200**

www.cartechbooks.com or 1-800-551-4754